Peacocks & Picathartes

Reflections on Africa's birdlife

RUPERT WATSON

Illustrations by Peter Blackwell

Published by Struik Nature (an imprint of
Penguin Random House South Africa (Pty) Ltd)
Reg. No. 1953/000441/07
The Estuaries No. 4, Oxbow Crescent, Century City, 7441 South Africa
PO Box 1144, Cape Town, 8000 South Africa

Visit **www.penguinrandomhouse.co.za** and join the
Struik Nature Club for updates, news, events and special offers.

First published in 2020
1 3 5 7 9 10 8 6 4 2

Publisher: Pippa Parker
Managing editor: Roelien Theron
Editor: Helen de Villiers
Designer: Janice Evans
Cover designer: Gaelen Pinnock/polygram.co.za
Typesetter: Deirdré Geldenhuys
Illustrator: Peter Blackwell
Proofreader: Thea Grobbelaar

The Publishers would like to thank David Chamberlain of
FH Chamberlain Trading for his permission to feature (and stylise)
illustrations from *Birds of Africa south of the Sahara* on the back cover.

Reproduction by Studio Repro, Cape Town

Printed by **novus print**, a division of Novus Holdings

Print: 9781775845607
ePub: 9781775845614

CONTENTS

ACKNOWLEDGEMENTS

This book owes a huge debt to the printed works of earlier authors and I have paid tribute to many of these in the final chapter. With regard to more specific accounts, where individual books or papers inform particular parts of my text, I have tried to acknowledge these as I go. Many were sourced on the internet, and no recognition is enough for the search engines that render them accessible; and no thanks are enough to those individuals or institutions who make their works so freely available for anyone to read without charge. In my experience, librarians always go that extra distance to help, and whether I was asking for help from the Witwatersrand Bird Club, the Cornell Laboratory of Ornithology or any other institution in between, I always got it.

A lot of my hard-copy reference material was found on the shelves of the National Museums of Kenya library in Nairobi, or on those of my neighbour and friend Tony Archer. I also received input and advice from many individuals, either over the internet or in conversation. Peter Ryan and Peter Steyn read large chunks of the book and Brian Finch read it all; others read and commented on different parts – Sidney Shema, Kariuki Ndanganga, Munir Virani, Charlotte Bildstedfelt and many more.

To the friends who have accompanied and inspired me all over the world as I went looking for birds, I say thank you, as of course I do to my wife Mary Ann who has all too often been asked to forsake the beach for the bush and the forest. And no-one gave me more encouragement to start this book, and continue it, than Pippa Parker of the publishers, Penguin Random House, nor help in its completion than consulting editor, Helen de Villiers.

PREFACE

Birds have loomed large in my life ever since my father infused me with his own lifelong interest during my schooldays. Indeed, it is no exaggeration to say that this contributed significantly to my searching for work in East Africa shortly after I qualified as a lawyer in England. The search was successful and I have called Kenya my home for the last 40 years, during which birds have taken up an ever larger part of my spare time, to such an extent that I increasingly find myself foregoing the fishing rod in favour of the binoculars.

As well as being a lawyer, I trained as a mediator and my work in teaching or practising mediation and conflict prevention has taken me to many different parts of Africa. I am self-employed, so I have almost always managed to find some post-assignment time to visit the wilder parts of any country where I was working. Doing so has contributed much to my gaining a broader perspective of the continent's birdlife, as have travels to southern Africa in the course of researching baobab trees for an earlier publication.

This book is intended as a celebration of the diversity of African birds, especially those peculiar to this continent. I have focused on families with little or no representation anywhere else and whose members are essentially only encountered here, and have also stretched this remit to include families, like sandgrouse and honeyguides, which are mainly, but not exclusively African. Finally, I have shamelessly indulged myself by covering six individual species, with close relatives on other continents, each of which seems, in its own way, to embody something of Africa.

I have written this book at my own comfort level. I have relied on terms such as 'close relatives' but also feel easy using the word 'congener', which is more specific in that it means 'within the same genus'. Elsewhere I may appear to eschew scientific terminology unnecessarily, using six words where one would do and for so doing I offer no apology. I am more at ease describing an evolutionary event as happening 'three million years ago' than 'at the start of the Pleistocene epoch', principally because I would have to look up 'Pleistocene' and so assume a lot of others would need to do the same. I do actually know what 'sympatric' means but I still prefer to say that two species both occur in the same particular area, and if I use a fairly technical word like 'allopreening' or 'pamprodactylous' I also define it in the text.

All this said, I hope that bird enthusiasts who have no idea what either 'sympatric' or 'allopreening' means will find the text informative and entertaining, and that those for whom the words are part of their everyday vocabulary will enjoy it too. It will become apparent that the studies of families or species are a combination of history, science and personal experience, and, as such, my further hope is that they will have broad appeal. Some readers may find that I stray too far from the basics of the bird, and would rather not read about the tragedy of the Bateleur's illustrations in *Roberts Birds of Southern Africa* or whether birds can count, but sometimes I find a story so fascinating, or a quote so bizarre that I feel it just has to be shared.

Writing about the birds of Africa first required a decision as to whether Africa meant the whole continent, or just sub-Saharan latitudes. And did it also include Madagascar and other outlying islands, which are all part of the Afrotropical region? There is no denying the fascination of Madagascar's flora and fauna, but somehow the island seemed too remote, from both geographical and ornithological perspectives, and it also became clear that the quintessential African birds were nearly all living south of the Sahara.

There is quite a lot of taxonomy in the book because, having settled to write about sub-Saharan bird families, I then needed to ascertain the component parts of each one. These parts are the genera and species, but I have kept away from any further subdivisions into tribes or superspecies, and there is very little in here about subspecies either. In reviewing a bird's taxonomic history, I often make reference to the 'type specimen' and to the individual author who first named it. I have also largely used English names for the birds, except where the Latin one is an essential part of the text.

There is certainly some original description in this work of bird behaviour so far unrecorded; the observations on Hadada feeding go beyond those reported in most accounts of this species, as do those on the solubility of turacin from turaco wing feathers. Generally, though, I rely on the researches of others, the results of which are often confined to specialised journals. I have done a lot of investigation into the early scientific history of the birds, and much of the quirkier or more historical content will be new even to the most professional of ornithologists. I am certainly in awe of the work done by the researchers in that epicentre of African bird study in the University of Cape Town, the FitzPatrick Institute of African Ornithology, but I am convinced that there is much of interest in this book for them too. Personal experience is, by definition, original and I hope that descriptions of time spent in earshot of Congo Peacocks or in the forests of Ghana and the Albertine Rift help to illuminate the texts where they appear.

My own level of interest in birds is that of the enthusiastic amateur. I take bird-watching friends on local safaris but have never had any pretensions or enough knowledge to raise my guiding level. I may spend half an hour looking at parent Rock Martins feeding young in their nest on our veranda, and twice as long when it is time for the chicks to try and fly. If I see a Secretarybird striding determinedly across the plains I usually try and keep it in view as long as possible in the hope of witnessing it catch a snake; and I would never move on from watching a visiting Osprey hovering over the lagoons at the coast until it either catches a fish or flaps out of sight. Nevertheless, these observations are generally for personal pleasure rather than in the hope or expectation of my being able to contribute anything new to the corpus of existing ornithological knowledge.

I do send in trip lists and reports of unusual sightings to our local Kenya Bird Map project, which has now taken on a pan-Africa dimension. Just after reviewing this preface in the quiet of my Nairobi home, I thought I heard the cry of an African Fish Eagle, which would be very out of place here. Having established it was not the ringtone for my neighbour's telephone, I rushed out to try and get a view into the distance and there, circling over a forested valley were two such birds, calling to one another. The nearest large expanse of still water is far away, and this sighting was quickly submitted, as was that of a Woolly-necked Stork which flew over the garden some weeks later.

I must admit that my enthusiasm for a lot of the minutiae of bird behaviour is limited, as it is for the whole question of whether a species really is a species. Ultimately, the birds are out there in their world, and whether there are two species of ostrich, or one with two subspecies, seems largely academic. So, despite what I said earlier about taxonomy, in practice I tend to ignore species splits until these are reflected in the next edition of whatever handbook I am using at the time.

I am keen to identify any bird (and not having much of a musical ear or musical memory, usually rely on sight rather than sound to do this) and I keep a list of those I see on a safari, or in my garden, or in Nairobi National Park, but I have no world or even country checklist. I usually make a note in my handbook when I see a bird for the first time, and maybe add in further sightings if these seem unusual, but seldom transfer such notes into any updated volume. There is no denying the excitement of seeing a 'new' bird, and not having a master list means I may get to experience this sensation more than once for the same species.

In writing this book I seek both to inform and entertain, and also to expand the reader's interest in Africa's birdlife. I have tried to balance the content so that there is no particular bias towards East Africa, but I am conscious of the fact that I have had much less first-hand experience of watching birds in some parts of Africa – particularly in West Africa and Ethiopia – than in others. This may be remedied in time, and in the case of the Cape's fynbos endemics, maybe even in the course of this book's publication!

In much of what is written here I have avoided the negative aspects of bird conservation. I am only too aware of all the pressures on wildlife and wild places consequent upon our continent's fast expanding human population, its increasing prosperity and the worldwide demands on our natural resources. However, I leave others to write about this and want my work to recognise and celebrate the birds we have here and now, and in so doing to generate an even greater awareness of their distinctiveness and diversity. So, if parts of the book seem overly optimistic, then all I can say is that this is how I mean them to be.

I am an early riser and usually go out for a walk just as it is getting light. Much of the thinking about what I hope to write that day happens then. The chain of thought is always punctuated by greetings to and from night guards heading home, or other neighbourhood staff coming early to work. It is also accompanied by the calls of three special African birds, which have become indelibly associated with both walks and thoughts – although I have only seen all three of them in the same morning twice. The first is that of the Montane Nightjar, whose crepuscular trill is usually uttered from a conspicuous perch on the internet lines. Soon after the nightjars have retired, I will often be lucky enough to catch the *kweek* of an African Goshawk, usually so far up in the sky that only by the call do I know it's there, unless the dawn has truly broken. Then, once it is well light, I may hear the distant near-croaking notes of the Hartlaub's Turaco, and very occasionally even see one hopping up a nearby tree before launching itself to glide across the track in front of me, flashing the crimson of its wings as it goes.

It is to these, and all the other birds of Africa, that this book is dedicated.

AFRICA

ACRONYMS USED IN THIS BOOK

BoA – *The Birds of Africa* (Vols I–VII)
BTO – British Trust for Ornithology
BOC – British Ornithologists' Club
K-Pg – Cretaceous-Palaeogene extinction event
DRC – Democratic Republic of the Congo
HBW – *Handbook of the Birds of the World*
IBA – Important Bird and Biodiversity Area

IOC – International Ornithological Congress
mya – million years ago
NGO – Non-Governmental Organisation
PTT – Platform Transmitter Terminal
RSPB – Royal Society for the Protection of Birds
SSG – Site Support Group
SABAP – Southern African Bird Atlas Project

Chapter 1

THE BIRDS
& THEIR LAND

Geological processes have divided the Earth into continents, the second-largest of which is Africa. Zoologists, originally at the instigation of Alfred Russell Wallace, prefer to identify zoogeographic regions on account of their distinctive biodiversity rather than physical boundaries. There are six of these: Palearctic, Indomalayan (or Oriental), Ethiopian (now Afrotropical), Australasian, Nearctic and Neotropical.

In the Americas the continental and zoogeographic regions roughly coincide – North America with the Nearctic and South America with the Neotropical (although this latter includes Central as well as South America). Africa is more complicated: the north coast, Atlas Mountains, Sahara Desert and lower Nile Valley are part of the Palearctic (the largest of the six zoogeographic regions, but with remarkably few bird species for its area – around 1,650). The remaining two-thirds of Africa, together with Madagascar, constitute the Afrotropical region and the home of the birds in this book.

It might have seemed more appropriate if the boundary between the Palearctic and Afrotropical regions had cut through the middle of the Mediterranean Sea, leaving the whole of Africa to comprise its own distinct zoogeographic region. However, the Sahara is actually much more of a natural boundary than the Mediterranean, and just how much good sense this demarcation makes does not take long to appreciate when visiting North Africa.

Some years ago, working in Tunis one spring, I was housed in an out-of-town lodging on the seashore, where my first surprise on walking down to the water's edge was to see a male Common Blackbird hopping along the ground between the bushes, in one of which was a Great Tit. With my northern European origins, neither of these posed any identification problems, nor did the European Robin, European Greenfinch or Common Chaffinch, which soon also appeared. Tunisia is in a bit of a no-man's-land when it comes to bird books, and I was armed with only the Royal Society for the Protection of Birds (RSPB) handbook on *Birds of Britain and Europe*. All the same, most of the birds I would see were covered in this book, and I was also able to use it to find less familiar Palearctic species like Spanish Sparrows, Mediterranean and Yellow-legged gulls, Serins, Spotless Starlings, Subalpine and Sardinian warblers and Black Redstarts.

While Tunisia is full of northern birds at the southern edges of their range, it does work both ways, at least for one or two species that are resident south of the Sahara but have somehow edged their way further north. The Nile provides a continuous flyway up the length of which food supplies are assured, so birds like the Common Bulbul have been able to ease their way out of the Afrotropical region. While this remained a single species, *The Birds of Africa* (*BoA*) described it as 'perhaps the most widespread and abundant bird in Africa'. Even so, I had never expected

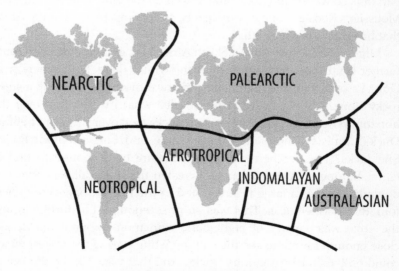

Zoogeographic regions of the world

to see it in Tunisia until one came and almost sat on my boot as I rested in the shade of the walls of an ancient town. There is a strange isolated bulbul population in northwest Africa, of which this was a member – a relic of cooler times, when the Sahara was savanna; and along the Maghreb coast, bird tours also hope to find the Black-crowned Tchagra, which, like the bulbúl, is also much better known further south.

Not surprisingly, with the border between the Palearctic and Afrotropical regions slicing through the Sahara, there are also birds in the Palearctic redolent of semi-desert wastes, with little or no European connection, such as Cream-coloured Coursers, Desert Larks and Buff-rumped (now Red-rumped) and other incredibly difficult-to-identify wheatears. However, the real prize birds are the one or two species endemic to North Africa.

Tunisia has wonderful Roman ruins, and few are more spectacular than those at the hilltop garrison town of Dougga. Here, having settled down under an olive grove on the edge of a grassy meadow, I heard a shrill piping from the other side of a valley, which heralded the arrival of a shepherd blowing his flute as he drove a flock of sheep between the ancient theatre and the remains of the city walls. Was a legion going to follow? Soon after that, I saw a bird hopping along a pile of Roman rubble; it wasn't in my RSPB guide, so I drew it in my notebook. Thank heavens *BoA* covers the whole of the continent, not just the sub-Saharan part of it, so when I got home and looked up the bird, it turned out to be Moussier's Redstart, one of very few birds endemic to continental Africa that breed only in the north.

Migrants find their way to North Africa, too, either pausing en route further south or spending much of the winter there. Somewhere near Douz I stopped for the night, and early next morning set off up a steep rocky slope near my hostel, with no idea what I would find over the horizon. When I was halfway up, two ducks flew over me, from behind. Ducks? Tunisia? Those ducks were large and buff-coloured: Ruddy Shelducks? No, not here, surely – these are hard enough to find in either Europe or Africa. Then, as I crested the ridge, all was revealed: down below was a large reservoir and in the nearest bay were indeed four Ruddy Shelducks. This was surprise enough, but further round the edge was a party of eight dark, cinnamon-coloured ducks, just close enough for me to see the shining white eyes of the males, which could only mean Ferruginous Ducks. And that wasn't to be the last of my wildfowl experiences. Tunisia is actually better watered than one expects, and further south are lush date groves, sometimes irrigated by springs, otherwise by fast-depleting aquifers far underground. Surplus water gushes out from these groves into man-made swamps, and on one of these was a large flock of Marbled Ducks.

Yes, that was in Africa, but in the western *Palearctic* – and this book is essentially about those birds that breed on the continent south of the Sahara.

Inevitably, with Africa being the second-largest continent after Asia, this land below the desert is one of huge topographical contrasts, characterised by relatively small areas of high mountains and comparatively little low-lying land. The continent's present outline can be traced back to the break-up of the ancient supercontinents of Gondwana and Laurasia. These formed and reformed, merged and separated, finally leaving us with the map we know today. More locally, massive underground activity set in train Africa's split from Arabia, as well as the formation of the Great Rift Valley, which now slices through two-thirds of the continent. Spectacular volcanoes erupted along the valley's edges, a few of which, like Ol Doinyo Lengai in northern Tanzania and Nyiragongo near Goma in the Democratic Republic of the Congo (DRC), are still active today. There is evidence of earlier volcanic activity all over East Africa – in the Ethiopian Highlands, mounts Kenya and Kilimanjaro and the Tanzanian Crater Highlands with, on the western side of the Rift Valley, the Virunga and Rwenzori mountains.

Climatically, tropical belts on either side of the equator run almost through the centre of the continent. Within these equatorial latitudes there are usually two rainy seasons: one from March to May and the other in October and November, although 'usually' is hardly a word applicable to climatic regimes any longer. On either side of the tropical belts are subtropical zones, each with one long summer rainy season. These are topped and tailed at both ends of the continent with strips of a milder Mediterranean regime at the Cape and along the Palearctic coast of North Africa, characterised by winter rainfall, short spring and autumn and dry summers.

The continent's present vegetation – or lack of it – can be defined in many different ways. *BoA* recognises six distinct habitats: montane, lowland forest, moist woodlands and savanna, dry woodlands, semi-desert macchia (essentially the bushed Mediterranean grassland at both ends of the continent) and desert. Each of these can be subjectively subdivided still further; for example, montane habitat might include both highland forest and open grassland with shrubby heathland in between.

Rivers and lakes, swamps and marshes drain these terrestrial habitats and provide homes or stopovers for a whole range of water birds. Lake Victoria is the second-largest freshwater lake in the world, Lake Tanganyika the fifth and Lake Malawi the eighth. Strings of freshwater and alkaline lakes have formed in both arcs of the Great Rift Valley, attracting millions of water birds, many of them local or intercontinental migrants. The Niger and Congo rivers drain vast areas of West Africa. In the south, the Limpopo and Zambezi nourish the surrounding lands as they wind their way down to the Indian Ocean. Further north, much of East Africa's water is actually taken by the Nile and it is somewhat counterintuitive to think that the dregs of a coffee cup emptied into a Serengeti stream in Tanzania will end up in the Mediterranean Sea.

Different habitats support different species. Some birds are particularly adaptable: Dark-capped Bulbuls, Helmeted Guineafowl, Klaas's Cuckoos, Red-eyed Doves and African Harrier-Hawks range far across a variety of different landscapes. African Jacanas, Black Crakes and Sacred Ibises peck around the edges of just about any still water on the continent. Other birds only survive in very specific environments, and then often in localised patches of these. At the northern extreme of the Afrotropical region, Blue-winged Geese, Spot-breasted Lapwings, Wattled Ibises and Abyssinian Longclaws are strictly confined to the grassy highlands of Ethiopia. At the southern tip of the continent, where Ground Woodpeckers hop around barren, rock-strewn hillsides with no trace of a tree, are other birds whose ranges are restricted by the Mediterranean climate and the vegetation this supports. Cape Rockjumpers, Protea Canaries, Orange-breasted Sunbirds, among others, cannot survive beyond the belt of fynbos growing along the coast. Between these two extremities of sub-Saharan Africa are the rest of its birds, mostly less localised and certainly less specialised, but no less fascinating.

At least that is how it is at present, as the planet continues to enjoy the warmth of the current interglacial period. Hanging over this are the unknown consequences of human influence on the world climate. On a far grander time scale, the Great Rift Valley could well become inundated with seawater from the Red Sea, eventually flooding its whole length and even carving a huge crescent of land off the eastern flank of the continent.

Birds, along with all other creatures on the continent, have been evolving since life on Earth began, largely in response to the climates and landscapes in which they found themselves. The Jurassic fossils of *Archaeopteryx* (from Bavaria) provided the first basic link between dinosaurs and modern birds; and much better and more recent evidence of their evolutionary progress has since been unearthed in the shale of northern China. However, perhaps the most significant milestone in bird evolution was around 66 million years ago (mya) when an asteroid (maybe several) slammed into the Earth off the Yucatan Peninsula of Mexico, an event referred to as the K-Pg extinction (somewhat confusingly, as K stands for Cretaceous, which was the period ending and giving way to the Palaeogene). Crucially, this set in train the annihilation of the large dinosaurs.

It is variously estimated that between half and three-quarters of the planet's species died out soon after K-Pg, yet frogs, crocodiles and other reptiles, as well as ancestral mammals, lived on; as did those direct descendants of smaller dinosaurs, of which there are today around 11,000 species on Earth – only today they are called birds.

No doubt the effects of K-Pg were felt varyingly in different parts of the world. However, with this huge emptying of ecological niches, the aftermath created rich opportunities for the adaptive radiation of the survivors into a mass of new forms. With the pterosaurs no longer competing with them for airspace, early birds had the skies to themselves, and, like everything else remaining on the planet, began a critical period in their evolution. Seldom can there have been such scope for new species to evolve as there was in the filling of these vacant niches, and the K-Pg avian survivors were ready to diversify. Bony tails were shed, breastbones enlarged to support stronger flight muscles, wings got bigger and legs smaller.

Research shows there to have been a frenzied burst of evolution during the 10 to 15 million years following the K-Pg extinction. The foundation species were relatively few, and probably closely related. However, by 30 mya the great expansion of perching birds (passerines) had long been under way, and doves, penguins, crows and owls would all have looked something like they do now. On the gradually forming continents, new orders of birds emerged, which since then have further branched into the families and species of today.

The birds most closely connected to this continent are those species whose entire families are endemic to Africa, with no close relatives beyond its borders. The world's bird families, the total of which is typically subjective, number around 250. Each family belongs to an order (the even thicker branches on the bird tree), by far the largest of which is the order Passeriformes (6,500 species), passerines being typified by three forward-facing and one back-facing toe, which enables the birds to perch. All the other 4,500 birds make up the remaining 35 or so orders of non-passerines. These include only two exclusively African ones – turacos and mousebirds.

Focusing on endemic, or sometimes near-endemic families means generally excluding the non-breeding migrants, which arrive in Africa as the northern winter sets in, and then leave again as the southern winter looms, to nest elsewhere. Some ornithologists opine that many of these birds actually spend more time here than on their breeding grounds, and are therefore African birds that leave the continent only to breed. My own feeling, though, is that nesting and raising young is what truly links a bird to its land, and those that breed in Africa are at the heart of this book. A few notable migrants – Black Storks, Booted Eagles and European Bee-eaters – have attempted to save themselves the effort, and danger, of the return journey and have successfully established breeding populations in southern Africa. Others, such as House Martins and White Storks, occasionally try this too, but generally with less success.

Many resident bird families, often with multiple species in Africa, such as bustards, bee-eaters, rollers, hornbills, parrots, weavers, barbets, drongos, sunbirds or cisticolas, may seem essentially African to anyone who lives with these birds every day. However, they are all also well represented outside this continent. Some have actually expanded eastwards from Africa, even as far south as Australia, while others may have had their origins in Indomalaya and spread west into Africa. I have nevertheless described several of these families in this book, even if they are not exclusively African.

Deducing the ancestral homes of bird families, and the direction of their spread, is particularly difficult. Jonathan Kingdon grappled with the same question from the mammalian perspective in the introductory chapters to his six volumes of *Mammals of Africa*: 'With 17 of the world's 20 orders of terrestrial mammals – more than any other continent – Africa certainly suits mammals. Does this imply that the first mammals were African? Is Africa the place to find evidence for the evolution of aardvarks, antelopes, apes, bats, giraffes and zebras from a common ancestor? On current knowledge [2013] the answer must be no.'

Tracking the movements of mammals in the distant past is no easy task, but at least it is simpler than trying to trace the ancient flyways of the far more mobile birds.

Modern birds inhabit a particular terrain either because they have colonised it from outside (easier for birds than for most quadrupeds), or because they evolved from ancestors that, for one reason or another, were already there. So, as the supercontinents of Gondwana and Laurasia began to fragment, and slabs of land drifted away from one another, they carried with them many of the ancestors of modern-day birds and animals. A lot of these have continued to evolve, in situ, all the while adapting to the changes going on around them. Others have spread far from their ancestral lands, in search of more suitable habitats, perhaps driven away by population pressures or the consequences of changing climates.

The Indomalayan region shares more families with Africa than it does with any other adjoining region, probably as a consequence of the intervening deserts of Arabia having once been thickly vegetated, and so allowing for the free westward flow of birds into areas well able to support them. When these vegetated areas dried up, easy movement was curtailed and new species began to evolve where the drier climate contained them. Now, the related families are still in place, but each has radiated within its own region into a variety of different species.

Easier to follow is the historic eastward movement of ancestral species out of Africa and into Indomalaya, as evidenced by the current numbers of related species in the different regions – although relative numbers in different regions is not an infallible guide to the direction of evolutionary spread. Of the 17 species of modern honeyguide on the planet, 15 are endemic to Africa, with the remaining two occurring in Asia, and not having been separated long enough to move out of the principal genus of *Indicator*. This almost certainly shows Africa as their ancestral home. Perhaps the same goes for the sunbirds: of about 130 species of true sunbird, over 90 occur only in mainland Africa or surrounding islands, most of the rest in the Indomalayan region, with only one, the Olive-backed Sunbird, crossing Wallace's line between the Indomalayan and Australasian regions, and making it to Australia.

Other examples abound. Of the 30 or so bee-eaters, almost 20 breed in Africa, rather fewer in the Indomalayan region, and again, only one, the Rainbow Bee-eater, in Australia. The family Ploceidae gathers up weavers, bishops, widowbirds and other similar birds, with over 90 per cent of its more than 100 species nesting in Africa. Nearly half the world's 60 hornbills are endemic to Africa, with the rest spread throughout Asia; and while the Papuan Hornbill has got close to Australia, it has yet to make it across the Torres Strait.

However, while Australasia is considered the home of early passerine ancestors, the real diversification of passerines occurred once they had spread away from their ancestral homeland. So, could sunbirds actually have evolved in Indomalaya and spread west into Africa? West-east expansions may be the exception, but that this is the case for pittas seems irrefutable. Nearly 50 species make up the pitta family, Pittidae, all in the Indomalayan region other than two that are endemic to Africa and one to Australia (which region two of the Asian species also reach). And drongos may have expanded in the same way; of 25 or so modern-day drongos, four are African, four more live on islands off Africa and the rest in Indomalaya, of which one, the Spangled Drongo, reaches Australia.

Even harder to chart are the movements of ancestral trogons, barbets and parrots, all of which are represented throughout the tropics. Barbets are now divided into separate New World, Asian and African families. Well over half of the world's 40-plus trogons make their home in the Neotropical region of southern and Central America, a quarter in India and Asia, and only three in Africa. Despite this, both DNA and fossil evidence support Africa as their ancestral home, and all the world's trogons are still in the same family.

Where a bird is widespread throughout different regions, with separate populations which themselves are not yet distinct enough to merit the status of species, its expansion is most likely to have been relatively recent. No better example of dramatic recent expansion exists than that of the Zitting Cisticola, which is described later in the book. Those populations that have been apart for longer are likely show more pronounced differences. Madagascar Fish Eagles clearly derived from African birds, which long ago found their way over the 500 kilometres of water, and are now quite different from their African congeners in both looks and behaviour.

Populations of birds continue to claim new territory. Africa shares very few species with South America, potential migrants being effectively deterred by the 2,800-kilometre journey from one continent to another. For some time there have been two subspecies of Cattle Egret – Eastern and Western. Probably originating from Africa, but possibly from long-established populations in southern Europe, some Western Cattle Egrets managed to cross the Atlantic Ocean to the north coast of South America in the late 1800s. This they used as a launch pad to move up into the Caribbean and North America, where they first bred in the early 1950s, quickly spreading all over the continent. Then, early this century, they established themselves as breeding birds in the UK.

The Eastern subspecies colonised Australia from southeast Asia, reaching New Zealand in 1963. The birds have always tended to migrate long distances after breeding, which clearly helped an expansion founded on the huge global increase in large-scale cattle rearing. Following a major ringing scheme in New South Wales and southern Queensland, written up in *Ostrich* in 1994 by M. Maddock and D. Geering, 11 of these banded birds found their way to New Zealand. Some may even have overshot because they have also been reported in the sub-Antarctic South Sandwich Islands, as well as in South Georgia, and are apparently now the least uncommon of the accidental visitors to the remote south Atlantic outpost of Tristan da Cunha.

Africa is home to a rich array of habitats, offering deserts, savanna, grasslands, rainforests, swamps and high mountains. With such diversity it is no surprise that Africa's fauna and flora are also immensely varied. However, large mammals excepted, it is actually nowhere near as diverse as that of South America. A lot of Africa is desert or semi-desert, and, as a whole, the continent is currently much drier than South America; aside from parts of Ethiopia, it is also much less mountainous. Most of Africa is hot, but rainfall varies enormously and is usually seasonal.

The South American climate is more stable, contributing to a much greater biological productivity that provides birds with year-round feeding and little need to fly away in winter. Three-quarters of South America's land is low-lying, well watered and hot. The Andes backbone runs down the whole length of the continent, providing great variety of habitat from the bare rocky summits through high desert and down to tropical lowland jungle. The Neotropical region, to quote Wallace, 'is distinguished from all the other great zoological divisions of the globe by the small proportion of its surface occupied by deserts, by the large proportion of its lowlands, and by the altogether unequalled extent and luxuriance of its tropical forests'.

So, it follows that bird diversity, at least when measured by numbers of species, is much greater in South America, where around 30 per cent of the world's bird species breed, with Africa nearer 20 per cent. The top seven countries in terms of numbers of bird species recorded within them are all in South America (Colombia, Peru and Brazil are first, second and third) with the DRC, Kenya and Tanzania the top three in Africa and 10th, 11th and 12th, respectively, in the world table. At the family and order level, the continental difference is much less marked, indicating perhaps that a lot of the Neotropical speciation has been fairly recent. Also contributing to this greater diversity may be the relatively late colonisation of South America by human beings (only around 12,000 years ago), while *Homo* has been shaping the African landscape ever since he became *erectus*.

Deciding whether a particular population of birds does or does not constitute a species is a highly subjective exercise, involving consideration of morphology, behaviour, call and genetic analysis. Nonetheless, species are the units of biological diversity and their numbers do at least provide a basis for comparisons, be these by the standards of history, geography, region, nation or any other. To facilitate such comparisons there is a need for a common reference point, and for this I have relied on the International Ornithological Congress (IOC) Checklist.

Comparing list totals over the years helps illustrate how fast reclassification is currently moving: from an initial description in the *Handbook of the Birds of the World* (*HBW*) of 9,972 species, just 20 years later in its 2016 Checklist, the number had risen to 10,964 (6,592 passerines and 4,372 non-passerines). In 1982 *BoA* described 1,850 species that could be sighted in Africa, remarking that none was resident all over the continent and that, somewhat perversely, the most widespread species were actually Palearctic migrants like Barn Swallows. Some thirty years later, BirdLife's 2013 *State of Africa's Birds* reported 2,335 species in Africa; but as the splitting of species continues unabated, a figure of 2,500 is probably more realistic – or just under a quarter of the world's birds.

20

Inevitably, the elevation of subspecies to full species seems set on an upward trend, neatly described as 'taxonomic inflation'. One of the benefits for the birds is that with full species status, they gain a much higher public profile than they ever do as subspecies, and are deemed far worthier of protection. Full species are, of course, also ticks on tens of thousands of lists.

Just one story will well demonstrate not only the taxonomic difficulties in deciding what should or should not join the list of full species but also the pressing need for some sort of universally acceptable classification. On 23rd October 1965, John Beesley was watching a large flock of larks on the dusty plains near Arusha in northern Tanzania. Among them was a party of eight birds that particularly attracted his attention. These had a very short tail, broad wings, and a long, extended neck supporting a large head, and they were active runners; each time he got near them in his car, they would scuttle away, stop, turn, stare and then set off again. Beesley had worked in different parts of Africa and had a continent-wide view of its birds, which was the main reason he was able to ponder whether he might have found an outlying population of Spike-heeled Larks (*Chersomanes albofasciata*). And quite a lot of pondering he must have done because, with the nearest known populations of these birds in eastern Angola or central Botswana, this was not a conclusion to be reached lightly.

A few days later, on 2nd November, he went back to the plains and collected a specimen. This he quickly despatched to England for examination by C.W. Benson, who had just retired from long colonial service in Zambia and Malawi and was soon to take over the management of Cambridge University Museum of Zoology. Benson had the advantage of being able to compare Beesley's specimen with skins of various acknowledged subspecies of *Chersomanes albofasciata* in the British museums. To him, there was no doubt that it was another such subspecies, and he it was who first officially described the bird as a subspecies of Spike-heeled Lark in the 1966 *Bulletin of the British Ornithologists' Club* (BOC), naming it *C. a. beesleyi*.

Benson based his identification largely on the smaller wings and a more streaked chest, reinforcing his opinion in a second paper, 'Further Notes on the Spike-heeled Lark in East Africa', in the 1971 *Bulletin of the BOC*, after receiving a further six specimens from Tanzania. There, Beesley had set about searching 'all the grass plains within a seventy mile radius of Arusha and ... found it on only one other locality'. And so it is today that, other than one further but unconfirmed sighting of the lark in Kenya's nearby Amboseli National Park, these remain the only populations, with a combined number of probably not more than 200 birds.

However, while the boundaries of the lark's known distribution have remained little changed over the last 50 years, its taxonomic status has certainly not, and following its fortunes from one publication to another gives an interesting insight into the promotion of a bird from subspecies to full-blown species – and back again!

The Spike-heeled Lark has always been known as a variable species in itself, with the Southern African Ornithological Society's 1980 checklist including no fewer than 16 subspecies within its range. *BoA* Volume IV, published in 1992, listed 10, of which one was *C. a. beesleyi*. However, when the next major classification appeared in *HBW*, Beesley's Lark was elevated to full species status in Volume 9, published in 2004; then named *Chersomanes beesleyi*, this species joined the Spike-heeled, *Chersomanes albofasciata*, in the genus *Chersomanes*.

So it remained, with some world checklists according it full species status and some not. In 2011 Paul Donald and Nigel Collar had another look at the bird, examining five specimens of *beesleyi* from the Natural History Museum in Britain and comparing them with specimens of other subspecies. In their 'Notes on the Structure and Plumage of Beesley's Lark' in the *African Bird Club Bulletin*, they seemed reluctant to endorse its elevation to full species, concluding that 'The rationale for elevating *beesleyi* to specific status therefore appears to require a more thorough presentation of the evidence'. This, they suggested, should include a detailed assessment of song variation, if any, and the publication of estimates of genetic differences, especially between *beesleyi* and other similar subspecies.

Two years later at least some of the detailed genetic information that had so far been missing from the equation appeared in a paper in *Molecular Phylogenetics and Evolution*, Volume 69. Clearly not intended for amateur consumption, 'Multilocus Phylogeny of the Avian Family Alaudidae (larks) reveals complex morphological evolution, non-monophyletic genera and hidden species diversity' was written by 10 named authors. One of its conclusions was to confirm that the Tanzanian population of *Chersomanes* had long been separated from those further south, 'adding further support to their treatment as separate species'.

However, there are two more chapters to the story. In Volume 2 of the 2016 *HBW Checklist*, *C. a. beesleyi* is back again as a subspecies of the Spike-heeled Lark, accompanied by a note admitting that the 'very rare race *beesleyi*, [was] treated as full species in *HBW* based on [a] suite of supposedly unique characters', when in fact many of these characters were shared with the Spike-heeled Lark. And thus it was, until version 8.1 of the IOC Checklist appeared in 2018, including Beesley's Lark, *Chersomanes beesleyi*, as a full species once again.

So here we have an outlying population of larks, similar enough to others nearly 2,000 kilometres away to assume that once upon a time, climate and vegetation allowed for the continuous distribution of the lark from northern Tanzania all the way down to southern Africa. This in itself is a fascinating thought, and whether we are talking about species or subspecies, this outpost of *Chersomanes* larks, so far from any other, is deserving of the highest degree of protection – something the community-managed Beesley's Lark Conservation Program of Engikaret is trying to accord it.

While the focus of this book is on families of African birds, there are a few individual species that have somehow come to epitomise Africa, even though they have relatives elsewhere, and commentaries on these appear too. Some are incredibly rare and hard to find. The revelation of the Congo Peacock to the ornithological community is one of the greatest bird stories of the twentieth century, followed not far behind by that of the Udzungwa Forest Partridge in northern Tanzania some 30 years ago. Other birds are included for the very reason that they are extremely well known. Familiarity may breed contempt for birds like the Hadada Ibis and Egyptian Goose, but it is just such familiarity that makes these birds so African. There are no endemic raptor families in Africa other than the Secretarybird, but the unmistakable silhouette of a Bateleur soars over the savannas throughout most of the continent, while the ringing cry of the African Fish Eagle lodges in the memory of anyone who hears it, and both these species are given space.

Madagascar, however, is beyond the reach of this book, notwithstanding its also being part of the Afrotropical region. Considering its size and variety of habitat, Madagascar is low on numbers of bird species but certainly not on the proportion of these that are endemic – over half of its 220 or so breeding birds. This is largely a consequence of the island having been isolated for so long and also difficult to reach, which neither woodpeckers nor barbets nor hornbills have ever done. The vangas are one of Madagascar's most distinctive and varied bird families, with some 20 species. Open up Volume 14 of *HBW* at page 165 and there is an array of birds that surely only a taxonomical aberration could have grouped into a single family. Yet they belong to just one, the Vangidae.

The Buffet de la Gare at Perinet Railway Station was a hotel when I first visited Madagascar over 20 years ago, as it had been in 1985 when it hosted Prince Philip, Duke of Edinburgh, then president of the World Wildlife Fund, and in 1990 when it welcomed author and conservationist Gerald Durrell (later to relate his adventures in Madagascar in *The Aye-Aye and I*). The Perinet Special Reserve (also referred to locally as Andasibe) is about three hours' drive east of Antananarivo and is best known for its sounds and sightings of one of the island's largest lemurs, the Indri. I remember, as if it were this morning, how their almost whale-like song rang out through the forest as we set off on our first walk. I also remember, just as clearly, the vangas.

All vangas live in forests and often travel in mixed multi-species parties that may or may not include other vangas. The Hook-billed was the first on my list, a less sociable bird than most other vangas; it is conspicuously black-and-white but one could never see the hook without having the bird in one's hand. The Red-tailed is distinctly shrike-like and it is no surprise to see that it was once known as a Red-tailed Shrike. The White-headed is plainer, slightly reminiscent of a crestless helmetshrike and was, I noted, whistled up most expertly by guide Patrice; Chabert's is small, also black-and-white with a pale blue wattle round the eye. The Blue is blue-and-white, the male looking out through eyes with pale blue irises to match, and is the only vanga to be found outside Madagascar, reaching two of the Comoros Islands. The Nuthatch Vanga behaves rather than looks like its tree-climbing nuthatch namesake, and the Tylas is a nondescript mix of black head, grey back and buff chest.

I had seen seven wonderfully different vangas in one forest, and a living tribute to the principle of adaptive radiation where many species evolve from a single founding population. I was also able to add to my list of Perinet birds a Cuckoo Roller (the only species in its family), which was surprisingly difficult to find, considering how vocal it is when one does find it. I went to Madagascar again a few years later and saw one more vanga, the Rufous Vanga, in Kirindy on the west coast, but I still haven't seen the two most magnificent ones – the much more localised Sickle-billed and Helmeted vangas.

The whole family evolved from an original founding population, which arrived from mainland Africa perhaps 20 mya. The vangas are now far removed from any of the African birds of today, for these, too, have been on journeys of change over the last 20 million years – as indeed they still are.

Evolution never stands still and few species are as they were many millions of years ago, nor as they will be so many million years hence. The subspecies of today are the species of tomorrow. The birds in this or any other book are like stills taken from the moving film of their own evolution.

Chapter 2

ONLY IN AFRICA

Here are stories of the most essentially African birds, introduced by way of their families. According to both my sources and senses, there are 24 of these families, all members of which breed in Africa. Some taxonomists would not give ground hornbills their own family, nor helmetshrikes, and others group some of the smaller birds differently. However, these are questions of systematics, and much more important is to focus on the birds calling sub-Saharan Africa their home, no matter how they are taxonomically grouped.

Saying that all members of a family breed here need not imply that they breed here exclusively. In one or two instances, breeding ranges stretch beyond Africa; so the Hamerkop is also resident in Madagascar and Arabia, and the nesting territory of the Black-crowned Tchagra stretches well into the Arabian peninsula. Until comparatively recently, ostriches, too, were running wild far beyond the borders of Africa – but sadly no longer do so.

For the sake of completeness, there is something written on each of these 24 families, although one or two of those further down the list, comprising lesser-known species, get much less attention than the more prominent ones.

The families are dealt with in taxonomic order. The first five need no introduction at all – ostriches, guineafowl, Hamerkop, Shoebill and Secretarybird. The Egyptian Plover has only recently been awarded its own family, which is certainly not the case with the turacos, mousebirds and wood hoopoes – all distinctive groups of birds with well-defined boundaries. Ground hornbills and African barbets are two families that were once part of larger ones. The components of the family of batises and wattle-eyes together are far from clear; there is agreement as to what is or is not a helmetshrike, but not on whether they are deserving of their own family, while the composition of the family of bushshrikes has varied considerably over the years.

The two species of picathartes are spectacularly different from any other bird in the world; less exceptional are rockjumpers, nicators, crombecs and their allies, yellow flycatchers and the Dapple-throat and its two allies. How to treat what are now the families of sugarbirds and hyliotas has long vexed taxonomists. Oxpeckers have posed fewer problems, as have whydahs and indigobirds, although the Cuckoo-finch has always been a bit of an outlier.

If families seem deserving of inclusion in this chapter, but are missing, then they are most likely in the next, which covers those that are almost, but not quite, endemic to this continent. That is where flufftails, honeyguides, cisticolas and other near-African families are given space. The sands of taxonomy are forever shifting, and deciding on the composition of bird families seems to be as much of a subjective exercise as settling on what does or does not deserve to be a species. Until a single, streamlined system of classification comes about, this is how it will be.

Ostriches
Struthionidae

It is hard to imagine birds any more different from all others in Africa than ostriches, the largest birds in the world. Most sources now describe two species, the Somali Ostrich of Ethiopia, Somalia and northeastern Kenya, and the Common Ostrich over the rest of the ostrich range. The two have repeatedly been split and merged, split and merged, and recently split again on the grounds mainly of the greyer skin and more vivid black plumage of the Somali bird. Apparently, the split is now also supported by genetic evidence, not available to earlier taxonomists who, in keeping them in a single species, might also have been taking into account that the two are known to have interbred successfully.

The ostriches have their own two-species genus, *Struthio*, and family, Struthionidae, which itself may even be so different as to merit its own single-family order – and this when there are only about 35 or so bird orders on Earth. Alternative taxonomy might group them into a family with the rest of the living ratites, which includes the rheas of South America, cassowaries and the Common Emu of Australia and New Guinea, and the tiny (by comparison) kiwis of New Zealand.

Sadly, other ratites have lived and died to prove that flightlessness is often incompatible with the spread of human beings and the animals that accompany them – domesticated or otherwise. One might think that being large would have provided moas with some immunity from persecution, but the first wave of immigrants probably reached New Zealand only 800 years ago, and not much more than 100 years later, all estimated nine species of moa had disappeared. Humans arrived in Madagascar from Indonesia rather earlier, perhaps 2,000 years ago, and took longer to exterminate at least seven species of the enormous elephant bird, but by 1700 they, too, had gone for good.

Ostriches have fared better than the moas and elephant birds, not least because their range was once far more extensive than that of either of these other ratites. That said, they owe their inclusion in this chapter on quintessentially African birds to the sad fact that it took the disappearance of wild ostriches from Arabia to confine their distribution within the limits of the African continent. And this, believe it or not, was only in the middle of the twentieth century, when the last of the Arabian birds finally succumbed to the same combination of firearms, cross-country motor vehicles and the perverted definition of hunting that sent the Arabian oryx and Saudi gazelle to extinction in the wild.

Ratites lack flight muscles as well as a keel on their breastbone to which these would otherwise be anchored (*ratis* is Latin for 'raft'). Their feathers lack the barbicels that on other birds zip together the strands growing from the quills, so giving their plumage the soft and fluffy texture that has made it such a success in the fashion industry. The birds do not need to oil such feathers, and thus lack a preen gland. Other features peculiar to the ostriches include legs ending with only two toes, making their feet particularly well adapted to running faster than any other bird in the world. They also have huge eyes (the largest of any terrestrial animal) and a unique breeding strategy.

Despite their flightlessness, ostriches retain substantial wings out of which grow 16 black-and-white primary feathers, as opposed to the usual 10 on birds that fly. Emus have no wing quills at all and cannot even flap what remains of their wings; and the moas' wings had also degenerated into useless little stumps by the time the birds disappeared. Male ostriches make the most of these vestigial wings, particularly during the breeding season, by spreading them out in mating display to females, or in threat to other males encroaching on their territory. These threats are often accompanied by neck swaying and loud hissing noises or booming calls.

Within his territory, a male may scrape out several nests in one of which, after mating, the female lays her enormous eggs – the yolk being the largest single-cell organism in the animal world. Despite their size, these still weigh less than two per cent of the adult's weight (in contrast to those of the Kiwi, which are proportionately among the heaviest in the avian world, at nearer 20 per cent of the weight of the bird that laid them).

The 'major hen', as the main mate is referred to, usually lays an egg every other day for up to a fortnight, during which time several other females ('minor hens') may also visit the nest – and possibly other nests too – to drop eggs. By the time all these visitors have finished, there may be far more eggs than the maximum of roughly 20 that any female can sit on – one nest in Nairobi National Park was recorded to hold 78 eggs of which only 21 were incubated. An intriguing aspect of this extraordinary behaviour is that the major hen seems able to recognise her own eggs from those of all the interlopers; these receive preferential treatment in that she ensures that they remain in the middle of the nest. Strange eggs take their chances on the periphery where there is not only very little likelihood of their being successfully incubated, but they will also be easiest for any predators to target.

Evolution could have done better than end up with off-white-coloured eggs, which are easily visible from afar. Perhaps they are on the way to becoming more cryptically coloured, but until then, the adults need to protect them at all times from the attentions of hyenas and jackals, as well as Egyptian Vultures, which have learnt to break open the shells using stones. Humans, too, have historically found a use for the shells. Once blown, they make excellent vessels for carrying liquid, as was discovered by the San and other Bushmen of southern Africa. Heaps of eggshell fragments in middens along the Atlantic coast of Namibia and South Africa also testify to their importance in decoration.

Incubation is shared by both sexes, the drab brown female doing most of the daytime sitting, leaving the black male to take over at night. The eggs, despite having been laid over a period of some two weeks, all hatch more or less simultaneously, and it is only a matter of three or four days before the adults are taking these football-sized balls of fluff out into the wider world. Sometimes their group of young meet up with and join other groups, together forming a substantial nursery gathering in which they remain as they grow.

Many African fossils of close ostrich relatives have been found, particularly in Tanzania and Namibia, which testify to the bird's long association with this continent. Fossil ancestors have also been unearthed in Europe, which is not surprising, considering that within the last 5,000 years ostriches thrived in and around the Middle East and that *Struthio asiaticus* seems to have been distributed as far as China, maybe even as recently as during the last Ice Age. More surprising is the recent find of a 50-million-year-old chicken-sized, ostrich-like ancestor in Wyoming, which, although similar, is different enough not to have ended up in the *Struthio* genus, but rather as *Calciavis grendei*.

While the final disappearance of ostriches from outside Africa happened little more than 70 years ago, humankind's influence on the bird goes back thousands of years, largely as a consequence of its remarkable feathers. There are fragments of nature that prove irresistible to human curiosity, and a feather is just one of these. Ever since people first shared the same expanse of Earth with flightless ostriches, they have stooped to collect the durable and decorative feathers.

So it was that most traditional societies living alongside ostriches decorated their headgear with moulted feathers, as and when they became available. Egyptian art evidences the use of ostrich feathers as adornment, and the unusual symmetry of the wing feathers made them appropriate symbols of justice. There was in these times probably no thought of killing an ostrich for its feathers, although with the gradual improvement in weaponry and hunting techniques it became much easier to target them for meat. As humans began to travel beyond their own home territories, the attractions of ostrich plumes were gradually revealed to those who lived far outside the bird's native range. Returning soldiers would bring back plunder and pillage, some of which astounded their compatriots who began to demand more of these objects from afar. Military might was often the precursor to commercial contact, and the Roman Empire created a ready market for both the feathers and the birds, which were also brought in to pull chariots round the track in the Circus Maximus.

Several centuries later, the Crusaders set forth from Europe under the banner of Christianity, and of all the loot they wished to carry home, ostrich plumes were the easiest to transport. These quickly found their way onto helmets, and later the hats and hair of their wives and admirers, and then even into the crest of the Prince of Wales. Inevitably, a time would come when demand could only be satisfied by killing the birds, and so their range began to contract. By the end of the nineteenth century, when feathered fashion was at its zenith, there were hardly any ostriches left in North Africa. At this point, serendipitously, the commercial feather industry came to the rescue of the remaining wild populations.

The first serious efforts to tame ostriches were made by European settlers in South Africa. As early as 1750, pet ostriches could be found grazing around the homesteads of Boer farmers in the Cape Province, but these were usually orphaned chicks, and not kept specifically for their feathers. Then, just over a century later, settlers in both Algiers and South Africa seem almost simultaneously to have succeeded in breeding the birds in captivity, followed soon by Australian farmers. From then on South Africa quickly gained pre-eminence in the industry, a status it has retained ever since, reaching its apogee in 1913 when an estimated 775,000 domesticated birds produced over one million pounds of feathers at an average price of nearly three pounds sterling per pound of feathers. Then, ostrich feathers were South Africa's fourth most valuable export after gold, diamonds and wool. But the First World War sent demand crashing and by 1930 there were only about 30,000 domesticated birds left. (Details of the ups and downs of ostrich farming in South Africa are found in *Ostrich Farming in the Little Karoo* by D.J. v Z. Smit, published as 'Bulletin 358' in 1963 by the Department of Agricultural Technical Services.)

Now, with farms also in the USA, Israel, India, parts of Europe and South America, as well as elsewhere in southern Africa, the ostrich-rearing industry has diversified into skin and meat production. The advent of feather dusters has helped sustain the demand for feathers, which still adorn headgear in Brazil's Rio Carnival. The skin has secured a reputation for producing one of the supplest leathers for handbags, wallets, belts, briefcases, shoes and cowboy boots, and often represents more than half the value of the carcass. The meat is particularly low in fat and cholesterol content. The best cuts come not from the breast – ostriches being particularly flat-chested – but from the fillets along the back. Blown eggs adorn dressers and tables; and even ostrich corneas and tendons are used in medical transplants or research.

Commercial ostrich farming has had its ups and downs, with a lot of busts after occasional booms, but given how fast the elephant birds and moas disappeared, it seems no exaggeration to say that the wild birds owe their continued existence to the success in domesticating their fellows.

Guineafowl
Numididae

The six (or, according to some sources, eight) species of guineafowl occupy just about the whole of sub-Saharan Africa. There was once an outlying population of Helmeted in Morocco but not any more. The heart rates of many bird watchers have been upped by the sight of guineafowl in Moroccan villages, but these are domesticated ones, carrying very few of the genes of the subspecies *Numida meleagris subyi*. The Helmeted is easily the most widespread and adaptable, absent only from the Congo forests and much of the West African coast, which are the domain of the Black, Plumed and White-breasted.

Crested are patchily distributed over a wide area of lightly forested country, such discontinuous distribution having given rise to sufficient differences in populations for some sources to split them into three

species – Western, Eastern and Southern. The splendid Vulturine Guineafowl are confined to Ethiopia, Somalia and dry terrain in eastern Kenya and northern Tanzania. One day, showing a guest around Tsavo West National Park in Kenya, we spotted, in quick succession, scuttling parties of Helmeted and Vulturine, and in the evening, at the foot a heavily treed slope, also found Crested members of the family.

Some characteristics of guineafowl behaviour are common to all species, wherever they live. The birds are essentially terrestrial and endearingly gregarious; they roost together in trees, and exhibit no obvious differences in male and female plumage. They are reluctant flyers but surprisingly mobile on the ground, particularly those occupying drier, more open country, which is far easier to run through than forest understorey.

The forest species are far less studied than the rest, and much of what is known about them is thanks to the work of James Paul Chapin. In the first volume of *Birds of the Belgian Congo*, Chapin writes of 'the difficulty of finding or observing the Black Guineafowl in its forested haunts', and how he relied on the birds being called up by his local aide imitating their soft whistle. The same ruse was used to attract Plumed Guineafowl, which responded to calls made by one of his scouts, Corporal Baginza, who 'closing both nostrils with his fingers ... gave a loud, nasal "kow!", repeated it several times, and then waited' for the birds to answer – which they did, ultimately leading to their 'dodging along beneath the undergrowth, directly toward their deceiver ... till they came within a couple of yards of the soldier'. Chapin could then collect specimens for further analysis of gender, diet and breeding condition, as well as of the taste of the flesh, which he claimed, for both species, was 'rather dry eating' with 'a peculiar strong flavour, due possibly to something they eat, such as the ants usually found in the crop'.

The Helmeted is the flag-bearer for its family. Being so widespread and living out in relatively open countryside, it is by far the best studied, and in the absence of knowledge to the contrary, its characteristics tend also to be attributed to other species. Its sequence of daily activities has been observed by many naturalists, from leaving the tree-top roost in the morning, through drinking, feeding – on a surprisingly omnivorous diet of seeds and insects and other invertebrates – dusting, preening, resting, becoming active again and then retiring back to the tree of roost.

Other than in North Africa, the Helmeted Guineafowl remains reasonably secure in its wide range, despite having been classed as one of Africa's premier game birds. Frederick Jackson (or William Sclater, who edited and completed *Birds of Kenya Colony and the Uganda Protectorate*) relates how a'Mr F. Holmwood, H.M. Consul at Zanzibar, bagged twenty-two birds with a double shot in the brown of a flock that he surprised from above ...'. Surprise is the essence of a successful stalk because guineafowl are actually quite difficult to get near on foot, with or without a shotgun, as they run so fast in front of anyone approaching. Those who catch birds to eat because they need the food – a common practice in both forest and savanna – usually fashion snares baited with seeds.

The nests of the White-breasted and Black have yet to be described, but there is no reason to think that they would not also scratch out a leaf-lined hollow on the forest floor, as does the Plumed. Chapin was brought eggs, or collected adult females with eggs inside them, but never found the nests themselves. Otherwise, all other guineafowl prepare a shallow scrape in the ground. At the risk of anthropomorphising, but without any apology for doing so, one can imagine that, having spent every night of their grown lives roosting in trees, guineafowl must be in for a nerve-racking shock as they begin the terrestrial existence of a ground breeder, suddenly surrounded by all the predators that a tree-top roost was designed to evade.

Incubation starts after the last egg is laid, which means that all the young will hatch more or less simultaneously. It is entirely the female's work, the male apparently guarding his partner while she sits, and perhaps bringing her occasional morsels of food. He will do his best to defend her against attacks from monkeys, various cats, birds of prey and mongooses, because a sitting guineafowl and her clutch of eggs are perfect prey for any number of predators. When the young hatch they are almost immediately ready to leave the nest, such early-leaving chicks being ornithologically described as 'nidifugous'. A whole range of different predators then threatens the brood. Keeping control of a dozen or more far-ranging chicks is largely the male's work, giving the female time to recover strength from her confinement to the nest, although she seems to take over parental responsibilities at night, allowing the male to fly back up to his tree roost. By the age of three weeks, the chicks are strong enough fliers also to be able to take to the trees for the night.

Guineafowl, particularly Helmeted, are easily domesticated and have long been farmed for their flesh, even though much of their bulk is feathers. They lay many eggs, a fact that has elevated them to symbols of fertility, and their feathers have always been in high demand for adornment. Vulturine neck feathers are much sought after in the fishing-fly industry: at one time I made earrings from fishing flies, and any number of fishermen in England would write asking where they could get these feathers, which were an essential component of a salmon or sea-trout fly, called an 'elver', tied to imitate a young eel.

Hamerkop
Scopidae

The Hamerkop is not endemic to Africa, living and breeding as it does in southern Arabia and Madagascar too. However, for all that it haunts the dry watercourses of parts of Yemen and Saudi Arabia, where it often has to nest on cliffs for want of a decent tree, it remains quintessentially a bird of this continent – and very widespread too. No hacking through the Congolese jungle or the papyrus swamps of the Sudd to find one, rather just head out to a shrinking muddy pool or the bare banks of a summer stream anywhere in sub-Saharan Africa, and there may be a Hamerkop.

Water – that is the bird's only essential, and occasionally it even seems prepared to forage on the seashore. Wetlands are being drained at alarming rates in Africa, usually to make way for intensive agriculture. However, if this involves a new rice scheme, it will not be long before Hamerkops turn up, at least until they are driven away by overuse of pesticides. Fish farms don't welcome them either, but that still leaves a great deal of watery habitat for the birds to exploit.

I know I am not alone in sometimes confusing a distant overflying Hamerkop with a Hadada Ibis, until one or the other chooses to communicate. Those who try bravely to reproduce bird sounds in writing must really struggle with the Hamerkop's call: it is variously described in the handbooks I use as 'a loud strident yelping', 'a far-carrying *kylp*' or 'a sharp *kiep*'!

Because it is one of the easiest birds for specimen shooters to collect, the bird was unsurprisingly christened earlier than most other African species. In 1760, from a skin obtained in West Africa, Frenchman M.J. Brisson coined its generic name, *Scopus*, and only later, after considerable taxonomic juggling, did it finally become *Scopus umbretta*, probably from the Greek *skopos*, a watcher, and French *ombrette*, which seems to combine both the word for 'shade' and also for the earthy brown colour 'umber'. Since then it has answered to 'hammerhead', 'hammerkopf', 'anvilhead', even 'umber bird', until finally the Afrikaans name 'Hamerkop' (with a single 'm') won out. Now two distinct subspecies have been recognised: *S. u. minor* from the coast of West Africa and *S. u. umbretta* everywhere else.

The essential role of European scientists in making some sense of the mass of information being relayed back from the front line of exploration can well be imagined in the case of the Hamerkop. Early West African specimens arrived in France, and from these the bird was named; then, many years later, some other centre of European learning received a skin from southern Arabia, whose collector was claiming a new species. Someone, somewhere had to link the two, although doing so made it no easier to decide how to classify the bird.

In due course, similarities were noticed in the ridges and hooks on the broad upper mandibles of Hamerkops, Shoebills (as they are now called) and the Boat-billed Herons of South and Central America. This had some taxonomists claiming they were all related; but were these really indicators of descent from a common ancestor or, as seemed more likely, simply a case of the independent evolution of similar beaks in the course of adapting to similar swampy environments? Certainly, the latter is probable as far as the heron is concerned. Molecular evidence now links Hamerkops more closely to Shoebills and also to pelicans than to any other birds, although some would argue that the Hamerkop's beak actually evolved as a tool for nest building rather than feeding!

The Hamerkop has another history that reaches further back than any European presence in Africa. Traditionally, probably more so than any other bird on the continent, it has inspired a combination of both dread and respect among local people throughout almost the whole of its range. This is probably the main reason for its being so seldom persecuted, which in turn must contribute to its widespread distribution.

Renowned Zulu sangoma Vusamazulu Credo Mutwa describes how, in his community, the bird's appearance is an ill omen. If one flies over a house, it is bringing a message of death or other impending misfortune. This news, suggest the Khoi of southwest Africa, may be divined by the bird as it stands motionless at the water's edge, gazing at the surface – a habit that has also turned it into a Zulu symbol of human pride and vanity.

36

The tradition of the mythical Lightning Bird – or *impundulu* in Zulu – is widespread throughout southern Africa. While the bird is envisaged in some parts as a large, dangerous, vampire-like creature, elsewhere it lives in all its flesh and feathers in the physical body of the Hamerkop (*uthekwane*). Sometimes the Hamerkop attracts lightning strikes to the very place where it was last seen; elsewhere it is held that Hamerkop nest raiders will be struck by lightning, while in eastern Zimbabwe, anyone burning such a nest is condemned to follow the displaced bird until dying of exhaustion.

Frederick Jackson was seldom short of a story about the more prominent birds in his book. He describes a nest on the Turkwel River in northern Kenya, which one of his gun-bearers was reluctantly preparing to pillage, when a porter hurriedly dumped his load and volunteered for the job. Initially baffled by the offer, Jackson was then struck with a possible explanation for the porter's enthusiasm: following the 'widespread native tradition that this bird, like the Jackdaw, carries off all sorts of things to its nest, such as knives or anything bright', might the porter be hoping to find treasure there?

In fact, the reward for the nest raider was a small stick, whitewashed with droppings, which he carefully removed, wrapped and placed in his pocket, seemingly well satisfied with his find. Still, the bird's habit of adorning its nest with odd plastic bags, bits of cloth or empty tins is widely recognised. Clarkson Tredgold, pre-independence Rhodesian lawyer and politician, presumably had to dismantle a nest to find that 'in the ceiling of the dome there were two tram tickets, red and blue, issued 100 miles from the nest, but presumably dropped there by some [passerby]'.

Constructing such a huge home has imbued the bird with magical powers for all sorts of reasons. To create a home that keeps its occupants both safe and hidden is seen as a major achievement in itself, easily comparable to similar human endeavours. However, at issue is whether the bird actually makes its own nest, or rather uses a gang of other unemployed Hamerkops, or even of other species, to do the construction work. Such organisation would be worthy of even more respect, and good reason for the Hamerkop to become one of many contenders for the title of 'the King of Birds'. This title, Chapin relates, was bestowed upon it by the Mangbetu people of eastern Congo, and Jackson heard of a similar accolade for the bird from the headman of a village near Lamu on the Kenyan coast.

Renowned Kenyan cinematographer Alan Root produced a masterly film on *The Legend of the Lightning Bird*, in which he showed several different species of bird visiting the Hamerkop's nest, either to pinch sticks for other nests (Silverbirds) or to see if the nest itself might be suitable for their own purposes (Verreaux's Eagle-Owls, Grey Kestrels or Egyptian Geese). If all these visitors were actually thought to be contributing materials to the nest, it is not hard to see how its true architect came to be hailed as the King of Birds. The mystique surrounding the Hamerkop was further enhanced by the sort of finishing touches it added to the roof, which included porcupine quills, animal hooves, bones and even a dead wildebeest's tail – trappings more usually associated with the activities of traditional doctors than birds bent on raising a family.

By its nest we know the Hamerkop, but why the bird builds such an enormous one remains a wonderful mystery. It is the only species in the genus, *Scopus*, which is the only genus in the family, Scopidae, so there are no clues to be gathered from the nest-building habits of close relatives. Some protection from sun and rain, as well as from predators, are certainly positive consequences of going to all that trouble, and there may be room to raise a larger clutch of eggs inside – nearer the maximum of seven – than could be done on an open platform of twigs and grass. An enclosed nest might also mean both parents can leave chicks in the nest and go off fishing, rather than one of them always having to stay behind to protect the offspring. And more time spent gathering food perhaps means being able to raise more chicks. However, none of this conjecture answers the simple question – why build so very big?

Could it be that it is actually the *process* of building that is important, rather than the end result? Is it the journey of construction rather than the completed nest that is at the heart of all this effort? Information on lifelong fidelity is sparse, but if Hamerkops mate for life, it doesn't take an anthropomorphist to imagine how building so many huge nests together must immensely strengthen any pair bond and sense of mutual understanding.

The first of surprisingly few detailed studies of Hamerkops actually building nests was that of R. Liversidge, published in the 1963 *Ostrich*, Volume 34. The nest he observed in the spring of 1959 was near Uitenhage in the Eastern Cape, and was sited in such a way as to allow easy access for bringing in building materials and ultimately also to enable smooth entry for the birds through the hole. It was notable for two inbuilt ledges within it, but no partitions between different areas. This countered the traditional wisdom of the Xhosa people who believed each nest to comprise three rooms: one for eating, another for raising the young and the third a day room.

Root's film appeared in the early 1980s and showed the complete construction of a nest in northern Tanzania, during which he calculated that, based on an average of 100 metres travelled for every collection of material, each of the birds flew nearly 500 kilometres to complete the nest. Then R.T. Wilson and M.P. Wilson produced a paper, *Nest Building by the Hamerkop*, for the 1986 *Ostrich*, summarising their observations of Hamerkops on an irrigated rice scheme in Mali from 1978 to 1983. Along the roadsides had been planted African mahogany trees in which the birds built their nests. The nest site was usually in the fork of a tree, and its suitability was certainly governed by factors other than height above the ground, this varying between 2 and 14 metres. The direction of the entrance hole also differed widely, seeming to depend simply on the structure and orientation of the supporting branches, so perhaps helping to counter the traditional belief that the birds wished to be woken or warmed by the rising sun. The nest must always be sited so that birds can enter it easily, which they do by neatly folding their wings at the last minute in what has been described as 'an upward dive'. This looks a tricky manoeuvre which, if the bird fails to 'hole out in one' – as C.F. Belcher put it in his *Birds of Nyasaland* – is traditionally thought to result in its abandoning the nest and building another one elsewhere.

Hamerkops are invariably most active in their nest building between dawn and 10 a.m. and then from 4 p.m. to dusk. The essential building materials obviously depend on availability; in Mali this was mainly rice straw, but birds nesting on river banks might make repeated visits to piles of flood debris, where sticks and branches of all sizes are stacked up together. Both sexes work on construction, although it is often impossible to distinguish one from the other, the only difference between them being that the female may be slightly larger. They build for anything between 25 and 60 days, with the nest that Liversidge watched taking 40 to complete. The last days are usually spent lining the inside with mud, leaves and grass, and perhaps adding decoration, whether in the form of tram tickets, coins, or more likely tins and plastic bags. In this instance, the male continued adding material even after the chicks had hatched. Nests have been reported to contain up to 8,000 items and weigh 25 to 50 kilograms. Size generally means strength, and strength means durability from one year to the next, so perhaps the last word is best left to Richard Meinertzhagen, who found in Yemen that 'An Arab standing on the nest and even jumping on it failed to make any impression'!

The Hamerkop's nest is so conspicuous, and its building efforts so protracted, that neither can go unnoticed. The Tswana have a proverb, *Bopelonomi bo bolayile mmamasiloanoka*, 'kindness killed the Hamerkop', in recognition of the number of other creatures that take advantage of its nest construction at one stage or another. Verreaux's Eagle-Owls may hijack the nest a few days into building, while other species, particularly Barn Owls, await its completion before moving in; at least Egyptian Geese only take over once the Hamerkop has finished breeding. Grey Kestrels have been known to rear their young on top of a nest, and sparrows at its edges, at the same time as the Hamerkops are raising their brood in the chamber below. Other animals – snakes, genets, monitor lizards – rest up in abandoned Hamerkop nests, and it is easy to see how Malawian tradition has it that the nest is full of partitions, creating separate 'rooms', one of which is always occupied by a snake.

Nest building is, needless to say, a precursor to egg laying, which means that any leftover energies are used for mating. Courtship displays can be protracted, often involving much 'false mounting' in which either bird jumps on top of the other's back without any attempt to mate, or make 'cloacal contact'. This may be a prelude to actual mating, but it also takes place well outside the breeding season.

Feeding is either a solitary or paired occupation. Amphibians, small fish, large insects, anything that might live in shallow water or the mud it covers make fair food. Particularly favoured are the widespread African clawed frogs of the genus *Xenopus*, so called from the claws on the end of their feet which they use to tear up scraps of food. This preference has given rise to one of the old Dutch names for the Hamerkop: *Paddavanger* – 'frog catcher'. In fact, there is such a strong correlation between the distributions of the Hamerkop and frog that the birds could be seen as specialist feeders on the frog or its tadpoles. Because they are so little persecuted, Hamerkops are often comfortable around humans, and while they are not normally social, I was astounded to see over 30 of them waiting for scraps of fish from brightly clad women cleaning and gutting tilapia and Nile perch at Mbita Point on the shores of Lake Victoria.

The beak upon which taxonomists have placed so much reliance allows the bird to probe around in water and mud, where it may disturb small fish and then snatch these up, unaccompanied by beak-loads of weed. Sometimes feeding is by stationary ambush, like that of a heron, but more often it involves swishing gently under the surface to disturb fish and grabbing them as they flee. Unusually, Hamerkops also feed by flying upwind across the water with slow wing beats and snatching prey such as tadpoles from just under the surface, almost as terns would. This is facilitated by the birds' having a very low ratio of body mass to wing surface area, which enables much more agile flying than the leisurely beat of their wings would suggest. At Lake Paradise, in Kenya's Marsabit National Park, I have watched at least six Hamerkops fishing together in this way, seeming to expend a huge amount of energy for very little return. However, in the lake lower down, one bird was finding plenty of food from its perch on the back of a buffalo while the animal wallowed in the shallows.

Remember, though, that if a Hamerkop crosses your path, you might be well advised to turn around and abandon any plans for the day.

Shoebill
Balaenicipitidae

'I have the pleasure of introducing to the notice of the Society on the present occasion the most extraordinary bird I have seen for many years, and which forms part of a collection made on the banks of the upper part of the White Nile by Mansfield Parkyns, Esq. of Nottingham. For this bird I propose the generic name of *Balaeniceps*.'

So John Gould, artist, taxidermist and ornithologist, and best known for his works on Australian birdlife, announced the identification of what is today called the Shoebill, in a paper in the 1851 *Proceedings of the Zoological Society*. He went on to complete the binomial as *Balaeniceps rex* – combining the Latin *balaena*, meaning 'whale', and *ceps,* the combination form of *caput,* 'head'; then, perhaps in true awe of what he had seen, adding *rex,* 'king', for the species name. Embellishing his description was a fine illustration of adult and chick, both with rather over-yellow bills, on a riverbank nest.

Gould was happy to acknowledge the provider of his raw materials – it was quite usual for travellers to collect and scientists at home to analyse and classify. Mansfield Parkyns had been in Egypt, Abyssinia and Ethiopia for three years, from 1843 to 1846, during which he integrated himself completely with the local people, possibly even marrying one. In that time, he either personally collected skins of the bird or otherwise acquired them from traders. He would later relate his adventures in *Life in Abyssinia – being notes collected during three years residence and travels in that country.*

The specimen that had so excited Gould was of a very large bird, weighing over five kilograms when alive, and standing nearly one-and-a-half metres tall. Its plumage was all blue-grey, paler on the chest; and on the back of the great head was a faint tuft of a crest, giving the bird its name 'whale-headed'. The most awesome of all its features was the huge beak, nearly 20 centimetres long. Gould was probably unaware then that the Arabic name for the bird was *Abu markub*, meaning 'one with a shoe'. He then went on to describe how the bird had 'toes four in number, all extremely long, and without the slightest vestige of interdigital membrane', adding that this aspect of the bird's morphology gave him reason to think its closest relatives were likely to be the pelicans.

Since then, the pronounced groove down the top of the Shoebill's upper mandible and the fearsome hook at its end have been advanced as further reasons for a pelican connection. The endearing habit of beak clattering to welcome back its mate has been considered enough to put the Shoebill in among the storks, but most storks (other than Marabous, which also have large, heavy bills) fly with their necks extended, and Shoebills don't. It has also been argued that the Hamerkop's beak has enough in common with the Shoebill's to support assumptions that the two are related, and it is now generally accepted that they are most likely each other's closest relatives. Of such arguments (and many more besides) is Shoebill classification comprised, and taxonomists have ultimately turned to that refuge of last resort: an independent family, Balaenicipitidae, in which there is room for only one genus with one species. And perhaps to steer the bird away from any stork connection, the literal translation of Gould's *Balaeniceps* – whale-headed – seems to have been abandoned, at least temporarily, in favour of Shoebill – not Shoebill Stork, but just Shoebill.

By the standards of the time, the bird's appearance above the horizons of the scientific community was very late. This was a reflection both of its remote Central African home – far from any of the well-travelled coastlines of the continent, or the settled southern tip – and of the impenetrability of its swampland habitat. The ancient Egyptians featured Shoebills in their illustrations, but perhaps these were based on captured specimens or descriptive reports of sightings, or even because the bird did actually find its way much further down the Nile in those days than it does now. Today, the northern limits of its range are fairly well established. The birds need a combination of open water and permanent swamp with seasonally flooded grasslands round the edges. These requirements confine Shoebills to an area stretching from South Sudan down the upper Nile basin through Uganda, western Tanzania, eastern DRC, and into Zambia, where there is a population in the Bengweulu Wetlands. The bird is easily disturbed, which may be why stragglers appear here and there, such as the wanderers that turned up in Kenya's Amboseli National Park in 1994, or on the Nyika Plateau in northern Malawi.

It is estimated that half the world's Shoebills probably live in the Sudd (from the Arabic *sadd* meaning 'barrier' or 'blockage'), which has long marked an impenetrable barrier to upstream exploration of the Nile, even for Roman soldiers sent south by Nero. It is the largest wetland in Africa, comprising clumps of often floating papyrus and a mosaic of different grasses and reeds. The Sudd evens out the river's flow, despite seasonal upstream rainfall variations, through a rhythm of rising and falling water levels, causing the extent of the inundated area to vary enormously. There is a permanent heartland within the swamp made up of open water channels and reed beds, edged by seasonal flood plains and wooded grasslands from which water advances and recedes. This ebb and flow is crucial to the livelihoods of the local Nuer and Dinka people, creating opportunities for frenzied fishing activity by both humans and birds as shoals of fish are confined to ever-shrinking pools.

Shoebills are opportunistic feeders, taking whatever they come across in their swamplands: fish, in particular, but also frogs, snakes, young monitor lizards and even newly hatched crocodiles. With so much inland water, Africa is blessed with a rich and diverse fish life, of which two particularly fascinating species are staples of the Shoebill diet. These are bichirs and lungfish, being the only surviving families of ancient lineages, with ancestors preserved in fossil records. Bichirs, which frequent tropical African waters, have long, eel-like bodies with a ridge of up to 18 independent spiny dorsal fins along their back, and are covered in thick, bone-like scales, giving them a primitive appearance. Most importantly, they have an air-bladder, which acts like lungs and allows them to gulp air from the surface.

Lungfish are also eel-like, and their distribution across Australia and South America as well as Africa suggests they were well evolved by the break-up of Gondwana. Their lungs are more than just modified swim-bladders, comprising many smaller sacs that maximise the surface area to improve oxygen absorption. Being air-breathers, both bichirs and lungfish are able to survive in warm, shallow de-oxygenated water – and there Shoebills wait.

With their enormous beak, Shoebills can handle prey much bigger than can any other water bird. They usually feed by ambush, standing quite still, looking downwards and so making the most of the binocular vision enabled by their forward-facing eyes. This facilitates a much more accurate strike at any fish or other aquatic animal that swims within range; otherwise they stalk, heron-like, through the shallows, seeking out basking bichirs; or, having spotted one, waiting until it comes up for a gulp of air. Stalking-style hunting may be helped by the long toes that once so impressed Gould, and often allow Shoebills to tread, like jacanas, on surface vegetation that would not support birds with smaller feet.

Having spotted prey, the Shoebill typically launches itself forwards in an ungainly movement, its head extended. This action is called 'collapsing' in the bird books; maybe 'lunging' is more appropriate, even if it ends in collapse, with the bird often overbalancing as it plunges its open beak into the water, almost on top of its prey, in the hope of grabbing a fish in its great gape. The reinforced beak acts as a shock-absorber, and the mandibles can work against one another to help eject any mud and weed before the fish is swallowed whole. It has also been suggested that the bird's reinforced beak enables it to dig up lungfish from the mud holes into which these creatures retreat to aestivate when the waters have disappeared.

Shoebills are essentially solitary birds, and pairs may feed at separate ends of their territory, although when waters are receding and lots of fish are trapped in shrinking mud holes, several may gather for the feast. *Clarias* catfish are also air-breathers and can survive in burrows for many months. Aggregations are often preyed upon by Marabou Storks and African Fish Eagles, and they are probably also important for Shoebills in the Bangweulu Wetlands of Zambia, where there are no bichirs.

The Shoebill I was lucky enough to see on a journey through Uganda was certainly solitary, standing so still that it was impossible to say if it was waiting in ambush or just resting. Anyone who has seen the great wide White Nile leave Lake Victoria will have trouble believing that almost all that water, and a lot more gathered on the way, could plunge through a seven-metre-wide gap. But it does, tumbling 45 metres down

Murchison (or Kabalega) Falls, into the swirling cauldron below, before weaving its way languidly past Paraa Lodge on its northern bank and out into the top end of Lake Albert. The first time I went there was on the way to Garamba in northern Zaire, as it then was (now the DRC). It was only a few years after the end of Idi Amin's disastrous rule, and the lodge at Paraa had been completely destroyed. A simple ferry still operated to take our vehicles over the river, before we drove on through the golden grasslands of the Murchison Falls National Park, but there was no talk, or thought, of seeing a Shoebill then.

The next time was a few years later; Paraa Lodge was still not functioning, so we camped above the falls, where the river flowed with beguiling calm, giving no hint of the maelstrom just below. My night was disturbed by our bedtime talk of initiation ceremonies supposedly requiring local youths to jump – yes, jump! – the width of the Nile at the top of the chute. The next morning, we idly tried to catch a Nile perch in the pool below the falls, which until the fish's inadvertent introduction into Lake Victoria had long acted as a barrier to its ever getting above them. Then we drove down to see how Paraa's rehabilitation was getting on and were delighted to find a small open boat available for rent, whose driver was more than happy to take us up to the falls, and yes, while he couldn't promise a Shoebill, he had at least seen one on an earlier trip that week.

We set off, and before long, there indeed on the northern bank was the upper half a Shoebill, protruding above the reeds, stock still, head down, facing upstream. We tried to hold our place in the current in order to watch the bird, but kept drifting towards it, so moved on rather than disturb it into flight. On the way back, an hour later, the Shoebill was still there, quite unmoved.

The bird is much sought after by bird watchers, although not many will go as far as Arnold Small of California and have their car number plate personalised as B REX. For those anxious to tick the Shoebill, the easiest place to go is probably Mbamba Swamp on Lake Victoria, less than an hour from Entebbe Airport in Uganda. A number of companies organise trips with a combination of car and boat travel. They often partner with community organisations in the search, and while they stop short of offering money-back guarantees, failure to spot the bird is unlikely. Various camps in Zambia also offer trips specifically aimed at finding the Shoebill.

Because these birds live in such inaccessible swamps and do all they can to minimise human contact, it is never going to be easy to count them accurately. In Volume 1 of *BoA*, published in 1982, the authors conjectured that 'total numbers may not exceed 1,500'. However, aided not least by the results of a survey in what is now South Sudan showing perhaps 7,000 there alone, world population figures from *HBW*, BirdLife International and other sources now vary from 8,000 to as high as 15,000. A combination of aerial surveys and fitting young birds with satellite tags is enabling scientists to reach a more realistic figure for numbers in Zambia's Bangweulu Wetlands. There, as in the Sudd, they face a range of threats – particularly disturbance from fishermen, the burning of desiccated vegetation as the waters retreat, and the trampling of nests by livestock or wild animals, of which there are many in both areas. The wild-bird trade also takes its share of chicks for sale to all sorts of dubious institutions. However, Zambia is at least able to dangle the carrot of tourism benefits in front of local communities in exchange for their help in conserving the birds, which is something the South Sudanese authorities will not be doing for the foreseeable future.

In the meantime, there is something the Shoebill could do to help itself! These birds construct their nests on floating mats of vegetation, or maybe on termite mounds in areas too wet for nesting on the ground. The female lays usually two, sometimes three eggs, which both parents brood and guard, repeatedly cooling them with mouthfuls of water or sodden bits of weed. Quite often two chicks hatch, perhaps two or three days apart, but very seldom have the parents been recorded raising both to maturity. Indeed, it is almost as if the second was a spare, and that is exactly what the BBC found when they managed to film a mother and two chicks on the nest in Zambia in 2016.

The film shows a healthy-looking three-week-old chick under the shade of its mother's wings, begging for a drink. A metre away is a smaller bird, weaker and helpless in the beating sun. Persuaded of the elder chick's thirst, the mother strides off to collect water, and while she is away the strong chick attacks the weaker one, driving its beak into the down on its sibling's neck. The weak chick flaps away on its own towards its returning mother, squawking softly in desperate need of water and protection. Mother must be perfectly aware of what has happened – the stronger bird still has sibling fluff on its beak. Despite this, she gives only the elder one a drink, bypassing her other offspring as if it were not her own and condemning it to inevitable death. If she ever needs a spare because the heir is dead, it will be too late.

Secretarybird
Sagittariidae

'Thereabove a demi-secretary bird displayed, charged on the breast with a stylized representation of a protea flower ...' reads the official blazon of the South African coat of arms, formally adopted on Freedom Day, 27th April 2000.

There is something particularly appropriate about the Secretarybird forming part of any coat of arms, because even in life *Sagittarius serpentarius* has an almost heraldic look: its shaggy, crested head and huge long legs would look impressive on any armorial insignia. Sudan had earlier adopted the bird to distinguish its arms too – a much more prominent black-and-white rendition, bearing an emblematic shield from the time of the self-proclaimed Mahdi and nineteenth-century revolutionary, Muhammad Ahmad. (Africa's newest country, South Sudan, has opted for a Fish Eagle).

The bird was originally christened *Falco serpentarius* in 1779, the author of which, in taxonomic terms, is still cited as John Frederick Miller, an illustrator. He is fortunate to have his name attached to such a magnificent species, merely as a consequence of having painted a specimen from the Cape of Good Hope. His illustration shows a bird with such a blue back, and a tail so finely barred in black and white, that one must either assume the skin was badly degraded by the time it reached the artist, or that the tail was made up of feathers from a different species. The picture later appeared in his 1796 work, *Cimelia Physica – Figures of rare and curious quadrupeds, birds, etc. together with several of the most elegant plants*. The Secretarybird's inclusion in this potpourri was perhaps appropriate because, for the next 150 years, no taxonomist knew quite where to put it. Even before Miller's work was out, the bird had been moved to its own genus, *Sagittarius* ('archer'), before, in 1935, finally being accorded its own single-species family, Sagittariidae. Recent DNA studies support the idea of diurnal birds of prey being the Secretarybird's closest relatives, and any likeness to cranes or bustards is seen merely as the consequence of similar adaptations to a terrestrial, grassland lifestyle.

Such uncertainty was not confined to the make-up of the Secretary-bird's family tree. There was also the whole question of why it was called what it was. Did the secretarial epithet derive from the dress of black breeches and tailcoat, supposedly worn by Victorian secretaries, or because the crest feathers may resemble the quill pens that secretaries would tuck behind their ears or under their wigs? Some suspect the word of being a corruption of the Arabic *saqr-et-tair*, translating literally as 'hunter bird'. Or is 'secretary' a corruption of the generic name *Sagittarius*, referring to early descriptions of the bird wandering around, somewhat haphazardly, like an advancing bowman?

Thanks to its being such a high-profile, widely distributed and generally protected bird, there is little uncertainty over its behaviour. It is most often encountered striding purposefully across open grasslands where, unlike any other raptor in Africa, it is actually hunting on foot. The birds usually live and hunt in loose pairs, sometimes so loose as to appear to comprise singletons – which they may indeed be, in the case of young birds that have yet to pair up, or males out searching for food while their mate incubates the eggs.

One September afternoon I watched two Secretarybirds in Nairobi National Park, surely a pair as their plumage differed slightly: one, presumably the male, with a shaggier neck and much larger and more pronounced crest that it held erect; the other with a smaller, sleeker crest, flattened against the back of its head. I first saw only one, and then picked up the other in my binoculars, far away both from me and from its mate. Gradually they closed in on each other, until they could almost have touched wingtips, walked together for a minute or two, but without seeming to be hunting co-operatively in any way, and then gradually separated again, back into their own worlds. This sequence was repeated twice before I finally lost them as they made their way together down a dried watercourse. I wondered how they would communicate if one of these mostly silent birds found prey when they were far apart. It then occurred to me that, as the birds usually swallow whole anything they catch, there may be little need to communicate hunting success, except perhaps when there is a swarm of locusts or grasshoppers, which can be shared.

Striding Secretarybirds may cover over 20 kilometres a day at speeds of up to three kilometres an hour in their search for food. To hunt like this on foot needs height and a powerful neck and legs. The evolutionary trade-off for being built in such a way is that the bird needs to bend its knees in order to pick prey off the ground, or to drink.

Seeking food on the ground has turned Secretarybirds into opportunistic feeders, so much so that just about any creatures they come across are acceptable fare. If the birds sense a disturbance that could signal the presence of prey nearby they break into a fast trot in search of what might be their next meal. Despite their Latin species tag of *serpentarius*, the importance of snakes in their diet is probably exaggerated, and smaller, more easy-to-swallow items are preferred, such as grasshoppers, lizards, eggs, nestlings, mice, young rabbits, even tortoises, crabs and mongooses. These may be flushed from the grass cover by the birds' stamping their feet, or otherwise intercepted as they scurry away from the advancing footfalls. Secretarybirds are not partial to carrion, except charred prey on the edge of burnt or burning grasslands, where individuals sometimes congregate. The charismatic naturalist, François Levaillant, is quoted by several authors, including Jackson, as having bagged a specimen on one of his South African journeys that contained 'eleven rather large lizards, eleven small tortoises, a great number of insects nearly entire, and five snakes as thick as a man's arm'.

Levaillant apparently did well to procure a Secretarybird because, as Jackson found when trying to shoot one: '… it is a very wary bird, and except under exceptionally favourable conditions can rarely be approached [on foot] within shot-gun range. Such an opportunity was afforded by one that was feeding on white ants close to a dry water-course … but the stalk was spoiled when almost within range by a leopard coming clattering down a tree just behind me.'

Writing in about 1910, he goes on to advocate the use of a .22 rifle for anyone wishing to secure a specimen for a collection, but adds that there is no other excuse for shooting one.

Much interest has been aroused by the Secretarybird's mode of killing its prey before swallowing. It usually kills larger rodents, lizards and snakes by stomping on them with its well-equipped feet, which have three thick, blunt toes in front and one behind, each ending in a short, curved talon. The force of the blow they inflict is prodigious, and the bird may deliver the final *coup de grâce* with a peck at the back of the neck. Thick scales on the front of its legs – and sometimes its outstretched wings – give protection from retaliation.

In 2016 a paper entitled 'The Fast and Forceful Kicking Strike of the Secretary Bird' by Portugal, Mum, Sparkes and Daley appeared in *Current Biology*. Hoping that their researches might, inter alia, be usefully applied to prosthetic limbs and rehabilitation medicine, the scientists teamed up with Madeleine, a Secretarybird at the Hawk Conservancy Trust in Hampshire, England. Madeleine had been trained to stomp on rubber snakes for the benefit of spectators, so a pressure plate was buried under the ground in her aviary, and a rubber snake pulled slowly across it while high-speed cameras recorded the action. The force of the stomp was equivalent to the weight of a 20-kilogram hammer, or almost four times the bird's weight, and, equally remarkably, the kick was timed to take just 0.15 of a second. The consequences for a Secretarybird of a badly aimed strike can be lethal, so there is no room for error – the kick must literally be deadly accurate.

These birds normally eat their prey on the spot as they are incapable of clutching substantial creatures in their talons and flying off with them. Therefore, rumours of Secretarybirds flying up high and dropping large prey on the ground to kill it, as both Lammergeiers and Golden Eagles do with tortoises, are probably unfounded. Secretarybirds carry food in their crop, and it is quite conceivable that either danger or discomfort would force a bird in flight to disgorge half-swallowed prey, such as a snake. Watching from a distance, no observer could distinguish this from prey being dropped deliberately; and, if the bird felt safe enough it would circle down to try and recover its meal.

Secretarybirds seldom fly from danger, preferring to run; a bird flying with a loaded crop is most likely bringing back food to its mate or young on the nest. Territories in East Africa are usually centred round flat-topped *Acacia* or *Balanites* trees, which often double as roost and nesting sites, with dense thorny branches that prevent predators from reaching the nest from below. On the flat nest platform of sticks and grass, the female usually lays two white or pale blue eggs, which she incubates for up to 45 days, occasionally aided by the male.

Once hatched, the chicks are fed for almost 90 days, both parents bringing back food in their crop, which they then regurgitate. Sometimes the adults tear prey up into smaller morsels and feed these to the chicks, otherwise the female may re-ingest the male's regurgitation, finally feeding the young partly digested and more easily swallowed nourishment. Chicks in the open-platform nests, often left unattended by either parent, are at the most vulnerable stage of their lives, and may fall prey to avian predators like crows, kites or even ground hornbills.

However, leaving the nest too soon also brings its dangers, because the young then risk being unable to fly back up to roost in the evening.

As a species, the Secretarybird is not remotely threatened: the shading on its distribution map stops at the edges of thick forest or true desert, but otherwise covers most of sub-Saharan Africa. It can survive anywhere between the semi-deserts of the Namibian Kalahari and well-bushed miombo woodland, as long as the grasslands are suitable for the birds' long daily hunts, and scattered trees offer roosts and nest sites. The grass itself also needs to be short enough for them to see their surroundings, and bushes should be sufficiently scattered so that, if forced to fly, they can take the few strides needed to get airborne. The birds have no real wild predators, and humans are generally protective, not least because of the benefits Secretarybirds are seen to confer on farming communities by controlling snakes and rodents. Does anyone, anywhere pass by one of these unique creatures as it strides across its territory, without exclaiming excitedly, 'Hey, look, there's a Secretarybird!'?

Traditionally, the birds were, and continue to be, revered or respected for any number of reasons, and valued far more alive than dead. Zulu sangoma Credo Mutwa (whose stories about the Hamerkop appear earlier in this chapter) recorded how Secretarybirds had come to symbolise victory over a demanding and pitiless world; and other elders see them as linking the realms of the ancestors to those of the living. Killing the birds seldom features in any tradition, an exception being the discovery by researchers Kioko, Smith and Kiffner that inhaling the smoke from burning Secretarybird feathers – presumably first necessitating killing a bird – was one of several traditional cures for epilepsy. ('Uses of Birds for Ethno Medicine Among the Maasai People in Monduli District, Northern Tanzania' – *International Journal of Ethnobiology and Ethnomedicine,* Volume 1, 2015).

However, there is no doubt that local populations are under threat and that the bird's range is shrinking, particularly with the expansion of intensive forestry and agriculture. Clearing thick bush for crops may actually attract the birds onto the land, as they can adapt easily to bare fields of cereals, but intensive agriculture is too often accompanied by the wanton overuse of agricultural chemicals, which will kill any suitable prey. The subdivision of large plots into smaller subsistence farms, enclosed with wire fences, drives Secretarybirds away, and power lines are a lethal danger for creatures that are so ungainly in the air.

In 2011 BirdLife in South Africa became so concerned over dwindling numbers that it began a satellite-tracking programme using GPS transmitting devices fitted to the backs of seven-to-eight-week-old chicks, which by then weighed just over three kilograms. These would record a bird's position (accurate to within 10 metres) every 15 minutes, emitting signals that could be downloaded on the cellphone network. Results showed how surprisingly far the young moved once they had fledged: a bird hatched in the Free State was followed for at least 100 kilometres east of where it was raised, while another from the south of Limpopo province left its nest and travelled 270 kilometres northwest to Makgadikgadi Pans in Botswana.

All of which brings this story back to where it started. The Secretarybird has a high public profile, and appearing on the coats of arms both of South Africa and Sudan – as well as featuring on a 25-Rufiyaa postage stamp of the Maldives – cannot but enhance the protection it receives. It is the national bird of Sudan – but, strangely, not of South Africa, whose national bird is the Blue Crane. As a letter to South Africa's *Financial Mail* of 11th December 2015 points out, the two have several similarities, to the extent that when flying high, or stalking across grasslands in the distance, one could be mistaken for the other. So, did the designers of South Africa's coat of arms, or President Thabo Mbeki's team of selectors, actually intend the Blue Crane to appear on the country's coat of arms, and not the Secretarybird?

Egyptian Plover
Pluvianidae

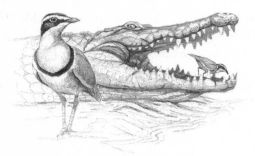

Fredrik Hasselquist was a Swedish traveller who had studied under the great Carl Linnaeus at Uppsala University. Hearing Linnaeus bemoan the paucity of knowledge on the natural history of Palestine, Hasselquist determined to remedy this himself and, having raised some money, embarked on a lengthy journey round the Middle East. Sadly, he was destined never to return home, and died, aged 30, in Izmir in Turkey in 1752. Nevertheless, his considerable collection of specimens did find its way back to Sweden, among which were skins of a bird that Linnaeus was able to include on page 150 of the 10th edition of his *Systema Naturae* in 1758 as *Charadrius aegyptius*.

These were Egyptian Plovers, for long alone in their own genus and only recently placed in their own family, Pluvianidae. Perhaps next they will need a name change, because even before the promotion, *Pluvianus aegyptius*, as they are now known, were deemed closer to coursers than plovers, and indeed sometimes known as Egyptian Coursers, Black-backed Coursers or Black-headed Plovers. In fact, any name for this bird with 'Egypt' in it could sensibly be abandoned as well, on account of its no longer being seen there (nor, even more perversely, is that icon of ancient Egyptian culture, the African Sacred Ibis).

One of the bird's other names – the Crocodile Bird – is equally questionable. It derives from the description by the Greek historian Herodotus, visiting Egypt in 459 BC, of how the crocodile is'... in the habit of lying with his mouth open, facing the western breeze; at such times the *trochilus* goes into his mouth and devours the leeches. This benefits the crocodile who is pleased and takes care not to hurt the *trochilus*'.

Whether *trochilus* refers to an Egyptian Plover is no more than surmise, and several other species have been said to behave in this way, including Spur-winged Plovers (or Lapwings). Solid evidence is still lacking, but it makes for a good story. In his multi-volume *Brehm's Life of Animals*, first published in German in 1879, zoologist Alfred Brehm was quite prepared to enliven the chapter on crocodiles by writing: 'When the crocodile has eaten its fill, it comfortably lies down on the sand and opens its huge mouth, well garnished with teeth, threatening dire peril to every disturber of its peace. Only one little bird is impudent enough to pick out the shreds of food remaining between the teeth.'

Richard Meinertzhagen never let an erratic memory get in the way of a good story and in his 1959 *Pirates and Predators* he would not only have us believe he had witnessed the plover in action, but that in his case there were three of them:'North of Khartoum I watched a large crocodile emerge from the river to a sandbank, flop down on its belly, close its eyes and open its jaws. Three *Pluvianus* who had been feeding nearby at once flew into it, one perching on the outer gums and pecking at the teeth, the other two remaining on the ground and inspecting the mouth, occasionally reaching up and pecking the teeth.'

Because something hasn't been witnessed does not necessarily mean that it didn't or can't happen. The present range of Egyptian Plovers is largely confined to areas little visited by ornithologists, so maybe the jury should stay out for now, continuing to consider whether to accept these stories or not!

What is much better documented is the bird's habit of burying its eggs in the sand before leaving the nest unattended. It nests on riverside sandbanks, excavating a shallow scrape without any added material. Covering the eggs seems to have the twin objects of concealment (even newborn chicks are sometimes covered over if danger threatens) and heat regulation. The temperature of the eggs is further controlled by the sitting plover, which frequently leaves the nest for a few minutes to wet its breast feathers.

My only experience with an Egyptian Plover was in Dungu, a small town in northeastern DRC, long before the town's residents were to suffer so horribly under the yoke of the Lord's Resistance Army. In a convoy of three vehicles driven from Nairobi, we stopped to stock up with provisions before setting off for our final destination of Garamba National Park. While my friends did their shopping, I wandered back down to the single-lane bridge over the Kibale River we had just crossed. Its construction as a double lane had apparently been approved by the Belgians in the 1940s, but the local colonial administrator diverted the balance of the bricks into a very fine 40-room colonial castle, the shell of which was still clearly visible downstream at the confluence of the Kibale and Dungu rivers.

As I reached the river bank and leaned over the bridge, a beautiful Egyptian Plover – totally unexpected and totally unmistakable – scuttled out of some short grass down onto the muddy edge of the river. 'Tame and confiding' is how the birds are often described, and that indeed is how this bird was. I had no binoculars with me but it made no effort to fly any further once it had reached the water's edge, and I could only marvel both at my good fortune and the beauty of its silver-grey wings, black-patterned face and buffy breast.

One of the lesser-known pioneers of West African ornithology was the American George Latimer Bates, author of *HBW*. Having settled in Cameroon, Bates became both familiar with, and fond of Egyptian Plovers, writing that 'one feels attracted to these nice little birds, not only on account of their beauty ... but also on account of their confiding ways as they run even among the feet of the people that throng the canoe landings'. He also describes how, whenever he thought he had found a nest by spotting a sitting bird, this was always empty of eggs, even though the plover clearly looked to have been incubating. After several false starts he managed to find eggs on a patch of ground that he had only recently searched. The thought then occurred to him that the birds had perhaps been sitting on buried eggs and 'what I took to be playing at incubation might have been the real thing'!

Turacos
Musophagidae

Call them louries or turacos, they are one of Africa's most distinctive bird families, both taxonomically and visually, with over 20 species spread around most of sub-Saharan Africa, excepting the drier, treeless areas of the south. There are all sorts of ways to classify turacos, and taxonomists split them into six different genera. The simplest division for watchers in the field, which also has some taxonomic justification, is into the brightly coloured forest species and the five or six drabber, open-country go-away-birds and plantain eaters (whose name is misleading in that they never eat plantains, and – to add insult to this failure of observation – the family name, Musophagidae, means 'banana eater'!).

The ancient history of turacos is complicated by the existence of fossil relatives of varying closeness from France, Germany and Egypt, and the Musophagidae family's current taxonomy is no less uncertain. Most sources now refer to the Knysna Turaco of the coastal forests of South Africa as a distinct species, as also are Livingstone's and Schalow's, although not long ago these were all merely subspecies of the Green Turaco. However, there is no denying that the most magnificent – and happily the most widespread – of the turacos is the giant of the family, the Great Blue, which enjoys its own genus.

The Great Blue ranges from the Kakamega forests in western Kenya to those of Guinea and Liberia on the west coast of the continent. Often silent, but not shy, it is always the most dramatic bird in its environment, even more so for its habit of travelling and feeding in small groups. While the Great Blue may be half as big again as any other forest turaco, it is also distinguished from the others by not having any red in its wings. Something that is indelibly associated with all the other forest-dwelling members of the family is a brilliant crimson flash as the birds glide smoothly from one tree to the next.

The turaco's red wing colour is due to a copper-based pigment known as turacin, which occurs naturally in the feathers of the Musophagidae family. Strangely, I have quite often found the remains of Hartlaub's Turacos while fishing up in the Aberdare forests of Kenya; perhaps their laboured flight makes them easy prey for sparrowhawks and other forest raptors. Their red feathers prove as irresistible to me as they do to any traditional elders who want to adorn their headdresses, and having collected some and kept them in a mug on my desk, I then read that the pigment was soluble in water. Anxious to test this assertion, I left a few feathers in water overnight to find the liquid had turned a pale pink colour, like rosé wine, the next day. A year or two later I repeated the experiment, with exactly the same result, and so was surprised to read in *BoA* that the 'persistent belief that they are water soluble and so washed out by rain is erroneous'. Well, the crimson feathers, which are primaries and outer secondaries, are only exposed as the bird flies, so washed out by rain they may not be, but yes, the pigment is water soluble.

Along with the red turacin, the green colour in many turacos' feathers is a consequence of turacoverdin, another copper-based pigment and also only found in turacos. The copper intake is derived from certain fruits, the principal component of all forest turacos' diets, including the fruits of species of the poison arrow tree, *Acokanthera*. Fruiting trees can be a magnet for the birds, and I have followed a group of over 25 Hartlaub's up a forested watercourse at Namanga in southern Kenya as they moved from one fig tree to another. The go-away-birds and plantain-eaters are more catholic than the forest species in their choice of food, as dictated by their environment, and add buds, leaves, seeds and pods to their diet, as well as occasional insects.

Their flight may be laboured, at best, but turacos are surprisingly agile in the trees, running quickly along branches and hopping from one to the other, giving them an almost prehistoric appearance. In so doing, they are aided by 'semi-zygodactylous' toes (as are some owls and ospreys too), which allow them to switch their fourth toe so that it points either forward, giving the birds four forward toes, or backwards, making three and one. This is also the arrangement of cuckoo feet – and the principal reason why turacos and cuckoos were once deemed close relatives. A further unusual feature is that the young of many species are born with a tiny claw at the joint on the front of their wings, which disappears as they mature. This was once considered enough to link them with South American Hoatzins, whose young have famously well-developed wing claws that they use to clamber back into the nest if some disturbance has sent them flopping into the swamps below.

While there is very little African forest that does not support a turaco of one species or another, it is seldom that more than two of the smaller species overlap; so, as long as one knows what to expect, identification can usually be assured. Some, the Great Blue and Ross's in particular, are widely distributed, and the Grey Go-away-bird's range stretches from one coast to another, but other species are extremely localised, often to the point of being classified as Vulnerable or Endangered. In Nairobi and the surrounding highland forests we are well used to both the sight and sound of Hartlaub's Turaco, but a glance at the distribution map shows that it is not far off being a Kenyan endemic, and possibly would have been if the Whitehall boundary-drawers had included a bit more of northern Tanzania in Kenya. Other species are even more localised, with Bannerman's just holding on in the dwindling forests of the highlands of Cameroon, and Ruspoli's limited to a shrinking area of juniper and conifer forests in southern Ethiopia.

There is something particularly romantic about any bird with a species name starting with Rwenzori – the fabled Mountains of the Moon, known even to the ancient Greek geographers but first observed by European eyes when Henry Morton Stanley's expedition passed by them in 1889. One of only three snow-covered massifs in Africa, and one of several sources of the Nile, the Rwenzoris are at the 'top' of the Albertine Rift; this is the western branch of the Great Rift Valley, with near-contiguous mountains and lakes stretching down from Uganda into Rwanda and Burundi, on one side, and the DRC on the other. Politically and socially the area is highly unstable, but its montane rainforests are host to amazing biodiversity, and perhaps one of the best places to experience this is in Rwanda's Nyungwe Forest, just up from the border with Burundi, and close to Lake Kivu on the DRC border. Among many other Albertine Rift endemics living there are the Rwenzori Double-collared Sunbird, the Rwenzori Nightjar (perhaps a subspecies of the Montane) and the Rwenzori Turaco, which can only be found well above 2,000 metres.

Work took me to Kigali one day, the spotlessly clean capital of Rwanda, and a Land Cruiser then took three of us on down an excellent tar road to the Nyungwe Forest. We had our list of endemic birds of the Albertine Rift, and a great guide, Godfrey, so as soon as I saw a turaco hopping through the forest on our first morning walk, I was ready to tick off the Rwenzori. But no, it was not to be that easy. Surprisingly, there are two more turacos in Nyungwe, as well as the ubiquitous Great Blue; and this turned out to be a Black-billed, with which I was familiar from Kakamega, but clearly not so familiar that it was instantly recognisable as such. I consoled myself with the thought that turacos are often just seen in silhouette or indistinctly among the branches, and so colours were unclear. As things went, it would be two more days before a very un-turaco-like call alerted Godfrey to the Rwenzori's presence, and three of the birds launched themselves out of a tree on a steep slope, actually gliding by at eye level, their red breast patches seeming especially bright as they passed.

As for the other Rwenzori birds, the double-collared sunbirds had not been hard to find, but we had almost reached the end of our visit without even going out to look for the nightjar. So, Godfrey was persuaded to stay on, and late in the afternoon we set out for some scrubland, my companions soon appeased by the extraordinary sight of a large party of ground-dwelling L'Hoest's monkeys cavorting around on top of the tea bushes in a forest-edge plantation. Watching these threatened to make us late for the nightjar, but actually we couldn't have timed it better, and by the time we reached the nightjar's territory it was already calling, and a few minutes later, with just enough light left to see by, one angled its way across the track in pursuit of insect food.

Next stop the highland forests of southern Ethiopia to try and find Ruspoli's?

Mousebirds
Coliidae

Mousebirds pose few taxonomic problems. Presently, there is one family, Coliidae, comprised of only six species, and other than in the arid north of the continent and its thickly forested heart, one or more of these are to be found almost anywhere. That said, around 20 distinct subspecies of the Speckled Mousebird have been identified, and it may not be long before some of these are promoted as candidates for specific status.

There is nothing quite like a mousebird, and at the risk of anthropomorphising again, no birds give more of an impression of the sheer enjoyment of being what they are. They truly seem to get pleasure out of their activities, and most of all out of each other's company. They are largely drab birds, but no less fascinating than turacos in their uniqueness, and familiarity should be cause for celebration rather than contempt.

The six species belong to two different genera. In *Colius* are the widespread Speckled, together with the White-headed, White-backed and the very localised Red-backed, which is endemic to northern Angola. The origins of the Latin name, *Colius,* seem lost in an extended game of taxonomic Chinese whispers. One suggestion has been a variation on the Greek words *keleos* or *kolios* for woodpeckers, although these have little in common with mousebirds. The Latin has itself been anglicised and 'coly' is a familiar name for any member of this family among Europeans living in Africa. The other genus is *Urocolius,* containing the Blue-naped and Red-faced.

The *Colius* species are often separated, if not by distribution maps, then at least by habitat within their ranges, but it is not uncommon to find *Colius* and *Urocolius* mousebirds together. Speckled *Colius* often overlap with Blue-naped *Urocolius* in East Africa, and with Red-faced further south. *Urocolius* are much stronger flyers, prepared to make longer flights with more rapid wing beats than the *Colius* species. The long tails and fly-glide flights of Blue-naped Mousebirds often remind me of pheasants, and I was happy to see that *HBW* was of the same mind. *Colius* species are inclined to make shorter journeys between bushes, and to hop around with great agility in search of fruits or leaves once they get there – behaviour not unlike that of rodents, and the reason for their colloquial name.

There is far more that unites the two genera than distinguishes them, and they share those essential characteristics that make mousebirds so remarkable. Despite their small size and stubby head and neck, they are not actually passerines, clinging to, rather than perching on branches, with feet described as 'pamprodactylous'; this means that of their four toes, the outer two can move forwards or backwards, so the mousebird can have all four forwards as it grasps a branch (like swifts hanging from the wall or palm swifts clinging on to leaf fronds) or two front, two back.

It is probably the long tail and forward positioning of the legs in relation to the rest of its body that give the mousebird its strange vertical hanging posture, which Jackson likened to 'a gymnast who has drawn himself up to his chest on a parallel-bar, the only difference being that it can remain in that position indefinitely and can even twist its head round and face backwards like an owl'. The long tail also helps them balance when trying to perch in more normal fashion, and they often rest their tail on a neighbouring twig. Mousebirds are remarkably agile on the ground too, on which they frequently land to dust-bathe, their toes then spread out in an 'X'.

Their social life is a joy to witness, and there is much more to it than 'follow-my-leader', which groups tend to play. Single life is not something any mousebird of any species experiences, and there is scarcely an activity in the mousebird's day that is not carried out communally. The birds often actively seek out physical contact: be they feeding, dust-bathing, or even roosting, they huddle together in groups for safety, support and warmth. Mutual preening (allopreening) helps birds groom those parts of their plumage they cannot otherwise reach themselves – something I first experienced when I saw an African Spoonbill tenderly nibbling a fellow bird's neck. Mousebirds take it one step further, and it is not unusual for two birds to preen a third.

Feeding is also communal, as commercial growers of exotic fruit will readily testify. The birds are almost exclusively vegetarian, relying on a diet of fruits, flowers, nectar and leaves. Fruit seems to be preferred and, glancing out of the window as I write, I see a party of Speckled Mousebirds exploring the ornamental berry bushes that edge the driveway. The success of mousebirds is due, in part, to their inclusive diet of both indigenous and exotic fruits and leaves. With such a range of vegetable matter on their menu, there is almost always something around for them to eat, even in a drought, and there is much overlap in the diets of different species where more than one is found. Fruit passes quickly through their short intestines, in not much more than 10 minutes; leaves, which seem to be part of their meals later in the day, may take longer. Eating so much fruit makes water intake less important, but when they do drink, mousebirds show one of their other unusual abilities: they can suck and swallow water without raising their heads, much like doves and pigeons.

Their diet and adaptability to human surrounds unfortunately brings mousebirds into sharp conflict with gardeners and horticulturalists. V.D. van Someren was in the forefront of ornithological study in Kenya, but in *A Bird Watcher in Kenya* even he seems to find that their destructive tendencies far outweigh any pleasure gained from their presence: 'Much to my wife's disgust, I could never bring myself to rob their nests, and in due course the masses would descend on the tomatoes, pea-seedlings and everything else and rip them to shreds. For sheer depravity of taste, they are hard to beat, and even unopened flower buds are fair game. The descent of a pack of colies always reminds me of a shower of meteors, with their long tails trailing behind them, and the damage they do is perhaps more selective but equally complete.'

Van Someren then goes on to advocate trapping as the preferred means of control over shooting, the latter method having been successfully used by one of his friends on a vineyard, until the Mau Mau emergency in the early 1950s forced the surrender of all surplus firearms. Another of his friends had started trapping the birds and caught several on his first attempt. Having pondered on how best to kill the birds inside the trap, he introduced his large tabby cat into the cage, which seems a strange story for Van Someren to relate, and perhaps the same could be said for this author too!

Breeding is less of a communal activity, in that the birds do not nest in obvious colonies like herons or weavers. Nonetheless, nests are often not far apart and are notable for being built not only by the couple, but also with help from outsiders, who sometimes even share incubation and caring for the hatchlings. Nothing in their life, it seems, is solitary.

Despite being so widespread, very little field research had been done on mousebirds before M.K. Rowan published her paper 'Colies of South Africa' in the 1967 edition of *Ostrich*. Many of her observations came from keeping captive birds, and her account contains charming vignettes of their interactions with wild ones; these would come to perch on the cages, attracted by their occupants' calls, and the two groups would even try to preen each other.

In her paper, Rowan observes that one of the consequences of the sparse research undertaken on these birds had been the reliance by one writer after another on such observations as they could find. So, in a letter written 100 years earlier, Thomas Ayres had told Edgar Layard he thought 'that when roosting they hang with their heads downwards, the whole family being nestled together; but those that I have seen have generally flown off so quickly that I could not be positively certain as to their position'. Despite the element of doubt, Layard had related the story in a later, 1884 edition of *The Birds of South Africa*, co-authored by Richard Sharpe. In 1961, Messrs Austin and Singer produced an ambitious compendium of the families of the *Birds of the World*, with a foreword by Peter Scott; and on page 174 they contend that 'several species sleep hanging upside down'.

Perhaps some individuals really do!

Wood Hoopoes
Phoeniculidae

Phoeniculidae – the wood hoopoes – is another family whose members bird watchers can find only in Africa. They are all distinguished by long curved beaks, either red or grey/black, although to frustrate identification, the young of all those red-billed species begin life with dark beaks. Wood hoopoes have long tails, often spotted white, and generally dark iridescent plumage.

Some sources argue for two separate families, others would put all the birds into a single genus, but most would now agree on two genera (*Rhinopomastus* and *Phoeniculus*) with varying numbers of species in each. *Rhinopomastus* contains the well known Common and Abyssinian scimitarbills, as well as the Black Scimitarbill, which used to be the Black Wood Hoopoe. The true wood hoopoe family, *Phoeniculus*, contains the lovely chestnut-headed Forest Wood Hoopoe and the equally striking White-headed Wood Hoopoe – both distinctive, if not widely distributed. It is the blackish ones with white in the wings and tail and usually red beaks that are complicated. The Black-billed, Green and Violet are all very similar looking, and fuel much taxonomic confusion, particularly the Violet, with two distinct populations, one in Kenya and the other thousands of kilometres away in southern Angola and northern Namibia. Almost the entire expanse between these two outposts is occupied by so-called Green Wood Hoopoes, so it came as no surprise to find the IOC creating a new species – Grant's Wood Hoopoe – for the northern population, while those in Namibia and Angola remain Violet.

Unlike the scimitarbills, the true wood hoopoes are generally gregarious birds, feeding conspicuously in noisy parties that move from one tree trunk to the next. They can creep up or down the trunks with short legs and strong-clawed toes, their long tails also helping them gain traction as they probe into cracks and crevices in the bark – far deeper than woodpeckers could ever reach – for insects or spiders.

The Green Wood Hoopoe is much the most widespread of the species, and its behaviour, having been carefully watched in both East and southern Africa (where it is also known as the Red-billed Wood Hoopoe), is often also attributed to the related species, about which less is known. However, there is no doubting that all wood hoopoes not only depend on trees for finding food, but also for breeding and roosting, both of which require holes. This was neatly demonstrated in South Africa by Morné du Plessis, who has studied these birds more than most in support of his Ph.D. thesis for the University of Cape Town on 'The Behavioural ecology of the Red-billed Wood Hoopoe in South Africa'. Du Plessis built artificial nest boxes in woodland where there were no wood hoopoes, not least because the trees lacked any suitable holes. Within two months, five groups of Green Wood Hoopoes had established territories in the woodland, always both roosting and nesting inside the boxes, never outside them.

Roosting is communal, even to the extent of a party of Green Wood Hoopoes at Naro Moru on the foothills of Mount Kenya allowing a White-headed to join them in their tree hole sleeping spot. Huddling together in these holes for warmth – especially for birds in colder parts of Africa – undoubtedly plays such an important role in temperature regulation that it is worth running the risk of predation from invading genets or even marauding columns of safari ants. Male wood hoopoes are significantly larger than females and often, if unable to fit into the same roosting holes, have to make do with inferior ones.

David and Sandra Ligon also studied Green Wood Hoopoes in great detail in the acacia woodlands on the shores of Lake Naivasha in Kenya. The lake is just south of the equator, but being at an altitude of almost 2,000 metres, it can get cold at night. The Ligons located roosting sites and captured birds in transparent plastic bags as they emerged into the morning, banding a total of 235 from 28 different flocks comprising, on average, six wood hoopoes. Being able to identify individuals made the researchers appreciate how territorial the birds were, the considerable lengths to which they would go to defend their territories and also how almost no territories with suitable cavities remained unoccupied. The Ligons wrote up their research in meticulous and very readable detail, including 'The Communal Social System of the Green Woodhoopoe in Kenya', which appeared in the 1978 edition of Cornell University's *Living Bird.* This showed Green Wood Hoopoes behaving in very similar fashion to those other classic co-operative breeders, the helmetshrikes, described on pages 77–81.

The Ligons concluded that both the male and female of the breeding pair were nearly always the oldest birds in the flock. Breeding is notable for the co-operative assistance of helpers, usually either earlier offspring or siblings of the breeding pair, but sometimes flocks would accept unrelated outsiders. Unlike the helmetshrikes, the wood hoopoes build no nest, the female simply laying in the bottom of the cavity she has selected. In Naivasha, this was nearly always in the trunk of an acacia, although one female nested successively in two different fence posts and then under a piece of heavy farm machinery, indicating both flexibility in site selection as well as a dearth of more suitable cavities. Nest holes may be naturally occurring, or first excavated by woodpeckers, and there is great competition for them, both from other groups of wood hoopoes as well as from species such as Lilac-breasted Rollers and glossy starlings – and even honey bees. Just as Du Plessis found, the availability of holes for roosting and breeding is the factor most limiting wood hoopoe numbers, and vacant territories that are suitably endowed are quickly occupied.

Having laid between two and five eggs (which are notable for being blue, grey or green – not white like those of most hole-nesters), the female alone will incubate them, although while doing so, she seems quite prepared to take food from her mate or from others. The more helpers there are, the less inclined is the mate to go foraging, and in the words of the Ligons, 'a significant inverse relationship exists between provisioning efforts of the male parent and the number of helpers; that is, helpers reduce the efforts of the male parent'! So it is too after hatching, when either the male or helpers bring food for the young, although during the first two weeks this is passed first to the mother who then feeds the chicks; or, if the caterpillar or centipede is too large, swallows it herself. After two weeks or so, the helpers, particularly females, start to feed the young directly, and once these have flown the nest, the whole flock takes on the responsibility of feeding and caring for the fledglings as they start to make their way in the outside world.

The Forest Wood Hoopoe may be the hardest of all the species to find, and has probably disappeared from Kenya as a result of habitat destruction. I found it in Mabira Forest in eastern Uganda, close to Jinja on the Nile, which is probably as far east as the species now reaches. There were three birds high up in the tree tops among the leafy branches, behaving quite unlike other wood hoopoes, and very hard to see as a result. They were particularly memorable for the fact that, a few minutes later, my guide identified a pair of Yellow-mantled Weavers, also in the tree tops and equally difficult to see. These weavers share the sad distinction with the Forest Wood Hoopoe of having once been found in western Kenya, but no longer.

The Black-billed Wood Hoopoe is mainly a bird of Ethiopia, but its distribution map still colours the wild lands of northeastern Kenya. Not long ago a terrific new tarmac road was completed, linking the border town of Moyale with the rest of Kenya. This was too good not to explore, so fellow bird enthusiast Ben and I decided to head up there to see what we could see. In the barren wastes north of Marsabit the dry-country birds began with a fine pair of Thekla Larks, easily contrasted with the softer-plumaged, sand-loving Crested Larks a bit further down the road. We found only a single party of Chestnut-headed Sparrow-larks and a single Rosy-patched Shrike, but Somali Bee-eaters and Somali Fiscals were not uncommon, and we spotted a fine male Somali Ostrich with two females that had escaped the hunger of the road-building gangs. Having been alerted to look out for White-crowned Starlings in Turbi, halfway between Marsabit and Moyale, we found a tree opposite the mosque outside the soda store in which a few of these prized sightings were chattering away – as they still were on our way back.

Reaching Moyale, we headed for the delightful campsite in the Kenya Wildlife Service compound, and the next morning sat drinking coffee and planning the day. 'Those look like scimitarbills,' said Ben, looking out over the valley. No, they can't be if there are lots of them, I thought, and rushed down the bank to get closer to the trees on the other side, in which the birds were hopping around. Indeed, they weren't. I captured five wood hoopoes in my binoculars just long enough for me to see their dark beaks.

Ground Hornbills
Bucorvidae

When are hornbills not hornbills? Perhaps when they are ground hornbills, which are so different from any other hornbills in the Buceroitidae that they may well be worthy of their own family.

Hornbills in general are renowned for their peculiar breeding habits, which involve the female sealing herself inside the nest cavity with droppings and mud, leaving only a narrow slit through which the male passes morsels of food. This state of incarceration lasts not just during the inactivity of incubation, but also for two or three weeks after the blind, naked young have hatched. Taking advantage of her immobility, the female also sheds her wing and tail feathers, all the while keeping the nest scrupulously clean by lifting out moulted plumage, uneaten food remains and other detritus. By the time she finally breaks back out into the wider world, exchanging her keyhole view for all-round access to forest or savanna, she may have been in the nest for anything from six weeks to more than double that.

Ground hornbills, however, neither seal up their nests nor clean them out. Moreover, they have 15 vertebrae in their necks rather than the 14 of all other hornbills, are almost exclusively carnivorous and feed more like Secretarybirds, stalking over the grasslands on long, strong legs with stubby toes. They are huge too, perhaps more than 50 times heavier than the smallest hornbills, which are those little-known inhabitants of equatorial African forests, Red-billed and Black Dwarf hornbills.

One other physical feature possessed by ground hornbills, and probably by no other bird in the world, let alone any other hornbill, are long curling eyelashes! Vernon van Someren pays the birds a truly double-edged compliment, remarking how 'their beautiful, long, curved eyelashes would be the envy of a mannequin but not their weird and waddling walk'; and so does Frederick Jackson, who describes them as 'far from prepossessing in appearance (except [their] really wonderful eyelashes), an awkward waddling mover when walking, and distinctly ungainly when running ...'.

So different are the ground hornbills that the IOC now gives them their own family of Bucorvidae, while the *HBW Checklist* continues to keep the genus *Bucorvus* in Buceroitidae. In following the IOC Checklist, at least in deciding what is an endemic family, ground hornbills are therefore no longer hornbills and must leave the other 60 or so true hornbills behind. However, all sources seem agreed on there being two species of ground hornbill – the Northern, *Bucorvus abyssinicus*, and the Southern, *Bucorvus leadbeateri*. The word *Bucorvus* is a hybrid of *Buceros* (so named by Linnaeus in 1758), a genus of Far Eastern hornbills, and *corvus*, the Latin for the even blacker-plumaged raven.

Abyssinicus at least tells us something about the bird that bears its name – that it must once have ranged across this northern part of Ethiopia. The first Northern Ground Hornbill to be viewed by Europeans was obtained in Gondar, but, as so often in those days, it would be left to museum-bound researchers to name the bird, in this case one Pieter Boddaert who happened to be working in the Dutch universities in 1783.

Leadbeateri, however, imparts no remotely helpful information about the bird. It is the Latinised name of specimen dealer and taxidermist Benjamin Leadbeater (his firm was later to change its name to Leadbetter), who also gets his name incorporated in that of a hummingbird and a cockatoo. The type specimen was taken from the Lower Bushman's River in South Africa, and somehow found its way to Leadbeater's premises in Brewer Street in London's Piccadilly. This was in 1825 and it is surprising that the relatively well-settled lands of southern Africa were slower to yield up their ground hornbill than was the little explored country of coffee and ancient Christianity.

Today, the two species are more or less confined to separate ranges – allopatric, in scientific terms – although in parts of Uganda and southern Kenya there is a chance of seeing either of them. The Northern strides across a belt of semi-arid land comprising the Sahel and latitudes just south of it, from Senegal right through to Ethiopia and East Africa, with the Southern occupying much of the African savannas further south that are neither too dry and treeless, nor too forested. The two species are distinguished particularly by the Northern's having a pale patch at the base of its upper mandible, and by the bare skin around the throat and eyes of both male and female being blue rather than red. Otherwise, the plumage of the two species is all black, except for the astonishing white primary wing feathers that show only when they take to the air.

Notwithstanding that they spend their days largely on the ground, the birds not only fly up onto the safety of a branch to roost at night, but also nest in natural tree holes, occasionally even excavating a hole in an earthen bank, or making use of some other ready-made cavity like an artificial beehive. Fifteen years ago, early one Tanzanian evening, I watched five Southern Ground Hornbills waddle down towards a baobab tree on the edge of Mikindani Bay, near Mtwara, and flap, one by one, up into the branches of the huge leafless tree. The next morning, I returned to the tree, in which I could now see a gaping hole at the top of the trunk, with an untidy mess of sticks protruding over the edge. Long before I got close enough to disturb it, a ground hornbill flew out of the hole, away on a mission of its own.

Breeding pairs of Southern Ground Hornbills, but seemingly not Northern, are often attended by several young acolytes. Not only do these help defend the nest territory, but the males also have the particularly endearing habit of bringing beakfuls of nesting material to the female, in each of which is wrapped a morsel of food.

If there are two eggs, these hatch in the order in which they were laid, the younger chick almost always dying of starvation. The survivor is fed by the whole group and, on leaving the nest, remains for many years to come with all those who reared it. Given that there are so many helpers doing the feeding, it seems something of a waste that their efforts are focused on only a single chick.

The food of a ground hornbill consists, in the words of *BoA*, of almost 'any animals it can overcome', to which could be added occasional seeds and even carrion. Grasshoppers and beetles are prime targets, but larger creatures, such as snakes, lizards and even hares, offer more worthwhile returns. Tortoises are particularly easy prey and the birds may be seen around the edges of burnt ground where smaller animals are trying to escape the heat. Food items for chick or female at the nest are often collected up one after the other in a bird's beak, and taken back whole, reminiscent of puffins returning to their nests with three or four fish gripped between their multi-coloured mandibles.

Not only do several Southern Ground Hornbills all bring food back to the nest, but these birds may also hunt as a pack. Thomas Ayres was one of the first foreigners to witness this potentially suicidal behaviour, and his description in the *Ibis* of 1861 is much quoted in subsequent literature, this version from the 1884 edition of Layard's *The Birds of South Africa*: 'On discovering a snake, three or four of the birds advance sideways towards it with their wings stretched out and, with their quills, flap at and irritate the snake till he seizes them by the wing-feathers, when they immediately all close round and give him violent pecks with their long and sharp bills, quickly withdrawing again, when the snake leaves his hold. This they repeat till the snake is dead. If the reptile advances on them, they place both wings in front of them, completely covering their heads and most vulnerable parts.'

Very occasionally, however, things don't all go the birds' way, as described in a report in *BoA* of the biter getting bitten: a snake brought back to a nest as food proved still to have enough life left in it to kill the chick it was intended to nourish!

The dynamics of co-operative breeding groups are generally poorly understood. For so many birds to be involved in raising a single chick, which itself may take up to five years to reach maturity and then not breed for several years thereafter, means the reproductive rate of Southern Ground Hornbills is inevitably very low. To sustain the population, even at current levels, entails the birds having to survive to a great age in bird – and even in human – terms. This, all other things being equal, they fortunately seem to do, and records of captive birds show them living for over 50 years. However, these days all other things seldom are equal, and the human impact on their habitat – the loss of breeding trees, overgrazing, land reclamation, electrocution and indirect poisoning – is inevitably having a deleterious impact on this highly visible species. Less well known is the persecution the birds have received on isolated farms for their habit of attacking their own reflection and smashing glass windowpanes to pieces.

Few birds – except perhaps the Hamerkop – are of such cultural significance among local people as are ground hornbills. The birds' role in traditional societies is mostly a spiritual one, and Boyd Alexander's description of the practical use of a ground hornbill's head is exceptional. In 1903 he joined an expedition to explore the area around Lake Chad, in which both his brother and one of his other two colleagues perished, but which he was still able to describe to the literary public four years later in *From the Niger to the Nile*. Travelling up the Niger, he tells how he watched a hunter of the Munchi people (today better known as the Tiv) in what is now northern Nigeria, who, in pursuit of a hartebeest, '… fastened on his head the head and neck of a [ground] hornbill ... and with arrow laid on bow, crawled on his knees close to the herd from which he singled out a male and started to approach it, swaying his masked head from side to side in imitation of the hornbill with masterly pantomime. By these means he got within twenty yards of his quarry, when he fired, [wounding] the animal in the shoulder. It sprang away a few yards, then spun round and fell, instantly killed by the deadly poison of the arrow.'

Often the bird plays a spiritual role as a bringer of rain. In Layard's *The Birds of South Africa*, H. Bowker relates how 'the bird is held sacred ... and is only killed in times of severe drought, when one is killed by order of the "rain-doctor" and its body thrown into a pool in a river.' He then follows this with a surprising description of catching the bird. 'It is very weak on the wing, and when required by the "doctor" the bird is caught by the men of a number of kraals turning out at the same time, and a particular bird is followed from one hill to the other by those on the lookout. After three or four flights it can be run down by a good runner.'

More recently, a comprehensive 'Exploration of Cultural Beliefs and Practices across the Southern Ground Hornbill's Range in Africa' by Coetzee, Nell and Van Rensburg was published in the March 2014 *Journal of Ethnobiology and Ethnomedicine*. Using interviews and group discussions to conduct their research, they divided their findings simply into traditional behaviours that generally had protective consequences for the hornbills and those that were most likely to be destructive.

A primary belief is that the birds are a bad omen, likely to portend loss, damage and death. This has both positive and negative consequences for the birds: in some parts of Africa they are spared for fear that killing them would precipitate misfortune, whereas elsewhere it is only by destroying them that adversity can be prevented.

The bird is also seen as a protector against drought or lightning, as well as against invasion by evil spirits. These are positive attributes, and yet, to take advantage of such protection perversely seems to require that a bird be killed, so that the bird's body (as described by Bowker above) or parts thereof can be used in rituals or mixed into concoctions. In South Africa a ground hornbill head may be dropped into a chief's bath before he bathes to strengthen his authority; or potions containing bits of hornbill body may be used to anoint a person or property in need of protection.

Another role for the bird – and one more likely to ensure its survival – is that of timekeeper, its call or appearance either indicating the start of the day or predicting a change in the weather. This function of daily timekeeper surely derives from the bird's resonant call, often uttered before it is even light; that of forecaster could simply be a consequence of their local movements, whether inspired by the onset of a breeding urge or some other stimulus coinciding with seasonal changes in the weather.

Both ground hornbills are renowned for their deep four-note boom (with slightly different spacing between the calls of the two species), the early hour of their utterance and the body contortions accompanying them. Jackson describes how when one he was watching began booming: '… he inflated his crimson pouch, lowered his head with the closed bill pointing vertically downwards, and with the tip either touching the ground, or very close to it, then trumpeted forth his deep sonorous notes'. Not for nothing is it known through much of southern Africa as the 'thunder bird', the name combining elements of the bird's call and its traditional role as a bringer of rain.

Today, the range of both ground hornbills is contracting rapidly. There is no longer any chance of encountering a Southern near the Lower Bushman's River, and one would now need to go far from the spectacular ancient castle of Gondar to find a Northern. I can remember seeing a party of four Southern birds within the city limits of Nairobi, about 35 years ago, on a grassy vlei now built over by the Law School;

today one would be unlikely to find one within 100 kilometres of the capital's boundaries. Ornithologist Alan Kemp has probably spent more time studying the Southern Ground Hornbill in South Africa than anyone else, and has continually pointed out how the bird's range is contracting dramatically, although they hold on in good numbers in protected areas, particularly the Kruger National Park. Some innovative conservation initiatives have been implemented, such as providing artificial nest sites where lack of natural ones is a limiting factor, or removing from nests the second-born chicks, which would otherwise starve to death, and raising them in captivity before release. The birds' reproductive strategy is against them, and they will certainly need a helping human hand to sustain them outside of protected areas.

African Barbets
Lybiidae

It may seem strange to include barbets in a survey of birds that only live in Africa. After all, it is hard to go for a walk anywhere in the woodlands and scrub of India or southeast Asia without hearing the repeated 'tink-tink' of a Coppersmith Barbet, while over in the Neotropics many other species are picking fruits in the forests of Central and South America. However, the IOC yardstick used to define endemic families in this book has now grouped the New World, Asian and African barbets into three distinct families, with about 40 species (including 10 tinkerbirds) in the African one, Lybiidae.

Not only are the often brightly coloured barbets easily recognisable as such, whatever continent they occupy, but they also share many of the elements of basic bird behaviour. Essentially frugivores, they usually swallow fruit whole – unless it is too big, as is often the case with orchard-grown tropical fruits (where barbets sometimes reach pest proportions), when they will peck away at pieces of flesh. The fruits of trees from the huge *Ficus* genus feature in the diets of barbets on all three continents, and with meals taking some time to digest, barbets are effective dispersers of seeds far from the parent trees. While the birds have evolved to eat fruit, no barbet will ignore insects it may come across, especially when collecting food to feed its young, and many species also try and catch hatching termites in flight.

Barbets the world over nest in holes in which they lay from one to six white eggs. The distribution of most species is largely controlled by the availability of suitable trees, particularly those with soft, dead branches, which are much easier to peck out. Barbets will, ideally, excavate their own new hole each year, rather than appropriating that of a woodpecker or some other bird, and by making their own nests they can ensure that the access hole is no bigger than it needs to be, thus minimising the possibility of unwelcome visitors gaining entry. As with most tree-hole species, the chicks are born naked and blind, spending comparatively little time in the egg (from which they emerge with the aid of a small egg tooth) and much more as a growing chick in the nest.

The greatest danger to successful barbet breeding comes less from snakes or birds of prey than from various honeyguides, which are all brood parasites. For the larger species of honeyguide, nests of the barbet and woodpecker are prime sites, which the female can be in and out of – having deposited an egg – in less than half a minute. Given time, the female honeyguide will also try and either puncture or eject any host eggs she finds in the nest. Once hatched, the honeyguide chick attacks any living chicks of its foster parents, using the hook on the end of its beak to lethal effect, and it is no exaggeration to say that each honeyguide chick represents a lost clutch of host young. Not all goes the way of the young honeyguide and it may struggle to develop on the fruit-rich diet with which barbets attempt to feed it, but by then the young barbets are dead.

African barbets occupy a much wider range of habitat than do others, perhaps as a result of changing climates that have shrunk their normal forest environment, thus forcing them to adapt to drier surrounds. Many are quite at home in low scrub, and three species of the *Trachyphonus* genus not only forage on the ground for seeds and insects, but also nest there. The Yellow-breasted and Red-and-yellow barbets excavate nests in banks or termite mounds; D'Arnaud's actually digs a hole in the ground, off the central shaft of which is a smaller breeding chamber, the whole structure allowing water and dirt to inundate the hole without flooding the actual nest. All these ground-nesting species are renowned for their melodic duets from atop small bushes, directed as often to other group members as to each other.

Other African barbets nest and roost colonially, especially the forest-frequenting species in the *Gymnobucco* genus. Pairs of Grey-throated, Sladen's, Bristle-nosed and Naked-faced barbets often excavate their own hole next to that of others in the same trunk. All members of a colony are not necessarily of the same species, and where more than one species of colonial nester overlaps, as for instance do the Naked-faced and Bristle-nosed, they might share a trunk. Some of these colonies can be quite dramatic, as in the much quoted example noted by John Elgood, a renowned expert on Nigerian birds, of 250 pairs of Naked-faced Barbets with holes in the same trunk.

Excavating nests in tree trunks and gripping large fruits in order to tug them from their branches requires a heavy beak, which is a characteristic of barbets worldwide. Some species actually have a serrated beak, with one or two 'teeth'. The species in the *Lybius* genus have a particularly stout bill, with the two notches of *Lybius bidentatus* being responsible for both its scientific name and the colloquial 'Double-toothed Barbet'. The beak of the more insectivorous ground barbets tends to be slimmer and pointed.

Round the barbet's face are bristles, which give the bird its name – from the French, *barbe*, meaning 'beard'. The placing and extent of these bristles varies much – in some species they grow only around the lower mandible, in others mainly the upper. They may be long or short, stiff or soft. These bristles are essentially feather shafts with no vanes, but their function is not clear. Whether or not they evolved to act as something akin to human eyelashes, they must certainly serve to protect the bird's eyes as it gouges out its nest or searches for insects. The tufts around its beak give the Bristle-nosed Barbet its name, as with the big red and black Bearded Barbet, whose hair-like feathers protrude underneath its lower mandible.

The calls of the barbet are usually very distinctive and carry far, although with their assortment of often harsh chattering or croaking, they must give those trying to transcribe them onto paper severe headaches. The tinkerbirds' calls jar less, with their classic metallic 'tink, tink, tink' or 'tonk, tonk, tonk', but these, too, can grate. Frederick Jackson described a common sentiment when he said of the Ugandan Lemon-rumped Tinkerbird (now, simply, Yellow-rumped Tinkerbird): 'No one, unless afflicted with deafness, can escape from its call ... and in the breeding season it may be heard in many directions and almost incessantly from early morning till sundown; to some people it becomes little less than maddening'. I remember, too, a much-loved uncle who had worked in the colonial service for most of his life, drinking his lunchtime gin on my veranda to the accompaniment of a Yellow-rumped, and telling me how this had driven more than one colonial administrator into insanity, much in the way of a dripping Chinese water torture. Short and Horne, authors of *Toucans, Barbets and Honeyguides*, listened to over 900 consecutive 'tinks' from a Yellow-fronted Tinkerbird before losing count.

One tinkerbird that will not be upsetting many listeners is the White-chested (*Pogoniulus makawai*). This recent addition to the tinkerbirds lifted the total number of species to 10, both the IOC and *HBW* checklists including it, notwithstanding its so far being 'known only from a single specimen' collected in Kabompo District in northern Zambia in 1964. Such deficiency of data was not enough to deter Zambia from celebrating the bird on a 20-Ngwee stamp – one of a series of six bird stamps issued in 1977 (the 25-Ngwee stamp featured another endemic barbet, *Lybius chaplini*, known either as Chaplin's or the Zambian Barbet). Rushing in to celebrate the White-chested Tinkerbird before the bird was even considered a full species by most taxonomists was perhaps a wise move. Further research could easily relegate it to a race of *Pogoniulus bilineatus,* the well-known and widely distributed Yellow-rumped Tinkerbird; or, alternatively, extend the range of the White-chested into nearby Angola or the DRC, thus rendering the bird no longer endemic to Zambia!

Batises & Wattle-eyes
Platysteiridae

Sources differ as to the precise composition of this family, but the general consensus is that there are around 20 batises in the single genus *Batis* and 11 or 12 wattle-eyes mostly in *Platysteira* – all small, insectivorous birds, some of which were known as flycatchers in the past. Two new arrivals in the family are the African and Black-and-white shrike-flycatchers, both more flycatcher than shrike and now appropriately included in Platysteiridae. The truly odd one out is the White-tailed Shrike (referred to in *HBW* as the Ground Batis), which is the only member of the family that is not truly arboreal.

Other than in the heart of the Congo Basin, there is not much of Africa south of the Sahara where a batis cannot be found, although a lot of the species have very restricted distributions. Reichenow's Batis is confined to a tiny corner of southeastern Tanzania, and the Rwenzori Batis to the Albertine Rift in western Rwanda and Uganda on one side, and eastern DRC on the other.

The first batises were formally named as early as 1766 by Carl Linnaeus in the 12th edition of his *Systema Naturae*. These derived from specimens from West and southern Africa – *Muscicapa senegalensis,* the Senegal Batis, and *Muscicapa capensis,* the Cape Batis. While Portugal and Holland were the first European countries to flex their empire-building muscles in West Africa, the French were not far behind and founded a trading station at the mouth of the Senegal River in 1638. From then on, whether by force or diplomacy, they continued gradually to expand their sphere of influence, as well as their general interest in the natural world, aided immensely by the development of museums, zoos and botanical gardens back home. To these were sent specimens of every kind of flora or fauna obtainable, whether skinned or alive.

Down at the tip of the continent, the Dutch settlement founded in the Cape in 1652 soon began to attract visiting naturalists, who ensured that Carl Linnaeus was acquainted with a batis by 1766. Interestingly, two of Linnaeus' students became pioneers of natural history study in southern Africa, although both – Anders Sparrman and Carl Thunberg – arrived there after the publication of their master's magnum opus. Britain's much later start in the scramble for influence in Africa is perhaps demonstrated by the fact that not until 1905 did Frederick Jackson formally describe the Rwenzori Batis in the *Bulletin of the British Ornithologists' Club* as the Rwenzori Puff-back Flycatcher, with the Latin tag *Batis diops*, as it remains to this day.

Batises are all very alike in shape, size and colouring, and separated mainly by micro-differences in plumage. Both sexes have soft and slightly 'erectile' feathers on their rump, hence their once having found a place in the bird books under the name of puff-back flycatchers. Not surprisingly, there is very little consensus over which of the variations on the batis theme merit full specific status. Is the Ituri Batis deserving of its own species, or is it merely a race of the Gabon Batis? Should the Eastern and Western Black-headed batises be split or not?

All batis species show varying degrees of difference in the plumage of the sexes; more often than not, the males are a mix of black, white and grey, while at least parts of the females are coloured some shade of chestnut brown. The Chin-spot Batis is probably the best known, being the most widespread, and is unusual in that its name derives from the plumage of the female, with her chestnut breast band and throat spot, which serve better to identify the species than does the plumage of the male. Seldom do two species of batis overlap, separated by altitude, if nothing else, so species identification is less problematic than the pictures in the books might have us believe. On a walk beyond Samburu in northern Kenya where, unusually, the Chin-spot and Pygmy can both be found, I had given up trying to decide whether a male batis was one or the other, until the arrival of a female with a chestnut breast band – but no trace of any chin spot – put the matter beyond doubt.

Occasionally, the sexes differ in iris colour too, so the males of the Rwenzori Batis and Boulton's Batis from Central Africa both have yellow irides and the females red. This difference in the colour of irides is unusual, the best known example probably being the Saddle-billed Storks, with the female's yellow and the male's dark brown. More usual is for eyes to change as birds age, as do those of the Superb, and indeed many other starlings, going from brown to yellow or red as the birds mature.

Wattle-eye males and females are also distinguished by differing plumage, and again, some of the species, like the Chestnut or Brown-throated, take their names from that of the females. The fleshy wattles apparently serve to enhance communication between individual birds, which can expand them when excited or attracted. Some species have red wattles just above the eyes, while others have blue, green or brown ones entirely surrounding them. The general function of wattles seems to be to attract mates, with larger ones signalling good health and perhaps high testosterone levels. They may also play a role in thermo-regulation, although this is perhaps confined to birds with larger wattles, such as plovers, starlings or cranes.

The ranges of several different species of wattle-eye may overlap in favourable habitat. Kenya is blessed with a wonderful remnant of the Congo Basin forest not far from the border with Uganda, and brimming with birds found nowhere else in the country. The forest is under huge pressure from tree-fellers, agricultural encroachment, illegal grazing and general exploitation, but bird watching here is spectacular and easily accessible. There is a good chance to see Brown-throated, Chestnut and Jameson's wattle-eyes, and the Yellow-bellied is also there, although it takes an ability to recognise its call, and probably also a play-back machine to have much chance of finding one. The Black-throated is recorded as only an occasional visitor to Kakamega but is probably the most widespread in the rest of East Africa.

By far the most unusual species in the family, the White-tailed Shrike, once sat, albeit somewhat uneasily, in its own genus in the Malaconotidae (bushshrikes) but has now arrived in this other all-

African family of Platysteiridae. A lovely grey, black and white bird, it seems more at home in the open than other batises – and more so than other bushshrikes, come to that. It is almost endemic to Namibia, and on my first visit there, I had only been in my Windhoek host's home for an hour before one came bounding down a dry watercourse at the end of his garden. It was hopping from tree to tree, investigating the lower branches for insect prey, all the while seeming to keep a bright yellow eye on its admirers. In hindsight, it is difficult to imagine it as a batis, and like so many other African birds, it seems short of any very close relatives, and actually in something of a taxonomic world of its own.

Helmetshrikes
Prionopidae

Human inhabitants of the southern tip of Africa are sadly deprived of the chance to watch large, noisy parties of helmetshrikes foraging through the tree tops; so are residents in parts of the Congo Basin. Anyone living in the rest of sub-Saharan Africa may find one of the eight species within a reasonable distance from home, although bird watchers will need to work hard to have either the Yellow-crested or the Gabela fill their binoculars.

The Yellow-crested is a dramatic-looking bird – the adults all black but for a bright yellow head (although it is much paler in the young). It is only to be seen in the highland forests of the eastern DRC, and according to Chapin, the type specimen, found on the summit of Mount Mikeno in Kivu district by Walter Ganshof van der Meersch in 1933, at an altitude of 4,400 metres, was dead. Chapin calls the bird King Albert's Helmetshrike, and while it has now shed its colonial moniker, it remains *Prionops alberti*.

The distribution of the Gabela Helmetshrike is equally restricted, and its territory only marginally more accessible – along the escarpment dropping down to the coast of western Angola. The Grey-crested is also very localised, and found only on the southwestern Kenya-Tanzanian border. It is genetically similar enough sometimes to interbreed with the most widespread of all the species, the White-crested, with which it could easily be confused, especially from a distance, when the presence or absence of yellow wattles or distinctive crests is not evident. All species of helmetshrike have yellow eyes, but in only the White-crested are they surrounded by yellow wattles.

The closely related Red-billed and Rufous-bellied were once treated as a single species and are respectively West and Central African birds. I had to have a large party of Red-billed pointed out to me in Ghana's Bobiri Forest Reserve; the 10 or so birds were strangely silent as they fluttered from branch to branch up in the canopy, dark silhouettes against a grey sky. Fortunately, the only other helmetshrike in Ghana is the White-crested, for which these could not possibly have been mistaken.

Retz's, Chestnut-fronted and White-crested occupy more open, accessible country, and as such can be found relatively easily within their respective ranges. Retz's and Chestnut-fronted helmetshrikes are not hard to see in the coastal forests of Kenya, particularly the Arabuko-Sokoke, where they often join up to form mixed flocks. They look, and sometimes sound superficially similar, both species exploring cracks in the bark on trunks and branches for food, or occasionally fly-catching from a perch.

There is little doubting what is or is not a helmetshrike, and all eight species occupy their own single genus, *Prionops*. However, as with oxpeckers, nicators and many others, taxonomists have found it difficult to decide whether to put this genus in its own family. Recently it spent time out among the vangas of Madagascar, the flycatcher-shrikes of the Far East – and, come to that, the shrike-flycatchers of Africa! Then, more recently, both the *HBW* and IOC checklists put them back into a family of their own: Prionopidae.

Helmetshrikes are intensely social, feeding largely on insects in noisy, close-knit family parties. This in itself is nothing unusual, and co-operative feeding behaviour is reasonably common in the bird world. Great White Pelicans group together in a horseshoe of birds, encircling fish which they drive into a tight shoal, each then scooping up beakfuls of water and fish. Verreaux's (Black) Eagles often hunt in pairs, one acting as a distant decoy to cliff-dwelling rock hyraxes, while the other pounces on them as they watch the bird in the distance.

Co-operative feeding among birds can also include feeding flocks of multiple species, which clearly gain from their togetherness. Different species assume different roles in the flock, and benefit in varying ways, either through improved feeding or better security, although the costs and benefits to each member of the flock are still the subject of much research. Outside of the breeding season, helmetshrikes often join mixed-species flocks, which may include members of other species of helmetshrike if these are in the vicinity.

However, helmetshrikes take their sociability several steps further than co-operative feeding, sharing almost every daily activity with fellow members of their party, even roosting together in a huddle, as well as preening one another. They are also one of the ultimate examples of co-operative breeders, in that the whole group helps build the particularly neat nest, incubate the eggs, and care for the young.

Although the dominant breeding pair chooses the site and does most of the construction, the rest of the group participates in the work as well. The nest's mottled grey camouflage in some way compensates for its unprotected, bare-branch setting, and Cecil Priest describes it as being '... made entirely of dead, dry, thin, fine-bladed grass and a large portion of very fine grass of similar aspect. The whole of the exterior is then tightly bound over with cobwebs, which just reach to the rim of this cup-shaped abode. ... placed in a fork in a tree, and tightly bound on to the spot where the two prongs met, but the whole structure was on top, and parallel with the branch.'

Incubation, too, is a communal task, as is feeding the young, but again the breeding pair seems to take on most of the responsibility, with non-breeding females next in order of importance. The defence of the nest against predation from snakes, monkeys or other birds is also group work.

The strategy of co-operative breeding poses many questions, none of which has yet been answered with any certainty. Here we have individuals helping to raise offspring that are not theirs, in the process often foregoing their own chances of reproduction and so flying in the face of one of the basic principles of evolution, namely that the urge to pass on genes dominates all others.

So why do they do it? Co-operative breeding parties usually consist of a dominant couple plus their previous year's offspring and sometimes also siblings of one or other of the breeding pair. All of these helpers share genes with the breeders, so by assisting in raising these offspring the helpers are, to some extent, contributing to the success of their own genes. This is an appealing theory, but one that has been seriously weakened by more detailed research into the 300 or so species engaging in co-operative breeding: many of these studies have revealed that helpers may actually be complete outsiders with no genetic connection to the breeding pair at all.

Current research seems to favour environmental pressures as the main driver of co-operative breeding habits, particularly in many of the drier parts of Africa and Australia, where the strategy is most common. Here, the climate is unpredictable, food is often in short supply and breeding opportunities limited by factors such as an uneven sex ratio, or shortage of territories. Young adults may therefore defer breeding until circumstances are more favourable, during which time the helpers advance up the ladder of seniority in anticipation of eventually acquiring their own territories. In the meantime, so current thinking goes, they might as well help others until getting the chance to pass on their own genes. Co-operation also avoids aggression from other birds and helps with overall security.

The White-crested Helmetshrike – being the most widespread, with a range including much of subtropical southern Africa where research is most advanced – has been studied more than any of the rest of the family. It is catholic in its choice of habitats, even edging into suburbia, and frequenting deciduous woodlands (where it is fortuitously easier to see). Perhaps one indicator of how much research has been done on the species is *HBW*'s description of recorded calls as including 'buzzing, chanting, chattering (on locating food or nest material), chipping, churring, clicking, gobbling, growling (during aggression), rolling, scolding, slurred twittering, whistling, winding and especially, nasal notes'. To these, of course, must be added their loud bill-snapping, which seems to be a feature of all eight species. Cecil Priest was never short of a good turn of phrase in *The Birds of Southern Rhodesia*, and likened the sound of what he then called the Southern Helmetshrike to a 'harsh grating noise, like a car being changed into low gear, and the driver making a terrible mess of it'.

Priest goes on to describe how the birds'... move in succession, one after the other, just like a flock of bush fairies' indulging in 'a continual sort of leap frog, the whole lot never still for a second'. He also quotes one of his correspondents, fellow resident and tsetse fly researcher, Charles Swynnerton, who had told him how the local folks regarded this helmetshrike 'as a bird of omen: should it cross their path, when hunting, from right to left, all is well, and they can proceed with full confidence of success; should it, however, cross from left to right, nothing but the worst of ill fortune can await him who is so foolhardy as to disregard the warning and the only sensible course is to go straight home'.

Despite the helmetshrikes' pronounced co-operative habits and all the activity engendered by so many helpers, Retz's Helmetshrikes, in particular, have a drastic problem with parasitism by cuckoos.

The Thick-billed Cuckoo is the only member of its genus, *Pachycoccyx*. Its species name is *audeberti*, from a Frenchman who collected the type specimen in Madagascar, and where, perversely, the species is now most likely extinct. It is a bird of more open savanna, particularly hawk-like, with a wide and fragmented range, the heaviest shading on its distribution map being in the southeastern segment of Africa. Its main claim to cuckoo fame comes from laying its eggs in the nest of a single species: this, wherever the ranges of the two birds coincide, is Retz's Helmetshrike, from whose pale, blotched eggs those of the cuckoo are almost indistinguishable. If there are no Retz's, as in Central Africa, other helmetshrikes, particularly the Red-billed, must provide nests for the parasite.

Like the African Cuckoo, which is almost exclusively dependent on the Fork-tailed Drongo to host its eggs, Thick-billed Cuckoos have evolved to lay in the nests of this one particular host, where it occurs. They might get away with dropping occasional eggs in the nests of other species that are little attuned to detecting strange eggs among their clutches, but fundamentally, the Thick-billed Cuckoo is now almost totally dependent on the sustained success of the populations of its host, Retz's Helmetshrike. So far down the path of deception have the cuckoos travelled that their nestlings now utter a two-syllable squeak exactly like that of a young Retz's Helmetshrike to attract the attention of its parents. And it was into the relationship between the host and parasite that C.J. Vernon directed his research in Zimbabwe, the results of which were set out in a paper entitled 'Breeding biology of the Thick-billed Cuckoo', published in 1984 in the *Proceedings of the Fifth Pan African Ornithological Congress*.

Vernon's researches showed that the level of parasitism was so high that two of the studied groups of hosts may well have failed to produce any of their own young for up to five years. Over half of a sample of 29 nests was parasitised, the helmetshrikes' energies being focused entirely on raising cuckoos rather than their own young. This may sound like short-term success for the cuckoos, but in the longer term, surely it is in no parasite's interests to drastically reduce the numbers of its host?

One of the great advantages of co-operative breeding is supposedly the added security provided by all the extra helpers. Yet, despite this, the cuckoos are clearly still able to gain relatively easy access to the nests of Retz's Helmetshrikes. In the continuing evolutionary 'arms race' between parasite and host, have helmetshrikes already begun to look for more secluded nest sites?

Bushshrikes
Malaconotidae

The mention of bushshrikes conjures up images of stocky, skulking birds, often brightly coloured, with large hooked beaks, and far more often heard than seen. However, the family embraces such a variety of other species in different genera (tchagras, boubous, gonoleks and puffbacks are all bushshrikes too), that it is actually one of the most diverse bird families in Africa.

The Brubru, currently alone in its own genus, has caused a considerable taxonomic headache, not least for looking and behaving far more like a batis than a conventional bushshrike, and its time among the bushshrikes may be limited. Widespread over most of sub-Saharan Africa, other than in the Cape and Central African forests, and very distinctive with its chestnut flanks, it is often spotted in the upper branches of acacia and miombo woodland, rather than flitting furtively from bush to bush. The nest is also very distinctive – lichen-covered cups instead of the much more twiggy creations of most other species in the family.

The Rosy-patched Bushshrike is also usually put in its own genus; it follows the familiar bushshrike pattern of duetting, but does so far more conspicuously than other family members. Two males, or a male and female, or even three birds together will call loudly from bush tops to one another, as may those of the closely related Bokmakierie. Both species are denizens of dry scrub and bush, flitting, or in the case of the Rosy-patched, often running from one clump to another.

Of the tchagras, the widespread Brown-crowned and Black-crowned are confusingly similar; and as they skulk, like most of the rest of the family, it is often hard to see the tops of their heads, which is the only sure visual way to identify them.

The Black-crowned Tchagra turns up in the field guides for North Africa and the Middle East, thus actually rendering neither its genus nor its family strictly endemic to Africa. Like the Hamerkop, it is to be found over in Yemen and Saudi Arabia too. These tchagras also grace the scrub along much of the northwest African coast, in Morocco, Algeria and Tunisia – surely relics of a pan-African distribution, when the Sahara was savanna, not desert, and they were found throughout most of the continent.

Neither Black- nor Brown-crowned get down into the southern tip of Africa, which is the domain of the Southern Tchagra (although towards the north of its range this overlaps with other tchagras; and even with a good view of its crown it is not easy to distinguish from the Brown-crowned, other than by the Southern's much longer bill). However, while the Southern Tchagra may be the least widespread of all its congeners, it can claim credit for both the Latin and the Anglicised names of the genus *Tchagra*, and for this we can thank that most distinguished of the early African ornithologists, François Levaillant.

Levaillant collected his specimen from the Eastern Cape near the Gamtoos River, later noting the bird's absence from more westerly regions. Because it is the only tchagra in the area, there can be no doubting the identity of the bird he named *Le Tchagra*, most likely following one of the onomatopoeic names conferred upon it by the local Hottentot inhabitants. Many of Levaillant's specimens still survive in the natural history museum in Leiden, and some of these will have helped Jacques Barraband paint the birds for his *Histoire Naturelle des Oiseaux d'Afrique.* So it is that, sandwiched between *Le Gonolek* and *Le Brubru* on Plate No. 70 in Volume 2 is a picture of *Le Tchagra* – actually two, a male and female duetting on a branch – perfectly illustrating Levaillant's description: '*Le male a un cri qui s'entend du loin, et qui s'exprime tres-bien par* tcha-tcha-tcha-gra' (the male has a far-sounding cry, well expressed as *tcha-tcha-tcha-gra*).

Boubous and gonoleks (the names often interchangeable) comprise most of the species in the *Laniarius* genus. Many of the boubous are entirely black, although, fortunately for anyone trying to identify one from another, their ranges are mostly very distinct. Tropical and Southern boubous together occupy much of sub-Saharan Africa and, like so many other bushshrikes, they are far more conspicuous aurally than visually. The former can become more confiding in garden habitat, and might even be persuaded to visit bird tables if these serve up insect fare rather than fruit and seeds.

The Tropical Boubous' duets are famous: like those of many other family members, they are uttered with such perfect timing that it is hard to believe the two calls are not from a single bird. The range of its other utterances is hugely varied, commandeering many column inches in the bird books, with perhaps its most familiar call giving rise to the 'bell bird' epithet. The duetting habits of many of the bushshrikes, and the reasons therefore, have been much researched. In the case of species living in thick undergrowth, being able to keep in contact with one another must be crucial. However, given that the Rosy-patched and Bokmakierie duet out in the open, reinforcing pair bonds or defending territorial boundaries are also likely to be important reasons for such calls.

Gonoleks are particularly striking, with their usually bright red chests, which they tend to display quite prominently. The Black-headed is fairly common in much of Central Africa, as is the Yellow-crowned in the west. The Crimson-breasted Shrike is widespread throughout southern Africa and sometimes travels under the name of Crimson-breasted Gonolek – or as Crimson-breasted Bushshrike or Crimson-breasted Boubou, or even as a race of the Black-headed Gonolek. What's in a name? Not much in this case!

Unlike most other bushshrikes, the Papyrus Gonolek has adapted to an aquatic environment, its waterside habitat rendering it particularly vulnerable to falling water levels, papyrus harvesting and swamp reclamation. A restricted distribution largely in and around Uganda makes it by far the most localised of the gonoleks – at least until the Yellow-breasted Boubou of southern Cameroon becomes a gonolek.

The six puffbacks are very different birds from other bushshrikes – more like brubrus both in size and their preference for the upper branches. Perhaps as a result of living more out in the open, they are less vocal, and also make much neater, better camouflaged nests. The plumage of the sexes differs to a greater or lesser degree, and the males all have different mixes of pied plumage. Puffbacks have feathers on their rump that they (and particularly the males) can puff up into thick white or greyish pom-poms.

If any birds can be called *typical* bushshrikes it is those of the *Malaconotus* and *Chlorophoneus* genera (once treated as a single genus), all species of which also have bushshrike in their names. They are skulking birds, and thus still have many secrets to reveal, particularly about their breeding habits.

The six *Malaconotus* species have big hooked beaks, mostly greeny-yellow plumage and grey or black heads. They don't duet, relying rather on deep whistles or whoops to stay in touch with each other. The Grey-headed is by far the most widespread, with three of the other five species being represented by the tiniest of dots on their distribution maps, none more so than the Uluguru Bushshrike, which is rated as Critically Endangered by the International Union for Conservation of Nature and found only in a small ridge of mountains in eastern Tanzania.

There are six species of *Chlorophoneus* too, all of which resemble *Malaconotus*, with their general green-and-yellow plumage. By far the most widely distributed of these is the Orange-breasted (once Sulphur-breasted – *C. sulfureopectus*). For me, this bird used to kindle uneasy memories. I was taught its distinctive call by a younger friend with whom I shared several happy bird-watching expeditions. One day, probably 15 years ago, he rang to say that he had the opportunity to go and ring birds in Ethiopia and would I lend him some money to enable him to travel; and it was urgent, so could I drive down to a hotel in town and give him the cash – which I duly did. For a long time, no amount of pleading would persuade him to repay that money, and of course the best thing to do would have been just to forget about it. But then I would hear the bird calling again – short, short, short, long – not only 'V' in Morse code, but also the opening theme of Beethoven's 5th symphony! Now, happily, repayment has begun.

Picathartes / Rockfowl
Picathartidae

There is much about Ghana to encourage the bird watcher. Surrounded by Togo, Burkina Faso and Côte d'Ivoire, all of which have had their recent share of turbulence, Ghana has remained stable over the past 20 years. The country is relatively prosperous and safe and is crisscrossed by a network of good roads. Visitor facilities are improving, and on the back of all this, tour operators have begun to exploit the demand for specialist bird-watching itineraries.

Ghana has its own bird book too, *Birds of Ghana* by Nik Borrow and Ron Demey, so bird watchers have no need to cart around a tome covering all the birds of Central Africa. And one of the birds in Ghana, and now in this book, is the White-necked Picathartes.

There are two picathartes – I would like to say Yellow-headed (as does the Ghana book) and Red-headed, but for consistency with most current lists they will have to be White-necked and Grey-necked. The ill-named White-necked has a bright yellow, near-bald head from which sprout little downy wisps of feather, and black patches on either side of its head, like a giant pair of headphones. The Grey-necked's head is a beautiful combination of red, black and blue.

They are long, leggy birds, which bound in huge hops along the ground like miniature kangaroos. As with a lot of the really interesting birds on Earth, taxonomists struggled about where to place them, agreeing on little more than that they are indeed passerines. That they have also been known both as rockfowl and bald crows gives some indication of how difficult they are to classify. The birds have been moved around in a game of taxonomical musical chairs from crows to flycatchers, via starlings, even Old World warblers, before coming to rest, as they now do, in their own family, Picathartidae, which in the IOC list comes right next to the rockjumpers.

Historically, the White-necked was first described by Dutch ornithologist Coenraad Jacob Temminck in 1825 from a specimen taken in Guinea, which probably landed on his desk in the Natural History Museum at Leiden, where he was the first curator. Initially named *Corvus gymnocephalus*, it was moved three years later into its own genus, *Picathartes*, by French zoologist R.P. Lesson, who remains the author. In rather ungainly fashion, the name now mixes derivations of both Latin – *pica* (magpie) and *cathartes* (vulture); and Greek – *gymnos* (bald) and *kephale* (head).

The Grey-necked lives in the forests of southeastern Nigeria, through Cameroon into Gabon. It is not uncommon in the undisturbed forest, but sites accessible to visitors are very limited and the best chance of seeing one is probably in Cameroon's Korup National Park. The White-necked inhabits the forests of southern Guinea, Sierra Leone, Liberia, Côte d'Ivoire and Ghana. It is most widespread in Sierra Leone, not least because, being linked with rock sites – many of which are sacred – the bird has come to be regarded as their guardian, thereby gaining protection itself.

In Ghana, it is least common, and for much of the twentieth century was assumed no longer to live there, until a team of ornithologists found it again in 2003. In the *Bulletin of the British Ornithologists' Club* of 2004 is a brief paper by Messrs Marks, Weckstein, Johnson, Meyer, Braimah and Oppong, titled 'Rediscovery of the White-necked Picathartes in Ghana'. 'Since the 1960s,' it reads, 'attempts to locate this species in Ghana have been unsuccessful. As a result it was widely believed that *P. gymnocephalus* had been extirpated from Ghanaian forests.' However, this was until the team set out a string of mist nets, in which they caught a single picathartes. Having released the bird, they then showed a video they had recorded to local hunters, who confirmed the bird's existence elsewhere as well.

All this took place in the Brong-Ahafo region of Ghana, and as word spread, other scattered colonies revealed themselves, one of which, in Bonkro, further south than where the birds were found in 2003, was eventually deemed suitable for tourists to visit. The hope was that, by focusing all visitor attention on a single population, after ensuring community participation in its protection, the other populations would remain safe, at least from bird-watcher disturbance. Now, having turned from poachers to gamekeepers, the community in Bonkro can almost guarantee to serve up one of the most remarkable birds in the world on a plate – no longer literally, those days are over – to any visitor prepared to make the journey to their village.

After some work near Accra I had met up with a Ghanaian guide, Francis, for a week's introduction to his country's birdlife. So far, the highlight had been a couple of hours on Kakum National Park's shaky walkway. Brown-cheeked, Black-casqued and White-crested hornbills had all hopped into good view through the canopy, until we and the birds were surprised by the arrival of a large group of American evangelists singing 'This Train is Bound for Glory' as they swung their way along the bridge.

The following day we were due in Bonkro, Francis having made all the necessary arrangements for a visit to the picathartes. Knowing that the best chance to see one was when it returned home to roost, we arrived in Bonkro in the early afternoon. 'Remains close to the nest site year-round. Secretive not shy', said the bird book. We would see. A large sign had alerted us to the village's conservation project on the way in, money changed hands, and a local guide was found to accompany us.

The first part of the journey took us through crop fields, not long cleared, with large tree stumps still in evidence. Then we dropped down to cross a small stream and headed off into true 'Upper Guinea forest'. The going was not difficult, and it was quite dry underfoot. Was this a bad thing? From what I had read, the birds built their nests in rock shelters to keep out of the rain, so presumably one of the trade-offs for a wet afternoon would be an increased likelihood of seeing them. I was trying to imagine what our destination would be like, the site where we would stop and wait for the birds if they were not yet there. Mindful of the alternative name of rockfowl, I imagined that cliffs or caves or jumbled boulders would feature somehow. Would there be a stream nearby? I knew the birds needed mud for their nests.

On the way I was discouraged from stopping to try and identify sounds or movements in the forest, and it was only by pure good fortune that, while scanning along a bare branch, my binoculars picked up a motionless, silent Narina Trogon. On we walked, and after an hour or so, reached a steep hill; having clambered up it, we were faced by a huge rock overhang, not quite a cave, but big enough to provide shelter for several bird watchers. Fortunately, it seemed we had the place to ourselves and, having scanned the area from a distance, and seeing no sign of any birds, moved on to the shelter and unshouldered our bags.

As we looked around, there, on the overhang, almost the roof, were two cup-shaped mud nests. Swallows and martins build mud nests too, but theirs are usually in a crevice or a right angle. These nests were not wedged into any nook or cranny, but almost slapped onto the flat surface of the overhang; and from what I knew, picathartes wouldn't fly onto their nests but would rather jump up to them. The mud hemispheres above us were way out of our reach, so how on earth had they built them? *BoA* muses: '... how bird begins construction on smooth ceiling of cave is not known', and then goes on to suggest that maybe old wasp nests form the starting blocks for the birds' nests. These ones looked little used for breeding, or even roosting; and the absence of droppings on the ground below did not bode well for our chances of seeing their occupants returning later.

It was now around 3 p.m. so we settled down silently to wait. I had no idea from which direction the birds were likely to appear, if indeed they did at all. There was a wide vista of forest in front, sloping down to a stream bed with big rocks on the far side, where I had been told the birds also roosted. I started scanning, left to right, right to left.

I suppose at least an hour went by, long enough for concentration to wane, and to have moved through the full range of positions for sitting or squatting on a flat rock floor. Then Francis gave a hiss and pointed back over my left shoulder: hop, bound, hop – there came a single, magical picathartes. Happily for us, it allowed curiosity to triumph over fear as it gave a wonderful display of locomotion. First it hopped up onto a low branch, paused – just long for me to wish momentarily that I had a camera – then down again onto the ground, bounding along right in front of us, even stopping to pick up some leaf litter and then toss it away. A few more giant hops, and it had disappeared into the undergrowth before reappearing – either the same bird or a different one – on the other side of the stream bed near the rocks. Then a second bird appeared from the same direction, and also set off up to the rocks and out of view. It had been a sublime five minutes, favoured with beautiful sightings of one of Africa's most extraordinary birds. That was all I needed to embed the birds in my memory. Maybe other picathartes were waiting for us to leave before they could return to the overhang we were occupying. It was time to go.

Away from their roosts, picathartes are seen only by lucky casual observers. The birds spend most of their day foraging on the forest floor, particularly around columns of army ants, where they feed both on the ants and on the insects these flush. Frogs, lizards and millipedes also contribute to their carnivorous diet, which is generalised enough to suggest that it is not a shortage of food that limits the populations of both species to the scattered small groups in which they are found today.

When I got home I looked up to see what Bannerman had to say about picathartes in his eight-volume *Birds of Tropical West Africa*. He particularly relied on the reports of G.R. Walker who, in May 1937, had taken time off from his research work in Freetown to explore an upland forest area called York Pass in search of strange birds. On his first day out he was clambering among some big rocks when '... a few yards away, I saw a strange black and yellow head peering at me round a rock. The bird came into full view and joined the other birds [bristlebills, alethes and ant thrushes] feeding busily on the little insects fleeing from the drivers.' Walker made several other visits up there, and only once more did he see the picathartes, and again they were in a mixed party following a trail of driver ants.

Picathartes are thought to mate for life, usually laying two eggs in the cup of mud they fashion, which is sited in such a way as to be safe from almost all predators other than forest raptors. They do not generally breed in large colonies, and competition for nest sites may be one of the factors limiting the size of their populations. Otherwise, the responsibility for falling numbers – if this is indeed the case – must lie with that perennial culprit, habitat destruction. Much of Central Africa's forest is being logged mercilessly, or otherwise degraded to such an extent as to be uninhabitable by these shy, yet inquisitive birds. That said, the difficulty in finding the bird makes estimates of existing numbers more guesswork than reasoned calculation, and without a baseline it is very hard to tell how the bird is really faring.

But to end on a more positive note, both species, and particularly the White-necked, now have very high public profiles. Their images appear on postage stamps and corporate logos, and in most of their range they receive some sort of legislative protection. The days when they were trapped and traded as cage birds are largely gone, and now they have become iconic, highly sought-after species, which visitors like me will gladly pay to experience in their natural habitat.

Rockjumpers
Chaetopidae

There are two rockjumpers, Cape and Drakensberg. Not long ago, however, they were lumped into a single species, *Chaetops frenatus.* These birds jumped around in the indigenous montane fynbos of South Africa and in the highlands of Lesotho and surrounding uplands. Actually, this lumping took a taxonomic step backwards because early versions of *Roberts Birds of Southern Africa,* which was first published in 1940, included both Cape and Orange-breasted (now Drakensberg). It also had a third species, the Damara Rockjumper, *Achaetops pycnopygius* (now living under the new name of Rockrunner). 'Affinities uncertain', says *HBW* and, as if to prove its own point, includes them as two of the 300 or so species in the babbler family, Timaliidae.

Since then they have been reassessed, resplit and deemed deserving of their own family; and while superficially they resemble chats with long tails, molecular analysis is now pushing them closer to picathartes. Thanks to the split, at least South Africa has gained an endemic species in the Cape Rockjumper, which retains the original Latin name, with the Drakensberg Rockjumper having become *Chaetops aurantius.* The ranges of the two species don't overlap, although at their extremities these are only 150 kilometres apart in the Eastern Cape, where the Drakensberg Rockjumper edges down below 1,800 metres.

These charming, charismatic birds are highly social, foraging on mountain slopes, raising and lowering their tails as they hop from rock to rock then disappear into the grassy gaps in-between, where they scratch away for insects. Distinctive plumage contributes to their appeal. The Cape Rockjumper has a rich chestnut breast and rump, as opposed to the more orangey hues of the Drakensberg species. The outer feathers of their long black tails are tipped white. Both have a distinctive black throat with white stripes on the sides of their face, and the iris of their eyes shines bright red.

The type specimen came from the Riviersonderend Mountains in the Western Cape and, like the White-necked Picathartes, was named in Holland in 1826 by the museum director, C.J. Temminck – he of courser and stint fame, and many more. Yet, despite its being relatively conspicuous, hopping around on rocks well below 1,000 metres, which it seemingly does at the holiday village of Rooi-Els (not far from Cape Town), the rockjumper's breeding habits were slow to be confirmed.

When Volume VI of *BoA* appeared in 2000, the authors tentatively alluded to the possibility that the rockjumper (then only a single species) gets help at the nest from birds other than its mate, describing it as a 'solitary nester, monogamous, but female often accompanied by two males'. However, this was as far as they would go in admitting that the bird might involve other members of the species in its breeding activities. Then a year later, R.T. Holmes et al. wrote up the results of three years of study near Cape Town in their paper, 'Breeding System of the Cape Rockjumper, a South African Fynbos Endemic', which appeared in *The Condor* 104(1). Apart from recognising two species, they were also able to confirm that 'breeding groups ... consisted of a breeding pair and often 1–2 additional individuals, which were usually, but not exclusively, offspring of the adult pair from the preceding breeding season. Supernumerary individuals of both sexes participated in territorial defence and alarm calling and in the feeding of nestlings and fledglings of the breeding pair. Supernumerary females also helped with nest building and incubation. The findings confirm earlier suppositions that the Cape Rockjumper is a socially monogamous, co-operative-breeding species, with offspring remaining in their home territory for at least one year during which they assist their parents in raising additional offspring.'

The plumage of the sexes differs markedly in rockjumpers (unlike in those other much studied co-operative breeders, the helmetshrikes), so it was at least easy for the researchers to identify the gender of helpers.

The Drakensberg Rockjumper is harder to find, although like its congener, it moves down to lower altitudes in the winter. Much of the range it occupies is in the mountains of Lesotho, and the best place to find it seems to be in the sub-alpine grasslands up towards the top of the gravelly Sani Pass, close to the border between KwaZulu-Natal and Lesotho.

With both species of rockjumper ranging over mountain tops, they are clearly susceptible to rising temperatures. Because they already breed high up in their stony strongholds, there is very little room for any upward expansion should average summer temperatures rise consistently. Such limited dispersal opportunities have caused recent research to be directed towards ascertaining the birds' response to warmer summers. The conclusion seems to be that they forage much less when it is very hot, and this is, of course, just when they need to be collecting food for their young.

The Second Southern African Bird Atlas Project began in July 2007, 10 years after the publication of the first *Atlas of Southern African Birds* in 1997. Plans are for it to continue indefinitely, but even now, effective comparisons can be made between the two sets of data. Sadly, both range and reporting rates of rockjumpers show serious declines. There could be other contributory factors than the warming world, but while the expansion of agricultural activity may have left its mark some time ago, and invasive vegetation could take over pristine grasslands, fires – without which a lot of the fynbos plants will not germinate – are the only likely threat to most of the birds' remaining habitat.

Nicators
Nicatoridae

Nicators have been bounced back and forth between bushshrikes (hooked bills and shy, solitary behaviour giving the two families much in common) and bulbuls, with which they share at least a superficial similarity. Eye rings and lores on the face are characteristics of some bulbuls, as they are of nicators, and nicator plumage is basically olive-green too. However, yellow spots on the wing distinguish nicators from all but faraway Spotted Greenbuls; and the gregarious tree-top partying habits of these bulbuls, which make them a gift to any bird watcher, easily distinguish them from nicators, or from any other bulbul, for that matter.

Nothing emphasises these taxonomic difficulties better than the situation in which the *BoA* editors seemed to find themselves. Plate 21 of Volume IV contains paintings of each of *Nicator gularis, chloris* and *vireo* among the bulbuls, but no accompanying text, merely a note below the illustrations that these species have been 'subsequently reclassified as *incertae sedis* [relationships unknown] possibly near Laniidae see volume VI'. Such are the problems that beset the editors of any series like this; volumes appear one after the other, over many years, and throughout the course of production, taxonomic rejigging suddenly renders the earlier illustration plans outdated.

Now DNA analysis suggests that nicators should be in their own family, and most sources today reflect this. Details of the analysis are beyond the scope of this book, but such distinction is enforced by the nicators' very loud and distinctive vocalisations, as well as their idiosyncratic behaviour, particularly when it comes to building nests. These are like neither the bulbuls' nor the bushshrikes', and are more akin to those of doves. They are minimalist constructions of crossed sticks, supporting smaller twigs which, at least in the case of the Western Nicator, appear to be selected for their state of decomposition, the invading fungi eventually acting as some form of glue. So sparse is this construction that eggs can easily fall through the gaps, perhaps explaining why the bird invests in only a single egg each brood – although, with such seemingly poor nesting success, might it actually make more sense to lay a larger clutch?

The other two species of nicator (Eastern and Yellow-throated) build marginally more robust nests in which they may lay more than one egg, although a description of the nest of an Eastern Nicator near Amani in Tanzania in the 1937 edition of *Ibis* – 'Biological & other notes on some East African Birds' by R.E. and W.M. Moreau – doesn't bode much better for the safety of any offspring: 'The middle was filled in perfunctorily with tendrils and a few slender twigs. The result was a lacy affair that one would have judged incapable of supporting a bird that weighs a couple of ounces.'

Crombecs, Longbills & allies
Macrosphenidae

This family is a recent creation, gathering up a potpourri of small African insectivorous warblers: crombecs, longbills, and then five other species, which are all single-species genera, namely Victorin's Warbler, Rockrunner, Cape Grassbird, Moustached Grass-warbler and Grauer's Warbler.

It derives from recent efforts to resolve classification conundrums, showing how difficult the task is, even with the input of DNA analysis. Many reclassifications of African passerines are a consequence of the partial dismantling of the babbler family; others, like this one, come from reassessing birds generally referred to as African warblers. Some of the family members may seem of little general interest – being small and seldom seen – but then, to other enthusiasts, this can be exactly why they are so deserving of attention.

There are sometimes nine, sometimes 11 crombecs – from the Dutch *krom* ('bent') and *bek* ('beak'), depending on the source – and all are distinguished by their almost total lack of any tail. They divide into two groups: forest- or scrub-dwelling species (Green, Lemon-bellied and White-browed), and the rest, which are at home in drier woodland, with Philippa's and Somali inhabiting particularly arid territory. The Long-billed is the only crombec in most of the southern part of the continent and, as such, is largely responsible for the crombec map's covering almost all of sub-Saharan Africa. At least half the species are a combination of grey above and some shade of chestnut or buff below, while the forest ones tend to have greener, more cryptic backs. The Green is a bird of both scrub and forest, and one of its subspecies was described and named by Frederick Jackson after his bird collector, Baraka (who appears again later in this chapter – see page 109) in search of the Pin-tailed Whydah's nest). Jackson collected the bird, which he named Baraka's Crombec, and today, as *Sylvietta virens baraka*, it remains a recognised subspecies.

Crombec nests are purses or pouches, usually with an entrance at the top, fabricated from lichen, grass, bark and spiderwebs, and suspended from a single branch. That of the Long-billed Crombec is particularly favoured as a suitable receptacle for the eggs of Klaas's Cuckoos, which occur throughout this crombec's entire range. The female cuckoo may lay a total of over 20 eggs in a season. She removes at least one host egg at the time of laying, and the nestling ejects any surviving eggs and young almost within hours of hatching. A single cuckoo can thus inflict significant damage on the population of its hosts.

Most of the longbills are canopy feeders, or creep around in vine tangles, and, as such, are not easy to spot. The only feature to distinguish them is their long beak – not as long as the sunbird's, and straight. They are mostly olive-green in colour, and being usually in the tree tops, often seen in silhouette or against leaves of a similar green, it is no surprise that little is known of their habits. Pulitzer's Longbill is extremely rare, hanging on in relict bits of forest in western Angola; Kemp's, Yellow and Grey are at home in Congolese and Central African forest, the ranges of two of the three often overlapping. The fifth species, Kretschmer's Longbill, might fill the binoculars of dedicated bird watchers in eastern Tanzania and Mozambique, where it is the only one, but they would be lucky –'… buries itself in thick vegetation; elusive and hard to see' is what *BoA* has to say about it!

Victorin's Warbler is a bird with very restricted distribution in damp mountain fynbos of the Cape, immortalising the Swedish traveller, Johan Fredrik Victorin, who arrived there in 1853, aged 22. Victorin was given the opportunity to leave Sweden in the hopes of relieving his tuberculosis, of which he was to die two years later, but not before he had completed a book of his travels, *Resa I kaplandet aren 1853–1855*. It seems surprising that, with the Cape area having been so extensively explored and settled, the bird had not been taken and named earlier; however, Victorin's collection of 517 bird specimens of 153 different species was always likely to yield something new. Certainly, the bird keeps to thickets along highland streams and to other rank vegetation, but its yellow eye and grey cheek are very distinctive; and while it is something of a skulker, it is not averse to singing out in the open on a rock or bush. Three years after Victorin's death, the bird was formally described in his memory as *Bradypterus victorini* by fellow Swede, C.J. Sundevall of the Swedish Museum of Natural History. Recently it had to be moved to *Cryptillas*, leaving *Bradypterus* to a host of other African warblers, including the localised and elusive Knysna Warbler, which Sundevall also described.

The Rockrunner, also once a babbler, is found only in Namibia and southwestern Angola, and seems to have caused the *BoA* editors similar difficulties to those of the nicators, its illustration on Plate 6 of Volume V bearing the inscription 'see volume VI'! There, this distinctive, chestnut-bellied bird appears sharing the genus *Chaetops* with the Rockjumper, which was then a single species. Later, the Rockrunner would be moved out of *Chaetops* to become the sole occupant of *Achaetops*, as it is today. A spectacular vocalist, its calls are reminiscent of those of the Cape Grassbird, but much more varied.

It is always a pleasant surprise when any bird with 'warbler' in its name proves relatively easy to identify. This the Moustached Grass-warbler certainly is, and it is also not usually too hard to find where it is known to occur once it has betrayed its presence by a loud – and even to my ears distinctive – song. Its plain breast and black 'moustache' stripes make it unmistakeable. The Cape Grassbird is also very distinctively plumaged, although it is sometimes reluctant to come out of the thick grass and scrub to display unless prompted onto a bush top to sing. There is a touch of the cisticola about it, with its chestnut cap and strongly streaked back, but it has a much longer tail.

Yellow Flycatchers
Erýthrocercidae

The three species of *Erythrocercus* used to be grouped into the monarch and paradise flycatcher family but are now, for the time being at least, out on their own. They are distinguished from other flycatchers probably more by habits than looks. Travelling in small parties, as they do, is unusual flycatcher behaviour and so is their foraging, warbler-like, among the leaves rather than taking insects in mid-air.

These are the Little Yellow, Livingstone's and Chestnut-capped fly-catchers, united together certainly by similarity of shape, all being small, lively birds with long tails. The Little Yellow Flycatcher has the most restricted distribution of the three but, when one gets into its territory, is probably the simplest to see. It is found along a strip of coastal and inland forest from southern Somalia, through Kenya, to northern Tanzania. In Kenya it is easily seen in the Arabuko-Sokoke forest near Malindi. The forest is a mosaic of *Brachystegia*, *Cynometra* and mixed woodland, and in any of these habitats parties of the Little Yellow may be twittering through the trees, so making them much easier to spot than more silent, solitary flycatchers.

Despite being fairly common within its home range, the Little Yellow was the last of the three species to be formally described, evidence of how relatively recent is a lot of the exploration of East Africa's biodiversity. The type specimen of this bird was only taken in 1901 by the German ornithologist Carlo von Erlanger on the Juba River in what was then Italian Somaliland.

Further down the Tanzanian coast is the territory of Livingstone's Flycatcher, much like the Little Yellow in habits and looks, except for a rufous tail with a black band near the end. Its range stretches much further inland, into Malawi and Zambia and even parts of northern Zimbabwe. This species was described 30 years earlier than the Little Yellow, from a specimen taken on the Mozambique-Zambia border. It ended up on the tables in the ornithological department of the British Museum, there to be examined and named by George Robert Gray, who worked in the museum for most of his life, writing in detail about insects as well as birds from all over the world.

Which leaves the West African representative of the trio, the Chestnut-capped Flycatcher, and perhaps the most interesting of the three. The chestnut cap itself is flecked with buff streaks, the tail is also chestnut, and this, together with a yellowish throat, make for an unmistakable bird. It is widely but patchily distributed throughout West and Central Africa, just reaching Uganda in the Budongo Forest close to Lake Albert. Birds often seem prepared to forsake the security of dense woodland for the edges of plantations and narrow strips of riverine forest, making them easier to find.

Mention of the Chestnut-capped Flycatcher provides an opportunity to introduce one of the most interesting characters in the history of American ornithology – John Cassin. Quaker, businessman, unpaid curator of the Philadelphia Academy of Natural Sciences, and much more, he described the Chestnut-capped Flycatcher in 1855 using a specimen taken in Gabon. He also described nearly 200 other new species from all over the world, many of whose common names are still prefaced by Cassin; those from Africa include a spinetail, honeybird, hawk-eagle and malimbe.

In the course of his work Cassin, who travelled little outside of America, showed how effective taxonomy relied not only on the efforts of collectors in the field, but also on detailed analyses and comparisons – in well-developed centres of science – of what they had collected. Most of those he named derived from his studies of skins, purchased by the academy and brought back to America (including a large collection from Central Africa, judging by the distribution of the African birds that bear his name). To preserve them, the skins were often treated with a chemical mixture that included arsenic, and there is a sad irony to his succumbing to arsenic poisoning aged only 55.

Cassin named the Chestnut-capped Flycatcher *Erythrocercus mccallii*, taking the contribution of Americans to African ornithology one step further by acknowledging his respect for fellow naturalist George Archibald McCall, also from Philadelphia. McCall was a professional soldier who indulged his passion for birds by writing to Cassin with descriptions of new ones he had seen on the frontier in the course of fighting and periodically being wounded or taken prisoner by Indians, Mexicans or Confederates.

Neither Cassin nor McCall knew anything of the habits of the bird they described, particularly that the Chestnut-capped Flycatcher is a communal breeder, as has now been discovered. J.P. Chapin didn't know this either by the time Part 2 of his *Birds of the Belgian Congo* emerged in 1939, nor did Bannerman by 1953. Today it is well established that groups patrol the edges of their territories together, and contribute to nest building. Helpers most likely also assist with incubation and raising the young. Not surprisingly, however, the breeding habits of this little West African bird are far less documented than are those of the more conspicuous and better-studied species of communal breeders, such as helmetshrikes or wood hoopoes.

Dapple-throat & allies
Modulatricidae

Another new family created for seeming loose ends comprises just three genera, each containing a single species: the Dapple-throat, Spot-throat and Grey-chested Babbler, all of which were previously in the babbler family and are no longer, despite the latter's name. Given their extremely limited distribution, any but the most assiduous ornithologist would be forgiven for querying whether there really are such birds in Africa, although the Grey-chested Babbler may have become familiar to some bird watchers under its earlier names of Grey-chested Illadopsis and Kakamega.

The Dapple-throat (once Dappled Mountain-robin) – a rare bird of eastern Tanzanian and northern Mozambican forest – is reasonably easily identified if its streaked chest is visible as it sneaks through the thickets, or otherwise by its distinctive early morning call, reminiscent of an oriole. With just a view of its back, it could easily be mistaken for the Spot-throat, whose even more restricted range covers much of the same areas of Tanzania. The Spot-throat has a rufous chest and a small patch of spots on its throat, and if ever encountered it is more likely to be on the forest floor than in the undergrowth.

The Grey-chested Babbler is best known of the three, not least for occurring in the much visited Kakamega Forest in western Kenya, from which it took an earlier common name. It is the size of a small thrush, shy and retiring – unless one can spot it pursuing columns of army ants, when it may be joined by several other species also bent on making the most of the bounty.

The bird's distribution map raises fascinating questions. Like many forest species, it occurs in two very disjunct populations: a Central African one in a small patch of mountain forest in southwestern Cameroon and southeastern Nigeria, and another much further east in the forests of the Albertine Rift in the DRC, Uganda and Rwanda, as well as just over the border into Kenya.

The Kenyan outpost of the eastern population may well be explained by Kakamega Forest being a relict of a once continuous swath of woodland, most of which has now been destroyed, and which originally joined that forest to the Albertine Rift. However, the western and eastern ranges are still almost linked by continuous Congo Basin forest; and yet in most of this forest corridor there are no Grey-chested Babblers. Were the birds once present in these heartland forests, and did they for some reason retreat, or otherwise spread, both east and west, to what were then more suitable climes? Did the vast forests contract, squeezing the birds into smaller refuges; and when they expanded again, were the babblers unable to colonise the new areas between their populations, perhaps because other competing species prevented them from getting a foothold there? Despite the vast distance between the populations, the two differ little, and at least not enough apparently for them to warrant subspecific status, suggesting that the separation was relatively recent.

Sugarbirds
Promeropidae

Like the rockjumpers, sugarbirds are specific to southern Africa; and, like rockjumpers, their genus comprises just two species, and is the only one in the family.

Sugarbirds, especially the much shorter-tailed females, bear a superficial resemblance to sunbirds. Their habits are similar, too, probing into the flowers for sugary nectar or searching around for insect protein, and it is not surprising that they have sometimes been grouped together. Other investigations even have the Australasian honeyeaters as the sugarbirds' closest relatives, particularly after it seemed that identical parasites were to be found in the blood of both. Now the parasites seem less conclusive evidence than was originally supposed, so the taxonomic jury is still in debate.

The Cape and Gurney's sugarbirds are similar looking, both with a distinctive yellow vent and plain brown back. Gurney's has a much brighter chestnut breast band, and the Cape male a far longer tail. They used to share a sliver of overlapping habitat in the Eastern Cape, but probably not any more, so with the range of each now quite distinct, there is little chance of confusing the two.

The Cape Sugarbird is one of six species described as 'fynbos endemics', all of which have very restricted ranges along the southern tip of the continent (although this hasn't prevented the sugarbird from finding its way onto the postage stamps of both Mali and Liberia!). The Cape Rockjumper is another such endemic, and so is the Orange-breasted Sunbird, both the male and female of which are unmistakable, the female showing a distinctive yellowy breast. The fourth fynbos endemic is the Protea Canary (sometimes the Protea Seedeater), a finch with a thick seed-eating bill, and actually with a much wider diet than just protea seeds. These birds often congregate around burnt areas for short-term feasting before the vegetation starts shooting, and have to wait up to seven years for a lot of the species to flower and produce seeds again. Another endemic seed-eater is the Cape Siskin; and the skulking habits of the final endemic, the Victorin's Warbler, make its precise distribution hard to ascertain.

With such restricted ranges, there is much concern over the future of these species, especially if the typically Mediterranean climate continues to change significantly. In their paper 'Endemic birds of the Fynbos biome; a conservation assessment and impacts of climate change' published in the March 2016 volume of *Bird Conservation International*, Alan Lee and Phoebe Barnard identify the Cape Rockjumpers and Protea Canaries as being particularly vulnerable and least likely to cope with rising temperatures.

Some of these endemics have adapted well to exotic vegetation, and have thus been able to expand their ranges out of immediate danger. Cape Siskins and Orange-breasted Sunbirds seem at home in gardens, and the first Cape Sugarbird I ever saw was in the Kirstenbosch National Botanical Garden, perched on top of a protea, on which the birds are largely dependent, before it moved on to a nearby aloe. I was quickly reminded of the Scarlet-tufted Malachite Sunbird, which, with its equally distinctive long tail, delights in feeding on the blooms of proteas on the moorlands of Mount Kenya. Both sugarbird species are important pollinators, although they can damage commercially grown protea blooms in the course of their visits, the birds' particularly sharp claws scratching the leaves as they probe into the flowers.

Gurney's Sugarbirds (J.H. Gurney was a Norfolk banker and Member of Parliament who appears never to have visited Africa, but worked a lot in the Natural History Museum in London) are locally common in areas further north. One of the most likely places to find them – as it is to spot a Drakensberg Rockjumper – is up the Sani Pass on the way to Lesotho. These sugarbirds also find proteas in their mountain homes, particularly *Protea roupelliae*, which attracts at least three species of sunbird as well. When the cold sets in and the pink proteas have faded, the sugarbirds drop down lower in search of the spiky blooms of the winter-flowering *Aloe arborescens*.

It may be something of a surprise to find that there is suitable habitat for Gurney's Sugarbirds in both Mozambique and Zimbabwe. It came as a surprise to Cecil Priest too, at least to find them,'… for the first time in our lives in May 1930 in Captain E. Allott's garden at ... Melsetter [a small town in eastern Zimbabwe] ... I did not notice any proteas in the vicinity, which I understand are a great attraction for these birds, but there was a profusion of other wild flowers, which had undoubtedly attracted them there.'

It would then have been getting on for mid-winter, and while both species of sugarbird often breed in the cooler months if those coincide with the flowering of the proteas, clearly in this case they were prepared to forego any breeding urges and forage further afield in search of alternative sources of food.

Hyliotas
Hyliotidae

The four hyliotas now comprise their own family, after being claimed by both the Old World warblers in Sylviidae and the batises and wattle-eyes in Platysteiridae. Some of their behaviour is flycatcher-like, and *BoA* remarked that they might even be diminutive bushshrikes and that 'DNA studies would be most revealing'. This they were, and it now seems that the family represents an ancient lineage of its own, with no close relatives at all, and so actually its members are a lot more interesting than they look or the way they behave.

Hyliotas are small, warbler-like birds of the tree tops, be these in miombo woodland or thicker forest. Their overall colour scheme is dark back and yellowy breast, with varying amounts of white on the wings. Where the ranges of the Southern and Yellow-bellied overlap, which they do in Malawi and Zambia, they are extremely difficult to distinguish. The Violet-backed is readily identified by the near total lack of white in its wings, while the endangered Usambara Hyliota is the only species in the forest canopy and edges of the Usambara Mountains in northeastern Tanzania. This was once considered a race of the Southern, but interestingly, and unlike the Southern, shows no obvious difference in the plumage of the sexes.

Hyliotas are essentially canopy feeders, searching leaves and bark for insects. Single birds or pairs often join mixed-species flocks of weavers, woodpeckers, eremomelas and others as they move restlessly about in the tree tops. Because they are usually high up, either backed by dark vegetation or silhouetted against a grey sky, hyliotas are seldom easy to view well; and, by uttering no more than a rather tuneless twittering to keep in touch with their fellows, give no help to anyone trying to identify them.

Oxpeckers
Buphagidae

Birds often take lifts on the back of other animals, usually the better to hawk insects disturbed by their hosts' progress through the grass. Carmine Bee-eaters are frequently photographed riding on Kori Bustards, noisy flocks of Piapiacs perch on elephants in the Ugandan national parks, while Common Drongos can be equally opportunistic. Cattle Egrets and Wattled Starlings also seem to prefer to hunt from the back of an animal, especially in longer grass when it is not easy for them to follow in its footsteps. These birds are all using the animal as a beater, waiting for it to flush out their food. However, for oxpeckers the host provides the food, sometimes even *is* the food, and that is why they perch on it.

Any visitor to one of Africa's great game parks is likely to encounter an oxpecker, with one or other species – sometimes both – occurring through much of the sub-Saharan savanna. At one time included among the starlings, the Red-billed and Yellow-billed are now deemed different enough from all other birds to be the only members of the genus *Buphagus*, which itself constitutes a family. The two species are genetically close enough for hybrids to have been reported from Zimbabwe, and can be found together in parts of East and southern Africa – even on the same animal.

The colour of the bill may be difficult to spot, not least because the Yellow-billed also has a red bill tip, and when first alarmed by approaching humans, both species are inclined to scrabble over to the far flank of their host, and so out of sight. If the bird is flying, the easiest way to distinguish between the two species is by the pale rump of the Yellow-billed. In general, they have surprisingly similar habits, differing little in diet, host preference or tree-hole nest sites. Some surveys have found Yellow-billed to prefer thinner-furred animals, particularly buffalo, while the Red-billed is more at home on an animal like a giraffe, with much thicker hairs on its hide. Otherwise, their respective habits give little indication of which of the two is crawling over the back of a large herbivore, where apparently both courtship and copulation also take place.

Although conventional wisdom has it that oxpeckers usually roost in tree cavities, there is circumstantial evidence for their actually roosting on their hosts. The 1982 *Honeyguide* journal from Zimbabwe contains a note from W.R. Thompson of Hwange National Park relating how he was repeatedly having to chase Greater Kudu from his garden: 'One moonlit night ... when a large kudu cow was noisily munching away at some cornflower plants in front of the bedroom window ... I was able to see quite clearly five birds on her shoulder and lower neck. They were not moving about but sitting quietly ... when I put on the outside lights the kudu stood stock still for several minutes peering at me through the glass. I could see the [Yellow-billed] oxpeckers were sound asleep with their eyes tightly shut.'

Most observers understandably focus on feeding behaviour, and it would be difficult to improve on Vernon van Someren's description in *A Bird Watcher in Kenya*: 'Oxpeckers are really rather unpleasant birds to watch feeding; they have the persistence of a swarm of bluebottles round a piece of meat. They slip and slide all over an animal's hide, often keeping to the side away from the observer, and cling closely to the hair with their long sharp claws. The beak is held parallel to the skin, and they wield it in a scissoring motion from side to side through the hair, two or three sweeps being made in one area before moving jerkily off to try elsewhere.'

He could have added that the birds also use their tail to help cling to their host's hide, rather as does a woodpecker on a tree.

While the Yellow-billed may prefer to feast on buffalo backs, it has shown itself to be flexible in its choice of host. In 1975, 12 Red-billed and 47 Yellow-billed were reintroduced into Matobo National Park in Zimbabwe. The Red-billed did not survive – maybe there were too few of them to begin with – but the Yellow-billed flourished, not least because of the large numbers of buffalo there. Then, in 1986, all the 600 buffalo were translocated because of a nearby outbreak of foot and mouth disease. Nevertheless, subsequent study showed the birds had continued to survive in the park with little difficulty, just shifting to a variety of other hosts – white rhino, zebra, giraffe and wildebeest – without any seemingly adverse effects. In his paper 'The Effect of the Removal of Buffalo on the Host Selection of Yellow-billed Oxpeckers in Zimbabwe', published in *Tropical Zoology* in 1992, James Dale then estimated a population of nearly 200, and quite possibly a lot more.

Over time, the birds have evolved along with their natural hosts, and only comparatively recently, at least in evolutionary terms, have the hides of domestic animals become available to them. Before the nineteenth century, the large herds of cattle provided ideal feeding grounds, and their African owners generally regarded the birds in a positive light for helping control unwanted ticks on their animals. However, for newly arrived European farmers, raising cattle as a commercial venture meant that breeding stock became increasingly valuable and the loss of any such animals to tick-borne disease was disastrous. Once the more reliable system of chemical control became a reality, most farmers would settle for nothing less; but for the oxpeckers, it not only reduced their food supply, but also proved toxic. This was probably why at least the Yellow-billed Oxpecker disappeared from South Africa. The dwindling herds of large wild herbivores throughout the continent also worked against the birds, but the development of game farms in southern Africa, along with careful oxpecker reintroduction programmes, has supplemented natural recoveries of populations of both species.

While cattle seemed to cope with the presence of oxpeckers, the birds had a very negative impact on the softer-skinned donkeys. Writing about nineteenth-century Uganda, Frederick Jackson described how 'to pack-donkeys and mules with a sore back, as all caravan leaders and transport riders can attest, it [the Red-billed] is one of the greatest curses. In the old caravan days, along the road between Teita and Mumias, the number of donkeys rendered unfit for service, the majority of which died, entirely through the attentions of this bird, and quite apart from other causes, must have amounted to many hundreds. The least little abrasion on the skin, when detected by one of these pests, was at once pecked into a ghastly sore.'

In his 1959 *Pirates and Predators*, Richard Meinertzhagen also has plenty to say about oxpeckers, including how 'donkeys resent them and have been seen to roll or run under bushes to rid themselves of the birds' – little wonder, if Jackson is to be believed!

These are serious charges against the oxpeckers: that they are sinner rather than saint, that it is less the ticks they seek, than the host's blood, and even flesh – after all, *Buphaga* (their generic name) means 'beef-eating'. Meinertzhagen recorded the birds visiting slaughterhouses in both Kenya and Somaliland to feed off blood from freshly flayed hides; and during an oxpecker reintroduction programme in South Africa, the donkey hosts were spared the aggressive attentions of the birds by the supply of a tempting counter-attraction – blood from recently slaughtered animals, treated with an anticoagulant. It is difficult to know whether a bird eating a blood-swollen tick is after the blood or the tick tissue, but whichever, the birds' love of both ticks and blood cannot be denied. The evidence for their picking away at existing wounds, especially in drier times when ticks are less abundant, seems overwhelming, although to what extent they actually open new wounds in an animal's hide is less certain; if this were the case one would expect to see them generally giving attention to thinner-skinned game and there is no proof that they do so.

W.L. McAtee wrote in 'Birds Pickaback' in the March 1944 *Scientific Monthly*: 'The perching of birds upon animals is not altogether an innocent and mutually advantageous arrangement; like so many relations, it has become perverted in some instances and has a sinister side.' Of the oxpecker, Jackson was convinced that 'beyond all doubt its favourite food, when it had a chance of obtaining it, is blood and meat, the latter being pecked away in minute particles'. Having examined the crops of several birds collected while they were feeding on both rhino and cattle hides, he became convinced that 'ticks, if at all, only form an infinitesimal portion of its food.' However, when Sclater came to edit Jackson's work, he was able to refer to the researches of R.E. Moreau (written up after Jackson's death), in the 1933 *Bulletin of Entomological Research*. Here, Moreau describes how he found a total of 2,291 blood-sucking ticks in 55 out of 58 oxpecker stomachs that he examined from birds taken in Amani in eastern Tanzania. Other items in oxpecker diets include lice, various fly larvae, mites and probably also ear wax (particularly from buffalos), but ticks still seem to dominate, and that is the wisdom that prevails today. So, while the oxpecker may occasionally act as a pure parasite, generally the relationship with its host seems to be one of mutual benefit.

There is another dimension to oxpecker behaviour, and that is one of 'watchbird' or alarm sounder, and regardless of whether the bird has eaten ticks or drunk blood straight from the animal, this other role is of undoubted benefit to the host. Before humans had begun to domesticate livestock, and still relied on hunting down their food, the birds would have been regarded as nothing but pests, given their habit of issuing loud hissing alarm calls and the flock's taking off into the air as a warning of impending danger. More recently, hunters for sport rather than sustenance have likewise found the presence of the birds favours the chances of the hunted rather than the hunter. Vernon van Someren was once tasked with canvassing opinions on oxpeckers among East African cattle ranchers and others, and his report stated that'... the bird has earned a bad reputation too among professional hunters. It perches frequently on the larger game animals, and its hissing alarm call clearly gives warning to the duller sighted beasts on the approach of danger.' He added that the general feeling was that any form of control was unnecessary, given that bird numbers had decreased as chemical tick control had improved, and there had been no noticeable increase in feeding on raw sores.

Meinertzhagen, who had done more than his share of game shooting, felt that the presence of oxpeckers lulled the animals into a sense of security – that they became 'conscious of an extra protection when accompanied by *Buphagus*. A rhinoceros is much more alert when without *Buphagus* than when they accompany him.' He also found that this might play into the hands of the hunter who, with the game's natural caution dulled by the oxpecker's presence, could sometimes get much closer than he otherwise would have done. Then, of course, there have been times in many hunters' lives when a flock of oxpeckers has flown off a sleeping buffalo, so warning hunters of the animal's presence – which may, of course, either result in the hunters beating a cautious retreat to safety or else loading up to try and shoot animals they would otherwise have had no idea were there.

David Livingstone's *Missionary Travels and Researches in South Africa*, published in 1858, contains many fascinating observations on the natural history of the areas through which he trekked. Here he describes birds, sitting on the back of a buffalo, that behaved exactly like oxpeckers, but which he named *Textor erythrorhynchus*, probably referring to what are now Red-billed Buffalo-weavers: 'On her withers sat about twenty buffalo-birds which act the part of guardian spirits to the animals. When the buffalo is quietly feeding, this bird may be seen hopping on the ground picking up food, or sitting on the mammal's back, ridding it of insects with which its skin is sometimes infested. The sight of the bird being much more acute than that of the buffalo, it is soon alarmed by the approach of any danger, and, flying up, the buffalos instantly raise their heads to discover the cause which has led to the sudden flight of their guardians.'

Later, though, there is no doubting his identification of the oxpecker: 'Another African bird, namely *Buphaga africana*, attends the rhinoceros for a similar purpose. It is called "kala" in the language of the Bechuanas. When these people wish to express their dependence upon another, they address him as "my rhinoceros", as if they were the birds. The satellites of a chief go by the same name. This bird can not be said to depend entirely on the insects on that animal, for its hard, hairless skin is a protection against all except a few spotted ticks; ... and while the buffalo is alarmed by the sudden flying up of its sentinel, the rhinoceros, not having keen sight, but an acute ear, is warned by the cry of its associate, the *Buphaga africana*.'

Whydahs, Indigobirds & the Cuckoo-finch
Viduidae

Ten indigobirds, nine whydahs and the Cuckoo-finch are the unlikely assemblage of species that make up this family, its members known colloquially as Viduids. All are African endemics and – much to the surprise of many, even seasoned bird watchers – all are distinguished by being brood parasites.

Of these 20 species, only the Cuckoo-finch does not belong in the *Vidua* genus. This bird has had a chequered taxonomic history. It was initially described in 1868 by German ornithologist Jean Louis Cabanis as a canary, before its superficial resemblance to the weavers took it to that family as the Parasitic Weaver. Finally, molecular genetics won out over basic morphology, propelling its move into a family together with the similarly parasitic indigobirds and whydahs.

The indigobirds were once considered a single species but have relatively recently been split, essentially on the basis of the various hosts they parasitise. Breeding males are all small, glossy black, finch-like birds, sometimes distinguished from other indigobird species by characteristic beak or leg colour or by subtle distinctions in their glossy sheen, otherwise only by song, which is influenced by whatever host raised them. In non-breeding plumage, males are drab brown birds with streaked crowns, as are the females all year round.

The breeding male whydahs are perhaps the most striking of all the continent's small birds, with a tail three or four times as long as their body. The five paradise whydahs are all very similar, and what was once deemed a single species, *Vidua paradisaea*, is now divided into the Long-tailed, Broad-tailed, Sahel, Togo and Exclamatory paradise whydahs. Their tails are extraordinarily cumbersome – surely an evolutionary triumph of mate attraction over survival – and distinguishing one species from another where two occur together, even in full breeding plumage, is not easy. Was the one I saw near Liwonde National Park in Malawi a Broad-tailed or Long-tailed? I still don't know, even though I am told they should not be that difficult to tell apart. The tails of the breeding males of the other whydahs are just as long, but much slimmer, and breeding male Pin-tailed, Steel-blue, Straw-tailed and Shaft-tailed are easily identified.

Twenty or thirty million years ago, what were to become the parasitic Viduidae began to split off from the Estrildidae finches – perhaps by first starting to drop casual eggs in finch nests and finding they got away with it. Even then, both parasite and host laid white eggs (apart from the Cuckoo-finch, which parasitises a different suite of hosts). So it is today that the Estrildids, in whose nests all Viduid species lay their white eggs, all also lay white ones, the only difference being that the parasites' eggs are slightly larger, as are the parasites themselves. This means that the parasites have never had to make any evolutionary effort to adapt their egg colour to that of their hosts – something that many cuckoos, and indeed the Cuckoo-finch, have had to do. The hosts are surprisingly tolerant of the usurpers too, even to the extent of sometimes remaining on the nest while a parasite female adds her egg to the clutch.

The journey to the final discovery that none of these species made their own nests was as fascinating as its conclusion, and it has also involved some of the major contributors to ornithology in anglophone Africa. That they took so long to uncover the true story was not eased by the fact that the parasites' eggs were so difficult to spot in the host nests. It was apparently not until the researches of Frederick Jackson in East Africa at the end of the nineteenth century, and Austin Roberts further south a few years later, that this family's parasitic behaviour began to be exposed – at least to European eyes.

In the third volume of their seminal work, *Birds of Kenya Colony and the Uganda Protectorate*, Jackson and Sclater explain how, while stationed in Eldama Ravine, in what was then Uganda but is now part of Kenya, Jackson spent a long time observing the activities of the Pin-tailed Whydah, not least because the breeding males were prone to displaying so prominently ('he will fleck and fossick about from bush to bush or other coign [sic] of vantage').

For 10 years, from 1885 to 1895, Jackson searched diligently for the nest of the whydah but without any success until, in desperation, he offered his helper, Baraka, a reward if he could find one. Jackson later wrote:'After several weeks of patient watching ... he one day announced his conviction that it did not make a nest but that the hen-bird laid her eggs in the nest of *Estrilda astrild* [Common Waxbill] as he had found the nest of the latter with four small white eggs and a larger one of a distinct creamy colour. Subsequently he and I found several nests of the Waxbill ... and I venture to claim that to Baraka, now dead, is due the credit of solving the mystery.'

Further south, and a few years later, the great South African ornithologist, Austin Roberts, reached similar conclusions, which he published in the 1907 Volume III of the London-printed and Pretoria-published *Journal of the South African Ornithologists' Union* under some 'Remarks on the Breeding-Habits of the Pin-tailed Widow Bird'. He began by referring first to the description of the Pin-tailed Widowbird (as the Pin-tailed Whydah was then known in South Africa) in Arthur Stark's *Birds of South Africa*. This describes how 'a somewhat openly woven domed nest of fine grass is suspended between the stems of a thick grass tuft a few inches off the ground, the ends of the grass being tied together over the nest so as to completely conceal it'. The writer then goes on:'The only nests that I have seen contained young birds, from three to four in number. The eggs have not been described.'There is no reference in this description or in those of any of the other widows or whydahs to any question of parasitism.

Roberts quotes some of this received wisdom on the habits of the Pin-tailed Whydah in his paper, in order to set the background for his own revelation, which begins with how he '... one day stumbled upon a clue to its peculiar breeding-habits'. When talking about birds to an old Natal colonist, the farmer happened to mention that 'the Zulus have a saying that a young "King Red-beak" [Pin-tailed Whydah] is reared out of every "rooibekje's" [Common Waxbill] nest'. Roberts then adds that 'it is well known how often the superstitions of the observant natives have been found to be based upon fact, and this, I have no doubt, is another instance'.

So, with the Pin-tailed Whydah's parasitic habits gradually exposed to newcomers to the region – although long known to the bird's Zulu neighbours – the next sources of study were the other Viduids. Gradually, the fact that they too were brood parasites began to be appreciated, often aided by the study of egg collections in museums: suspicions that a particular species of finch might play host to a parasite could be confirmed by finding a slightly larger egg in the clutch, although this would not necessarily reveal the specific identity of the parasite. In due course, the paradise whydahs were found to parasitise various species of pytilia; and it is now known that what would eventually become the Exclamatory Paradise Whydah visits the nests of both Red-winged and Yellow-winged pytilias. The Shaft-tailed Whydah has been recorded laying in the nests of at least three different species of waxbill, but these are the exceptions proving the rule – that most Viduids are host-specific and rely on a single species of Estrildid to accept their eggs and raise their young.

The breeding habits of indigobirds took longer to establish. In his notes in the description of the Kenya Purple Indigobird, Jackson first mentions how one of the doyens of early East African natural history, V.G.L. van Someren (father of Vernon van Someren), 'found them breeding in Kisumu ... the nest was placed in a thick spray of Cape lilac, about seven feet from the ground'. It would take courage to disagree with someone as distinguished as Van Someren, so Jackson would only say: 'There is some evidence that this bird is parasitic in its habits; at any rate it frequently adopts the nests of other birds for its own use. Whether it actually leaves its eggs to be incubated by the owner of the nest appears to be less certain. Careful observations on this point would be most valuable.'

Like all his peers at the time, Jackson identified and named only one species of indigobird, although he, or more likely his editor, Sclater, was aware that different races might exist. That these races were actually separate species was left largely to the work of Robert Berkeley Payne from the University of Michigan. His researches in the 1970s, aided by DNA analysis and an increasing tendency to split rather than combine species, culminated in the naming of several distinct ones, defined less by appearance than by the identity of the birds in whose nests the females laid their eggs.

The most widespread is the Village Indigobird, which principally (but not exclusively) parasitises the nests of the similarly widespread Red-billed Firefinch. Other species focus on much more localised hosts, which obviously makes their distribution equally restricted, and also renders them much more vulnerable as a species. The incredibly sparsely distributed Jos Plateau Indigobird from northern Cameroon and northern Nigeria, of which very little is known, seems to depend exclusively upon the nests of the equally localised Rock Firefinch. On the other hand, the Quailfinch Indigobird's very limited and disjunct distribution in West Africa and South Sudan contrasts with that of its much more widespread African Quailfinch host. This is also the case in the paradise whydah world, in which the very localised Togo is also thought to depend upon the nests of the more common Yellow-winged Pytilia.

As Robert Payne's research revealed, the male indigobird learns its host's song while in the nest, and once ready to breed will sing that song as his own, thus proclaiming the identity of his species of indigobird, if feet or beak colour is not enough. The female indigobird has also learnt her host's song, and so is ready to be attracted by a male of her own species, and only of her own species. The field observations that initially prompted these notions have been subsequently enforced by intricate aviary experiments, in which every effort was made to trick females into accepting the attentions of males raised by different host species, but without success. A female indigobird raised by a Chaffinch will need to find a male indigobird singing the song of a Chaffinch. Nothing else will do.

Not only do the songs of the adult male indigobirds match those of their hosts – and have helped researchers identify these hosts – but the markings inside the mouths of the young bear a remarkable resemblance to those of the young host nestlings. Most Estrildid nestlings have multi-coloured gapes marked with distinctive spots and streaks, unique to their species. So, presumably in order to render the intruder indistinguishable from the host's own chicks, its gape has evolved to match theirs and thereby benefit from equal rations of regurgitated seeds. On the face of things, the Pin-tailed Whydah and those few others that parasitise several different hosts might upset this idea that the foster child nestling needs to be indistinguishable from the nest's genuine occupants. However, it appears that most waxbill nestlings have fairly similar mouth patterns, so the usurper is acceptable in the nests of more than one species.

Occasionally, a parasite female indigobird may eat a host egg to make room for her own, but generally, neither makes any effort to evict the eggs of the other. Notwithstanding the difference in size, the parasites' eggs hatch more quickly, but whether they hatch before or after the host's young, the usurper has no instinctive urge to kill or expel its step-siblings – as, for instance, does a young honeyguide – and all of them are raised together.

So the total dependence of one species on another continues, although tying its future to that of a single host species renders the parasite particularly vulnerable to any misfortunes that may befall its host. The Green Indigobird was once considered a race of the Village, and then as conspecific with the Dusky, their ranges overlapping. Later, on the basis of their parasitising different hosts, Dusky and Green became species in their own right. On such distinctions are indigobird species now built.

In East Africa, we are particularly familiar with the Village Indigobird, not least for the males being, as Jackson described them, '... found near human habitations, about houses and farms ... a familiar, bold bird, with the male often sitting on a twig or branch in a conspicuous position'. For twig or branch now read 'television aerial' where, at least in the Nairobi suburbs, the male is to be seen more often than not, and when not, most likely because it is on the bird tables, frequently with the species that raised it, the Red-billed Firefinch.

The final member of the family is the peculiar Cuckoo-finch, and again it is Austin Roberts who contributes his insights, penned a few years after he had published his contributions on the Pin-tailed Widowbird. In the 1917 *Annals of the Transvaal Museum* he writes about the Rendall's Seedeater, which was the name he used for the Cuckoo-finch: 'In a recent paper on "Egg-collecting in the Bushveld"... I mentioned some cases which seemed to indicate that Rendall's Seedeater (*Anomalospiza imberbis*) might also be parasitic. I have just obtained proof that my supposition was correct. On Sunday last (24th January 1916), I searched for a nest of a pair of Black-chested Wren Warblers [now Black-chested Prinia], (*Prinia flavicans*), which had been observed for some days to be very busy carrying grubs and insects to a nest somewhere in my garden. The nest was discovered and to my delight was found to contain a young Rendall's Seedeater. During the day I showed the nest to quite a number of friends and relations, but for fear of scaring the birds too much we did not do more than peep carefully into it; the young bird filled the whole of the bottom of the woven nest, and this accounts for overlooking the presence of a young warbler as well, which must have been hidden under it.'

Then follows a description of Roberts's efforts to get his brother down to photograph the nest and the birds, and of the ensuing frustration when he only arrives after the young have flown. Nevertheless, they seem to have no difficulty in catching the young seedeater and prinia, putting them in a cage and then watching the parent prinias come and feed them both through the bars!

112

Not only does the Cuckoo-finch look nothing like any other member of its family, but its parasitic behaviour is also markedly different. The females lay pale blue, sometimes lightly marked eggs, in the nests of any of several different species of prinia or cisticola, giving rise to the notion that there are probably different races of Cuckoo-finch, each of which searches out its own specific host. A female will try and remove all the host's eggs before depositing her own. Should the host lay more later, the parasite chick, which looks very different from the host young, may try and evict its step-siblings, although it is more likely simply to dominate them to death in the nest. Roberts's experience of finding both parasite and host young together is certainly the exception, although sometimes two young Cuckoo-finches find themselves in the same nest and both fledge successfully.

So indeed, a 'finch' the bird may be in diet (although the young are raised largely on insects by their adoptive parents), but very much 'cuckoo' in behaviour; then how assured is the place of this extraordinary bird in the Viduidae family? Apparently, after recent genetic studies, it is unlikely to move any time soon.

Without a family

If there has not been enough in this chapter to show how fraught can be the science of taxonomy, then consider this: there are still three African species whose places in the tree of life are so uncertain that the IOC has refused to commit them to any family. Each of the Tit Hylia, Green Hylia and Grauer's Warbler has its own genus, but the IOC finds these taxonomic loose ends so loose that they are simply described as being *Incertae sedis* – of uncertain relationship.

Rudolf Grauer lent his name to Grauer's Warbler (once 'forest-warbler' before the 'forest' was dropped). With its barred chest, it looks more like a wren than a warbler, and the *HBW Checklist* put it in with crombecs and longbills. For ages it had no tick beside its picture in my book, despite a diligent search in a segment of forest understorey close to the lower-level Bwindi Impenetrable Forest camp, where it was known to live. Then, some years later, I was shown one in tangled understorey in the Nyungwe Forest in western Rwanda.

Grauer was an Austrian zoologist who organised expeditions in Africa, including one to the little-explored eastern Congo in 1909, during which he collected hundreds of specimens. Seemingly not one to shun immortality, he also has a swamp warbler, broadbill, cuckooshrike and subspecies of ground thrush to his name, as well as a subspecies of gorilla – the Eastern Lowland Gorilla. Grauer's Swamp Warbler is much easier to see than Grauer's Warbler, in that it is less afraid to show itself above the vegetation. Sitting beside a swamp in the upper levels of Bwindi Forest, I watched several popping up out of the pale brown reeds to display above them, or singing from their tops before sinking back into cover.

The Green Hylia and Tit Hylia are patchily distributed throughout West and Central Africa. The Green closely resembles a palearctic warbler, complete with pale eye stripe, so would be identified with most certainty when the migrants have returned north to breed – which is perhaps why I was so sure of having seen it in Mabira Forest in eastern Uganda one July. There I could also have found a Tit Hylia, but didn't, despite these moving around tree tops in small parties. Reaching Uganda, but not Kenya, this most appealing little bird has a very short tail, dark distinctive streaking on its chest and head, bright yellow underparts and orange legs.

In time, maybe any of these three extraordinary little birds will have to be allotted its own family; and maybe other birds whose affinities are still uncertain will come back to spend time as *Incertae sedis* while their DNA is further analysed and more appropriate slots are found for them.

Chapter 3
MAINLY IN AFRICA

Some families of birds seem so closely associated with Africa that they demand to be included in a book about quintessentially African species, notwithstanding that they have members outside the continent. In this chapter I have described some of them. Of the world's honeyguides, all but two of the 17 are endemic to Africa. In other families the proportion of endemic African birds is less, perhaps showing them to have left Africa much longer ago, with time to have evolved outside the continent into distinct species, even genera. I must admit to some degree of subjectivity in the selection of these families, but all are particularly distinctive in their own ways and as African as all those already treated, other than that they have overseas relatives.

There is always scope for more; I could also have covered, for example, sunbirds and rollers, but have settled on bustards, flufftails, sandgrouse, coursers and pratincoles, bee-eaters, honeyguides, cisticolas and weavers.

Bustards
Otididae

Bustards surely evolved from African ancestors and then spread out eastwards, mainly overland, given that the birds are, at least now, essentially ground dwellers. Of the 26 species of bustard, korhaan and florican, 19 are essentially African, three Palearctic (Great, Little and

Macqueen's), three Asian (Great Indian, Bengal Florican and Lesser Florican) and one Australian.

Some bustards, like the Kori, White-bellied, Black-bellied and Denham's, are widespread, but others, such as Southern Black or Little Brown, have very restricted distributions. The two epicentres of bustard diversity are East and southern Africa. We are blessed in the tiny area of Nairobi National Park to be able to see Kori, White-bellied, Black-bellied and the very similar Hartlaub's, but the presence of all of these seems sporadic, suggesting that they indulge in local migrations. All bustards can fly, although the larger they are, the more reluctant they seem to leave the ground, and their lumbering take-offs must use up an enormous amount of energy.

Of the many distinctive physical features that characterise members of the family, one of the least obvious, but actually most fundamental, is their small feet, with no back toe — only three forward-facing ones. This renders bustards unable to clasp their feet round a branch, evolution thus confining them to open, largely treeless ground on which they roost, feed and nest. Being so terrestrial, it befits the birds to be cryptically camouflaged, particularly the females. Males take no part in incubating eggs or raising young and so can better afford vivid splashes of black, white or chestnut, particularly noticeable in flight.

The family's most famous African representative is the Kori Bustard, not least because of its habit of striding across the grassland and scrub of both the east and south of the continent. It also has the reputation of being the heaviest flying bird in the world, although in fact the Great Bustard of the Palearctic is also a contender, occasional males of both species topping 18 kilograms (females are much lighter). (A Mute Swan in Poland apparently weighed in at 23 kilograms, and while this may be a record for a species that can fly, it seems likely that this individual was actually too heavy to take off!)

Frederick Jackson described Kori Bustards as 'game birds' but, in this case, it seems that colonial hunters probably made little impact on the population, the bird being '... almost impossible to approach ... within shot-gun range, it is mostly killed with a rifle, and as it is generally on the move when approached within reasonable range, it is none too easy to hit'. Unpalatability may also have helped spare the birds. B.G. Lynn-Allen, author of *Shot-gun and Sunlight: The Game Birds of East Africa,* 'tried one for our Christmas dinner – and infinitely preferred the most scraggy turkey'.

Bustards have short, stout beaks, ideal for foraging for both animal and vegetable matter. These flexible eating habits enable them to adapt well to changes in their environment, as when wild grassland is brought under cultivation and the bustards need to develop a liking for the planted crops. They are also readily able to take advantage of short-term abundance, like swarms of hatching termites or invasions of locusts. Lizards, snakes, frogs and small mammals also feature on their menus and the birds often peck around the edges of grass fires. As much of their territory is very dry, a lot of their water requirement must be obtained from food. Diet is best monitored in captive birds, several of which have shown a marked attraction for bright objects, something well supported by Jackson who relates, without irony, how 'a splendid cock [Kori Bustard], shot at Naivasha [Kenya], had steel and rolled-brass bases of five Snider cartridge cases in its gizzard'.

One of the most renowned features of bustard behaviour is the males' extravagant courtship displays. Larger species like Kori, Denham's, Heuglin's and Arabian, for which flight is a major effort, tend to show themselves off on the ground, the males using a combination of puffed-out neck feathers, cocked tails and fanned wings as they strut or shuffle around their patch. A lot of the smaller bustards, some inhabiting thicker scrub, indulge in aerial spectacles of self-promotion, in which the males fly steeply upwards, then glide slowly down before parachuting almost vertically back to Earth with wings held over their back. The Black-bellied is particularly well known for its airborne ostentation, often accompanied by raucous croaks; these also have the advantage of advertising the male's presence far further afield than if it confined itself to displaying on the ground.

Some species appear to be monogamous, particularly in the genus *Eupodotis* (White-bellied, Blue, Karoo and Ruppell's), establishing flexible territories that both sexes defend. However, the males of most of the others whose breeding habits are known congregate on leks (from the Swedish word for 'play'), where they parade around competitively before mating, often with several females. Thereafter, these males play no further part in nest protection, incubation or raising the young, the only resource they provide being genes. Some bustard leks seem to differ from the conventional and often long-established parading grounds, in that the males congregate over a much wider area, giving rise to the expressions 'exploded' or 'dispersed' leks. With an expanded area, the males can display much further apart, resulting in less aggression between them, although the strongest and most flamboyant still tend to dominate. It is conceivable that some form of bond continues after mating, because males of both Kori and Denham's bustards have been observed feeding females.

Now, in most of sub-Saharan Africa, colonial game laws have been replaced by other legislation providing bustards with much better protection. Further north, Nubian, Arabian and Savile's bustards, as well as the African Houbara, all run the gauntlet of life on the Sahara's edges, and, as such, are particularly vulnerable. Where food is scarce, both the birds and their eggs make welcome additions to any diet, and as if that were not danger enough, bustards still fill the definition of game birds as targets for trained falcons and their retinues of handlers using super-technological support systems that totally redefine the word 'sport'.

Flufftails
Sarothruridae

The primary requisites for finding flufftails are patience and an ability to recognise their calls. The forest-dwelling Buff-spotted Flufftail is widespread throughout a lot of sub-Saharan Africa, but it would be quite unrealistic to expect to come across one without first having heard, and recognised, its 'far-carrying, hollow wail, with the resonance of a tuning fork' as one book puts it, or 'low, foghorn-like "dooooooooooo"', in the words of another. Bates, writing in 1927 about his experiences in Cameroon, investigated the source of 'this mysterious sound I have known for many years; it is a long-drawn-out, mournful whistle, heard about dark thickets of second-growth', but got little satisfaction from the people living around him. He finally realised that, clearly allowing imagination to triumph over observation, they just'... do not know what it is that makes the sound, but have local traditional lore about it, varying in different parts of the country. It was attributed among the Fang to the large snails that are found on trees; by the Bulu in one district to the chameleon mourning for its mother; in another district the people confessed their ignorance ...'

Once heard, and memorised, the distinctive calls proclaim the presence of the flufftail species with some certainty. So, it seems unlikely that the Chestnut-headed's 'series of moaning notes increasing in intensity in the middle and trailing off with a grunt' could ever be confused with the call of any other species. Unfortunately, this bird is so localised that most of us will never hear it calling, and nor will we hear the 'very deep oooh, oooh' of the White-winged Flufftail (of which more later), which is actually the exception proving the rule that flufftail calls are easily identified with the makers. This species' call has been so confused with that of the Grey Crowned Crane that it has frustrated efforts to prove the flufftail's presence in Rwanda!

There is one flufftail that observers might just find without first hearing it. The White-spotted is less retiring than its fellows and also renders itself more likely to be seen by seeming to adopt a particular patch of wetland as its home range. If, in the late afternoon, one waits silently and patiently on the tiny little artificial pond below the Rondo Retreat in Kenya's Kakamega Forest, as often as not one of these delicate little creatures will edge its way tentatively out of the bushes onto the mud at the water's edge.

The chances of seeing any flufftail would be multiplied many times by the use of playback to lure them out of their thickets. I don't like using this, but with an illogicality shared by many others, am quite prepared to try and summon birds with my own vocal version of their calls – usually with conspicuous lack of success. Nor can I spend too long on my high horse because when I look at the notes of my first visit to Madagascar I find written next to the Madagascar Flufftail 'Perinet – found with the aid of a tape recorder'!

There are nine flufftails – all only in the Afrotropical region – of which the Slender-billed and Madagascar occur only on that island. That leaves seven true flufftails in Africa (by 'true' I mean those in the genus *Sarothrura*, because these have been joined in the family recently by three rails of the genus *Canirallus*). The seven mostly thrive in forest (White-spotted and Buff-spotted) or marshland habitat, but within these parameters, one or more species can, with much difficulty, be found in a lot of sub-Saharan Africa. The Striped Flufftail is something of an exception in that it is also at home in montane grasslands, from the uplands of Kenya all the way down to the fynbos of the Cape, but in extremely isolated populations.

Every flufftail male has varying amounts of chestnut on its head, throat and chest, and then stripes and streaks on the rest of a black body. The stubby, cocked, eponymous tail is actually more of a feature on the bird than it is on most crakes and rails, and in the males of the White-spotted and Striped is uniquely uniform chestnut. If representatives of every flufftail species were to present themselves for an identification parade, there would be many causes for confusion, but in the wild they tend to separate out by habitat preference and, to a lesser extent, distinctive distributions. Where ranges overlap, visual identification can be particularly difficult as the birds are often seen so fleetingly on short, quick flights from one patch of rushes or thicket to another – and are reportedly almost impossible to flush a second time.

Further confusing the distribution maps of several species are the migratory journeys flufftails are said to undertake, causing occasional birds to crop up far outside their breeding areas. There is something counterintuitive about flufftails and their kin migrating even short distances. Few birds look more ungainly in the air, legs dangling as they flap their way across the surface of the water or struggle to take off from the ground – often out of long rank grass, like the Corncrake I surprised one rainy April in a Nairobi vlei. However, a lot of these birds are strong flyers, migrating at night, close to the ground, and there is no doubting that several species of flufftail, particularly the Streaky-breasted, at least make local post-breeding migrations to more suitable environments once their breeding grounds have dried up.

In addition to the Striped Flufftail of the African uplands, the Chestnut-headed is also notable for a very disjunct distribution, with scattered dots and crosses on its map all over Central Africa, where it is at home in grassy forest clearings. It might be tempting to attribute these scattered populations to the birds' migratory tendencies, but they seem more likely to be relict populations from former times of very different climate and vegetation. No such explanations, though, account for the extraordinary distribution and suspected migrations of the White-winged Flufftail.

This flufftail is known from several small patches of boggy upland in Ethiopia, and from similar habitat in South Africa, but scarcely from anywhere in-between. It is quite distinct from the rest of the flufftails, with its white secondary feathers, so is unlikely to be mistaken in flight for any other, and irregular sightings have certainly been recorded from Zimbabwe.

Writing about 'The occurrence near Salisbury of the White-winged Flufftail' in the 1977 *Honeyguide*, G. Hopkinson and A.N.B. Masterson described three separate sightings in January and February of that year. These were far from being quick flashes of birds in overhead flight, but good views by two experienced ornithologists of flufftails flushed from damp grasslands, which then flew on for quite long enough to show their distinctive white wing patches. The first was of a flufftail put up from a damp habitat on the outskirts of Harare, and in the second and third cases, the birds were flushed just below the drive-in cinema!

These reports fuelled speculation that, after breeding in Ethiopia's rainy season between June and August, the birds migrated every year down to South Africa, where almost all sightings have been between December and March, and that they then went back north again. As flufftails go, the White-winged is a strong flyer and so could quite possibly make the 4,000-kilometre journey. Providing further support for these migrations have been the proven similarities, both physical and genetic, between birds from Ethiopia and those from South Africa, suggesting that the populations are not yet distinct.

Now known as *Sarothrura ayresi*, the White-winged Flufftail was first described by Thomas Ayres, communicating from South Africa with banker and amateur ornithologist J.H. Gurney (of sugarbird renown) in England. Gurney arranged for the publication of Ayres's 'Additional Notes on the Ornithology of the Republic of Transvaal' in the 1877 *Ibis*, in which this description appeared: 'This pretty little fellow we call the White-winged Rail from the white patch on the wing, which is very conspicuous when it is flushed and making away. I have only noticed this species here the last two seasons; it is very scarce; the two sent are the only specimens I have obtained, though I have seen one or two others.'

This was Ayres writing, but back in England Gurney then adds his own note: 'On receiving the two Crakes above mentioned I was unable to refer them to any species with which I was acquainted, and I therefore sought the kind assistance of Mr. Salvin [one of the *Ibis* editors], who confirmed me in the belief that they belong to a species hitherto undescribed, which I propose should bear the name of my valued correspondent Mr. Thomas Ayres, to whose researches we are indebted for this interesting acquisition.'

So it was that both Ayres and Gurney contributed to the bird's name, but there is more to be extracted from Ayres's description. He also writes that 'the bird shot the 4th October contained water-insects in its stomach' and later that it was 'apparently immature'. Early October is far sooner than most other sightings in South Africa, and with Ayres also referring to its apparent immaturity, was this an early clue to the flufftail's breeding there? Having only just experienced the bird, he would not have considered finding a young one in October anything unusual; nor, of course, would he have any idea that it would take another 140 years for its breeding in South Africa to be confirmed.

Even if Ayres's hints of possible nesting in South Africa were largely ignored, it was long suspected that this was the case. In 1983 J.M. Mendelsohn found two young birds in late September, but some doubters still remained to be convinced – until the 2017/2018 breeding season. After much trial and error, two South African ornithologists, Robin Colyn and Alastair Campbell, developed a remote camera trap, which finally managed to photograph newly hatched chicks, as well as older ones of up to four weeks in Middelpunt wetlands near Belfast, due east of Pretoria. This constitutes one of the most sensational ornithological revelations in recent years, but does not in itself provide evidence that flufftails do or do not migrate between Ethiopia and South Africa.

Recently, the call of the White-winged Flufftail was identified, but for fear of playback abuse, has not been made generally available. BirdLife South Africa has been particularly active in other flufftail research and now focuses on raising funds for habitat protection as well as for further population studies. It has also come up with innovative schemes that combine research with fundraising, while at the same time creating opportunities for bird watchers to sight the bird. These are 'organised flushing events', particularly the Flufftail Festivals at Dullstroom, which allow 120 or so paying enthusiasts to watch while a team of a dozen or so 'flushers' walk the target area in an attempt to put up the birds. Occasional events like these have minimal impact on the wellbeing of the flufftails, while contributing much to knowledge of their numbers. Most of the funds raised have been used to provide social benefits for communities living around the Berga Wetlands in Ethiopia, where the particular danger to the breeding birds is from the hooves of grazing cattle.

Successful conservation measures increasingly involve thinking outside the borders of national boxes, and none more so than in the case of the White-winged Flufftail.

Sandgrouse
Pteroclidae

There is a fast-shrinking pool somewhere out in the stony semi-desert. A few stunted bushes edge its high-water mark, now far from the distant remains of the lake. A churr, chuckle, even a melodic whistle signals approaching – yet still invisible – birds. The calls get louder.

Not only are they closer now but there also seem to be more of them. Black dots appear in the distance, hundreds of them in many separate groups; each group wheels high over the pool – maybe a safety check – before alighting, still calling, some distance away from the water's edge. Now silhouetted dark brown against the paler desert sands, they are sandgrouse and this scene is repeated in the dry lands all over Africa, at hundreds of different waterholes, every day – morning, evening, even after dark.

Only four of the world's 16 sandgrouse species are not to be found in continental Africa, implying that their common ancestors were African, and that powerful flight, as well as an ability to cross barren country, helped their dispersal north and east. Of these four, one is endemic to Madagascar, two (Tibetan and Pallas's) belong in the Palearctic, and the fourth, the Painted Sandgrouse, is at home throughout most of India. Black-bellied and Pin-tailed sandgrouse are also clearly Palearctic species just stretching their breeding maps into North Africa. Others, the Chestnut-bellied, Spotted, Crowned and Lichtenstein's, are spread around the north of our region and also drop in at the waterholes of the Middle East. This leaves the Four-banded, Double-banded, Black-faced, Yellow-throated, Burchell's and Namaqua as truly and exclusively African species.

The Palearctic pair share their own genus, *Syrrhaptes*, distinguished by feathered toes, and by lacking the stumpy little back one, which is present on all other sandgrouse legs. The rest are in *Pterocles*, although this grouping is still open to much debate. However, what seems beyond doubt is that they all belong in the same family, Pteroclidae, although where this itself belongs is also far from clear. The 'grouse' in sandgrouse implies a clear affinity with other game birds, but their pointed wings are more redolent of pigeons and doves (Columbidae), with which they were once grouped. Nonetheless, their connections to these were tenuous, not least because of the totally terrestrial lives of the sandgrouse, compared to the committed tree-dwelling and branch-perching existence of pigeons.

A particularly intriguing distinction between sandgrouse and the pigeons and doves is that the latter do not need to raise their head when taking in water, rather sucking it up as if with a straw. The birds in Columbidae, together with mousebirds, are the only ones that appear to drink like this, and all others, including sandgrouse, fill up their mouth with water and must then tilt their head up to swallow it. As recently as 1966, in Issue 83 of *Auk*, T.J. Cade and others were reporting their observations in an effort to convince doubters that sandgrouse really did not drink in the way of doves. They watched flocks of Burchell's and Namaqua sandgrouse at waterholes in the Kalahari, noting that every one of the birds had to raise its head to swallow the water it had sipped. They referred to each head raise and swallow as a 'draft', and for the Namaquas, drinking sessions comprised, on average, just fewer than 10 drafts, while for Burchell's it was seven or eight. Their waterholes were also visited by Ring-necked, Namaqua and Laughing Doves, as well as by Speckled Pigeons, none of which needed to do more than 'stick their beaks into the water and suck to satiety before raising their heads'!

To a lot of amateur observers, sandgrouse are best divided by tail shape, the long pinfeathers of those like the Namaqua (sandgrouse, not dove) clearly distinguishing them from the stumpier-tailed species. Others – often hunters – split sandgrouse into those that drink when the sun is well up in the sky, and those that go to water at first or last light, or even later, particularly Four-banded, Double-banded and Lichtenstein's. Jackson relates how 'Towards dusk it [Lichtenstein's] assembles in large flights, and arrives at its favourite drinking-places when almost ... dark ... flying very low, silently, and almost ghost-like'. He also quotes one of his sources, a Mr W. Lowe, recalling how '... numerous flocks of this sandgrouse came to drink after dark in the wells in the river-bed. It is most interesting to watch the steady stream of birds entering and leaving these deep holes, and that there were no collisions was marvellous.'

Their affinities with game birds go much further than just in name, and sandgrouse have long been high on the list of many hunters' target species. Living where they do, the birds have never been easy to study, other than when flying in to water, and it is the observations of those with guns that originally provided much of the knowledge we have today about the birds' drinking behaviour. Everyone must make their own judgements on the practice of shooting sandgrouse round waterholes, and can decide if the word 'sportsman' is appropriate for those who indulge in it. Such hunting still continues, where the law allows, although, as noted with Egyptian Geese, it is difficult to dictate close seasons for birds that have flexible breeding regimes – as sandgrouse often do. At least shooting is subject to much more rigorous control than when newly arrived colonial officers fired blindly into the middle of flocks to see how many they could kill with a single shot; or when the Maharajah of Bikaner and his party apparently killed 5,968 migratory Black-bellied Sandgrouse in a two-day shoot at his estates in Rajasthan in 1920.

Most sandgrouses' daily intake of food contains very little moisture. In fact, they can be described as 'obligate granivores', meaning that they eat seeds exclusively; and to accompany this diet, they need to drink lots of water, especially in the summer months. Moisture loss is high, particularly for females, who are the ones to sit on the nest in baking daytime sunshine. Drinking, therefore, is often a daily requirement, and while this may sound extreme for birds living where water is so scarce, their strong, fast flight makes hour-long journeys to distant waterholes, even up to 70 kilometres away, perfectly possible.

With such short legs and necks, the birds are ideally designed for foraging on the ground, and do not even need to use their feet to scratch around in the dirt for food. Considering the sparse environments that sandgrouse inhabit, it is extraordinary how discerning they are in their diet, when one would imagine they could not possibly afford to be: these beggars are often choosers, as Penn Lloyd showed in his 1998 Ph.D. thesis on the 'Ecology of the Namaqua Sandgrouse'. His studies in the Northern Cape province showed, after analysing the stomachs of 130 birds, that they much preferred seeds of legumes, with leaves and fruits making up less than one per cent of their diet. More than 75 per cent of what they ate derived from the Fabaceae, or pea family, and the succulent plants of Aizoaceae. A full crop can hold a lot of seeds, and in one particular case, of a phenomenal 40,456 seeds, all but 11 were of the sprawling succulent, *Gisekia pharnaceoides*. Most stomachs also held a few tiny pebbles, which the birds had ingested to help them break down the seeds. Clearly, preference is dictated by availability, and it is often a case of feast or famine, perhaps perversely famine being most likely just after the rains have prompted most of the seeds in the ground to germinate.

When the time comes to breed, sandgrouse disperse all over their territories in pairs, although by still flocking to drink they give a misleading impression of continuing a colonial existence. In keeping with their terrestrial lives, all sandgrouse nest on the ground. From this follow various consequences, such as the more cryptic plumage of the female, who does most of the daytime incubation of the equally cryptically marked eggs. The nest is nothing more than a barely lined scrape in the ground, sometimes even just an unimproved animal hoofmark, in which almost always a clutch of three eggs is laid. As Lloyd remarks, any nests with fewer eggs could well have lost the missing ones to predation, perhaps following the slithering arrival of a nocturnal toothless rhombic egg-eating snake or the unwelcome attentions of yellow or Cape grey mongooses. The more distinctly plumaged male sits on the nest most of the night and also at first and last light, giving the female a break to feed and drink. The incubation period is three weeks almost exactly, and as soon as the young are hatched, the attendant adult removes the telltale pieces of eggshell and deposits them up to 20 metres from the nest, presumably to divert predators away from the chicks.

Difficult though it must be to synchronise, hatching would ideally be timed to coincide with the end of any flowering season, when seed supply is at its maximum. The clutch all hatch together and the young are immediately out and away from whatever constituted their nest. Right from the start they are able to feed on the same food as their parents, although not without a lesson or two in finding, identifying and dealing with seeds. Often a parent picks up seeds and repeatedly drops them in front of the chicks until they eventually learn to fend for themselves. Nonetheless, while being able to forage independently straight away, the chicks still need water every day, perhaps for up to two months, and there is seldom any of that within walking distance of where they hatched.

Anyone who has watched, either in life or on film, male sandgrouse soaking their breast and flying back to water their chicks cannot help but be emotionally touched by this life-sustaining practice. The phenomenon was first publicised by the splendidly named Edmund Gustavus Bloomfield Meade-Waldo, born in Hever Castle in Kent, England, where he lived most of his life. Unlike the archetypal colonial administrator-naturalist (although he was no less observant than many of these were), his birds lived in an aviary rather than out in the African wilderness. In the 1896 issue of *The Zoologist*, this note from him about Pin-tailed Sandgrouse appeared on page 298, and is fascinating for much more than the revelation that male sandgrouse soak their breast feathers in order to water their young: 'The number of eggs laid were ... four and ... I removed one egg ... knowing that three eggs are the proper complement. Incubation was commenced by the cock, who went on the nest the evening of the day the third egg was laid, his place being taken next morning by the hen ... and this arrangement was kept up all during the incubation, which lasted twenty-three days, *viz.* the cock sitting all night and the hen all day. To my mind this is an extremely interesting fact: the brightly plumaged cock sitting during the dark hours, and the hen, with her protective colouring, sitting during the day ... As soon as the young were out of the nest (when twelve hours old) a very curious habit developed itself in the male. He would rub his breast violently up and down on the ground, a motion quite distinct from dusting, and when all awry he would get into his drinking water and saturate the feathers of the under parts. When soaked he would go through the motions of flying away, nodding his head etc. Then, remembering his family were close by, would run up to the hen, make a demonstration, when the young would run out, get under him, and suck the water from his breast. This is no doubt the way that water is conveyed to the young when hatched far out on waterless plains. The young, which are most beautiful little creatures, and very difficult to see even in an aviary, are very independent, eating hard seed and weeds from the first, and roosting independently of their parents at ten days old.'

Yet, despite further submissions by Meade-Waldo to other publications detailing other examples of this breast saturation, few were convinced that wild birds behaved the same way. This was quite apparent when, on Wednesday 11th January 1922, none other than Richard Meinertzhagen asked Meade-Waldo, at the 262nd meeting of the British Ornithologists' Club held in Pagani's restaurant, Great Portland Street, London, 'if there was any direct evidence to show that water is carried to the young in the feathers or was it a myth?' Meade-Waldo reread his 1896 letter, as well as adding further information derived from 20 more years of captive breeding, but his magnificent observations continued to be regarded with scepticism at best, not least by Meinertzhagen. Never one to bow willingly to the superior knowledge of another, as late as 1954 he was stubbornly describing in *Birds of Arabia*: 'Between 1895–1897 I kept several pairs [of Chestnut-bellied Sandgrouse] in a large aviary in Hampshire, where they bred for two years in succession. Water was taken to the chicks in the crop, whence it was regurgitated, and though the belly was often wet, there was no sign of chicks taking water from the abdominal feathers.'

Oh ye of little faith!

Amazingly, it was not until 1967, when T.J. Cade (again) and G.L. Maclean finally produced enough evidence to satisfy the most intransigent of non-believers that what Meade-Waldo had observed in captivity 70 years earlier was mirrored by behaviour in the wild. They published their eminently readable paper 'Transport of Water by Adult Sandgrouse to their Young' in the July/August issue of *The Condor*, detailing observations of Namaqua Sandgrouse in South Africa's Kalahari Gemsbok National Park. As well as documenting males both collecting water and delivering it to their young – it is one thing watching masses of birds soaking themselves in a waterhole, but quite another catching a single male in the act of delivering liquid to his offspring – they also tried to find out how they did it. What was it that enabled them to keep on providing their chicks with water, often for as long as two months, until the young were finally able to fly off with their parents for a first drink of their own?

The basis for this ability seemed to lie in the modified structure of the birds' breast feathers, particularly the barbules that fringe the edges of the barbs, and which have a unique sort of springy coiled structure. This allowed the male Namaqua Sandgrouse's breast to absorb twice as much water as could a synthetic kitchen sponge or paper towel. Such structure seemed totally unlike that on any other birds' feathers, and when they examined museum specimens they found that all other species of sandgrouse, except the Tibetan, had similarly modified barbules, and that the same applied to the breast feathers of females, although over a much smaller breast area. Tibetan Sandgrouse live at altitudes up to 5,000 metres, and so water loss is much less significant. This, coupled with their perhaps less granivorous diet, means the birds drink much less, and evolution has favoured insulation over any adaptations to soak up water.

When sandgrouse arrive to drink at a waterhole they may first land on the ground some distance away, either a short flight or a longer walk from the water, before venturing forward to drink. At this stage, watchers often record that in fact not all birds actually visit the water, and even if they do, a lot of them leave without drinking, at least in the cooler months and when there are no young to sustain. In his thesis, Lloyd suggested that Namaqua Sandgrouse may actually go two or three days without drinking, perhaps joining in the party to learn about food sources – or, dare one say it, just for the pleasure of communal activity?

Males collecting water paddle into the pool, four or five centimetres deep, swaying to and fro, ruffling their feathers to soak up as much as they can, sometimes drinking at the same time. Some water evaporates in flight, and if the nest is far away, the male may make more than one journey in a day. Females can carry small amounts of water, although they seldom do so.

Sandgrouse seem to focus on preferred drinking holes, even after rains that may have left puddles right next to where they are breeding or roosting. A very gentle slope round the edge and minimal vegetation are essential prerequisites. In hot weather, when even favourite drinking holes have mostly dried up, thousands of birds may congregate around the remaining areas of water and there is much jostling for space. At the other extreme, floods can change the usual configuration of well-used waterholes, making familiar banks or shallows no longer accessible. Thoroughly confused, sandgrouse may then resort to drinking on the wing. This is a risky strategy, often ending in waterlogged plumage, which can even prove fatal: birds can drown, or otherwise their struggles attract the attentions of watchful predators such as Lanner Falcons, or even lurking crocodiles – a particularly unfitting end for a creature so perfectly evolved to survive in the most barren of arid environments.

Coursers & Pratincoles
Glareolidae

Coursers are like many of the plovers – long-legged denizens of dry country. They are usually solitary birds, feeding on insects and sometimes seeds they collect as they scuttle along the ground. Pratincoles are essentially water birds, although their name has a more terrestrial connotation, deriving from the Latin *pratum*, meaning 'meadow' and *incola*, 'inhabitant'. They have much shorter legs than do coursers, and forked tails. They are gregarious, breeding colonially too, and hawk much of their food in the air. It would be hard to imagine two less alike birds sharing a family, but for once it is not a case of DNA evidence trumping morphology and behaviour; rather, all species of both groups have arched beaks, and it is this distinction that brings them together into the same family. This alignment was formed in 1831, and it once also included the Egyptian Plover, until this beautiful bird was recently cast out into a family of its own.

Coursers and pratincoles most likely evolved in Africa and, like bustards, then spread eastwards through the savanna that once joined Africa and India, or, in the case of the pratincoles, hopping from one wetland or estuary to another, or maybe just following the coastline. Once the common ancestor was established in Asia, the African and Asian populations each began to evolve in their own ways. Two examples of this are Africa's Temminck's Courser and the Indian Courser (which look very similar and presumably diverged from a common ancestor), and the Grey (Africa) and Small (southeast Asia) pratincoles.

Of the nine coursers, two (Indian and the Critically Endangered Jerdon's, which was thought to be extinct for nearly 90 years until being 'rediscovered' in 1986) live in India, and the others principally in Africa. Pratincoles, with their long, slender wings, are much more mobile; most species migrate long distances, and so, unsurprisingly, they have spread further. Both the Small and the Oriental are all over southeast Asia and down into Australia, where they join the other family representative, the Australian Pratincole. This is an odd-looking bird, which seems to bridge the gap between coursers and pratincoles – not an original thought, apparently, as it also flies under the alternative name of Australian Courser. Its legs are much longer than those of all other pratincoles and it appears at home in dry, barren country, where it feeds, courser-like, on the ground.

If I were blessed with the opportunity to write a monograph on a family of birds, it would be on the coursers and pratincoles. They seem wonderfully adrift in both looks and habits, occupying quite distinct niches. True, the coursers have much in common with a lot of plovers – the Egyptian Plover has also flown under the name of Egyptian Courser – but pratincoles, while showing something of both the tern and the swallow, bear little resemblance to either. Having decided that they deserved a few pages in this book, I was happy to see *HBW* comment: 'Both pratincoles and coursers have great aesthetic value, and bird watchers tend to place them high on their lists of special birds to see in the regions where they occur.'

One of the habits for which the Egyptian Plover is particularly noted is that of burying its eggs in the sand, both for concealment and thermoregulation. The Three-banded Courser does likewise, although to a lesser extent, because half or a third of the egg is often still showing if the parent leaves the nest. Two eggs is the norm for most courser species, but strangely the Double-banded Courser always lays only one. Both sexes contribute to the incubation of the eggs, sitting very tight and enhancing the birds' reputation for being tame and approachable.

Pratincoles, in particular, have certainly rewarded me with wonderfully memorable sightings in some of the remotest parts of Africa, and elsewhere, usually when least expected. My first Rock Pratincoles were hawking insects over the Epulu River, in the Ituri Forest in eastern DRC, where James Chapin may well have seen them too. His book mentions many sightings of what he called White-collared Pratincoles, including finding a completely unlined nest in a rock depression in the Nepoki River, which flows close to the Epulu. Seeing many of the birds around Stanley (now Boyoma) Falls, but no nests, he concluded that 'egg laying did seem correlated with the level of the water in the rivers, so that they might be all but absent when it was high'. This is a recurring concern today, especially with so many dams on large rivers, but the upper reaches of the Zambezi are less threatened and we were able to watch a lot of these lovely birds in the Zambezi region (formerly the Caprivi Strip) on the rocks below the bridge at Katima Mulilo.

One of the many joys of visiting Amboseli National Park can be finding Collared Pratincoles in the swamplands backed by the towering bulk of Mount Kilimanjaro; there may also be Double-banded Coursers on the plains. The excitement of thinking I had found a flock of Madagascar Pratincoles at the mouth of the Sabaki River was short-lived (they turned out to be the much more widespread Collared) but very real nonetheless. In southern Tunisia I watched a Cream-coloured Courser bobbing and running and bobbing and crouching, and the odds of seeing a Somali Courser on a visit to Tsavo East National Park are better than evens.

Other experiences await: Madagascar Pratincoles should not be hard to find on the East African coast, with the entire population arriving every year from that island, nor are they hard to recognise, with their lack of any black throat ring. The Black-winged Pratincole nests in large colonies round the Black and Caspian seas, most of the birds migrating down to South Africa in the northern winter, largely unseen on their journeys, probably because they fly so high. Many of them end up in the Free State or on the Vaal Dam south of Johannesburg, where 72,000 of these birds were counted in 2011.

However, while the Black-winged Pratincoles may be safe on their journeys, or even in their wintering grounds, Rooks, grazing livestock and droughts or floods are all taking their toll on the breeding birds, and numbers have fallen dramatically. Even allowing for some exaggeration, the report that appeared in the 1884 second edition of Layard's *The Birds of South Africa*, from a surveyor working for the Colonial Engineering Department near the Fish River, paints a dramatic picture of a scene that is no longer: 'The principal enemy of these great swarms [of locusts] and the valued friend of the Cape farmer, is the small locust bird *Glareola melanoptera*. These birds come, I may say, in millions, attendant on the flying swarms of locusts; indeed, the appearance of a few of them is looked upon as a sure presage of the locust-swarms being at hand. Their mode of operation, as I saw it, was as follows. They intercept a portion of the swarm and form themselves into a ring of considerable height, regularly widening towards the top, so as to represent the appearance of a revolving balloon or huge spinning-top. When they have consumed this portion of the swarm, they follow up the main body and commence another attack, and so on, until night sets in and the birds happen to lose the swarm or the locusts are all devoured. I should not forget to mention that the beak of these birds is exactly of such a shape and such dimensions that when they seize the locust the snap cuts off the four wings, and a passer-by sees a continual shower of locusts' wings falling on the ground.'

The book draws heavily on reports from correspondents all over the country, like the one above, although sometimes accuracy seems sacrificed for entertainment. A Mrs Barber is also quoted, writing that the bird referred to as the Locust Bird is 'well known in South Africa as a friend of the farmer, and ... always builds its nest in the neighbourhood of swarms of young locusts, so that they may have plenty of food for their young ones ...'! The second edition was 'thoroughly revised and augmented by R. Bowdler Sharpe', who never actually visited Africa, so was probably unable to verify a lot of the reports he received. Or maybe Mrs Barber was confusing the Black-winged with the Collared, which does breed in South Africa?

Perhaps when I come to write my treatise, I need to visit Madikwe Game Reserve on South Africa's border with Botswana, which advertises not only wintering flocks of Black-winged Pratincoles but also the presence of Temminck's, Double-banded and Burchell's coursers, as well as occasional visits from the Bronze-winged.

Bee-eaters
Meropidae

Bee-eaters, too, mirror the distribution patterns of most other families in this chapter, probably also once having taken advantage of the continuous swath of vegetation – where the dry deserts of Arabia now are – to spread out beyond the borders of Africa.

The family has some 25 or so species, of which all but three are in the same genus, *Merops*. Most of these *Merops* are essentially African, two Palearctic and three southeast Asian, with one, the Rainbow, breeding only in Australia. As with almost any bird family, the pace of species' splitting is picking up, so now most authorities agree on both Northern and Southern Carmines, where once there was only the Carmine.

While they may not be exclusively African, bee-eaters are still essential components of so much of natural Africa, and there is scarcely a corner of the continent south of the Sahara where a bee-eater of one species or another is not busy showing itself in pursuit of insect prey.

Most of these birds need open country with tallish trees from which they can search the skies around them for food items. The smallest of the family, the Little Bee-eater, is at home on small bushes or even tall grass stems. There are bee-eaters in dense forest too – the Black, Black-headed, Rosy, Blue-headed and Blue-moustached – although these all find it easier feeding in the open above clearings or tracks.

The birds often sit in pairs, tails wagging, watching, before one sets off in pursuit of a tiny speck in the distance. A bee-eater catches almost all its prey in the air. It can swallow small insects on the wing, which then allows it to fly straight on to find others. Larger insects cannot be eaten in flight, and after the bird has closed its beak on such prey, often with a clearly audible snap, it then swoops gracefully back onto its perch. There it may swallow its quarry whole, or if it has caught bees or wasps or other poisonous members of the preferred order of Hymenoptera, the bird first neutralises their venom by pounding and rubbing the insect along the branch or wire – apparently closing its eyes to avoid any contact with the poison.

Worker honeybees do indeed make up a large proportion of some bee-eater diets, although, of course, this depends on bee availability. Over the last 2,000 years or more, much has been written about the damage the birds can do to domestic beehives. The subject of such writings was, and still is, almost inevitably the European Bee-eater, given this species' extensive distribution and its long-distance migrations. Yet, despite its being watched for thousands of years, there still seems no real consensus on how badly it can damage bee populations.

Greek philosopher Aristotle set the tone in his *Historia Animalium*, around 350 BC, writing: 'Bees are attacked most by wasps and by the birds called titmice, also by swallow and bee-eater'. More than 300 years later, the Roman poet Virgil continued the theme in his poem, *Georgica*:

'First find your bees a settled sure abode ...
Let the gay lizard too keep far aloof ...
And the bee-eater ... for these roam wide
Wasting all substance, or the bees themselves
Strike flying, and in their beaks bear home, to glut
Those savage nestlings with the dainty prey.'

A 1792 English compilation entitled *The Natural History of Insects* may have drawn more on later observations, because it went some way towards exonerating bee-eaters by identifying a different, and unlikely, culprit as the bee-keeper's worst avian enemy: 'It is also said, that among the Birds, that those called Bee-eaters, Swallows, and Titmice, feed greatly upon Bees; but the bird that does most mischief among them, and destroys more than all the rest put together, is the Sparrow. They swallow them like grains of corn, and they have been seen to carry three Bees at a time to feed their young with, that is one in their bills, and two others in their claws.'

Today, European Bee-eaters are shot and trapped mercilessly on their migratory journeys through the southern Mediterranean, and are still persecuted elsewhere for the damage they are perceived to inflict on apiaries. No amount of research, either highlighting the other bee predators that the birds usefully destroy, or the limited numbers of bees they actually consume, seems likely to change already made-up minds. Paolo Galeotti and Maria Inglisa published the results of a survey 'Estimating predation impact on honeybees by European Bee-eaters' in Sardinia in *La Revue d'Ecologie* of 2001, concluding that 'the economic impact on apiculture by bee-eaters was in general negligible'. More recently, in Issue 2 of the 2016 *Journal of Apicultural Research*, Pablo Farinos-Celdran and others described their studies on 'The Consumption of honey-bees by *Merops apiaster* ...' in southeast Spain. During the birds' visit for summer breeding in 2009, they found that a single bee-eater consumed, on average, 1,333 bees, which was far below the theoretical regeneration capacity of a beehive. So they, too, concluded that the effect of bee-eater predation on local apiaries appeared negligible.

My very limited personal experience also exonerates the bird. We had three beehives in our Nairobi field, and bee traffic had to cross a lot of open grassland. Easy pickings, one might say, and Cinnamon-chested Bee-eaters are common in the area for most of the year. However, the bees seemed to offer the birds no great attraction, and the bee-eaters never looked to be taking up stations to intercept the insects on their way to or from the hives. Now and again, Little Bee-eaters visited the field, and they appeared no more interested in passing bees either, and nor did the flocks of Europeans that occasionally stopped by on their northward migrations to roost in the tall eucalyptus trees.

One of the habits of the bee-eater, which fortuitously makes research both easier and kinder, is that of regurgitating pellets containing the indigestible remnants of their meals. Birds of prey are best known for doing this, but far more birds, including kingfishers, herons, gulls and swallows, cast pellets than is commonly supposed. Bees, and a lot of other bee-eater prey, particularly beetles, have hard exoskeletons, and careful analysis can reveal the food preferences of the birds. One of the genuinely negative consequences of bee-eaters consuming bees may be that microspores from those insects infected with 'colony collapse disorder' or other disease may be cast up in the birds' pellets, where they could possibly remain viable for long enough to spread the infection.

All bee-eater species nest in earthen holes that they excavate themselves; some, such as the Red-throated, in huge colonies and others, like the Little, in solitary burrows. Pairs of Cinnamon-chested nest on their own or in loose aggregations, often in the embankments beside forest tracks. Many species breed, somewhat surprisingly, on the ground. My first experience watching breeding bee-eaters was of what are now Northern Carmines in frenzied colonies on sand cliffs above a coastal estuary; and it was a real surprise to find just as big a colony of Southern Carmines nesting on the ground in Botswana's Okavango Delta. Their burrows were in a slightly raised earthen mound, high enough to keep out floodwater, but not predatory snakes and rodents.

A lot of bee-eaters are local migrants, to a greater or lesser extent, but none travel so far as the European, which breeds throughout southern Europe and east into Asia, where the Blue-cheeked also nests, the two often migrating together. European Bee-eaters from the west of the continent tend to migrate down to West Africa for the winter, while those from further east pass through East Africa on their way further south. Their arrival in Kenya en route south is as sure a sign of summer as is the coming of the swallows or cuckoos to Europe, and is announced with loud, melodious trills from the flock as it passes overhead, usually about the second week of September.

One of the joys of the bee-eater family is its diversity of species, different ones turning up in one part of the continent or another, including just one record of a Swallow-tailed here in Kenya. In the course of researching baobab trees for an earlier publication, I passed by a huge, but failing tree in Botswana, in the bark of which a caravan of so-called Dorsland ('Thirstland') Trekkers escaping British colonial dominance and threats to their freedom of worship had carved '1883'. Not long after this, Germany, realising that the only way to secure what is present-day Namibia was to run it as a true colony, dispatched

Schutztruppe to enforce its occupation. A detachment of these passed the Dorsland tree too, at least three of them, 'H Gathemann', 'E Heller' and 'D Hannemann', engraving their names and '1891'. I felt an easy sense of contact with them in seeing the work of their hands exactly where they had left it. The tree was bare, backed by a watery evening sun setting behind the cracked mud of a waterhole. Skinks scurried in and out of holes in its trunk, and, to add to the wonders of the evening, a Swallow-tailed Bee-eater darted from a perch at passing insects – not a rarity to those who live in southern Africa, but something new to me.

Some years later, I found time to escape from training Uganda Wildlife Service wardens and head down to the Semliki forest in western Uganda. Godfrey was my wonderful guide, and while guides certainly help spot far more birds in a new area than one would manage to do without them, having every ornithological sight and sound identified by someone else creates a certain feeling of inadequacy. Still, in this eastern remnant of Congo forest we saw some wonderful birds, a few – very few – distinctive enough for me to identify alone.

On my third day there, under overcast skies, we headed west towards the Semliki River (different territory from the first two days), where most of the fishermen greeted us with the *bonjours* of Congo immigrants as often as in local Lukonjo. Six boggy kilometres down the river path Godfrey and I reached one of the oxbow lakes – remnants of the river's abandoned course. We called a halt there and ate some early lunch, during which Godfrey pointed out the flash of a Shining-blue Kingfisher. As we set off back back to the car, the sun came out, seeming to press an activity switch in the tree tops; and looking far up into the canopy, in a tiny patch of blue sky between the leaves, a red throat caught my eye – just mine, and unaided. Kingfisher was my first thought. Was there some exotic forest species that rested out on open branches? Then a dark breast showed below the throat and, with a twitch of a tail and a flutter of black wings, it all fell into place: a Black Bee-eater, *Merops gularis*, all my own, no Godfrey involved. Now, with all the chats, alethes, greenbuls and illadopses merged into one composite blur, no more than ticks on the list, that bee-eater is still out there on its perch, and on my Semliki list, illuminated by my own store of cerebral sunshine!

Honeyguides
Indicatoridae

Honeyguides – drab, grey-green-brown birds, usually flashing white outer tail feathers to distinguish them from other drab grey-green-brown birds, but that is where the drabness ends. Beneath it, they are perhaps the most interesting birds in Africa, not only for their diet of beeswax, and the way some of them find it, but also for their need to lay eggs in other birds' nests, with brutal consequences for any true offspring of their adopted parents.

The family name of Indicatoridae may imply that all its members guide, but in truth it seems only one of them does, and this one's habit seems to have been bestowed not only on the family name but also that of the principal genus of honeyguides – *Indicator*. The genus comprises 10 species, with its flag-bearer, *Indicator indicator*, the Greater Honeyguide, being the one that actually lures humans to bees' nests.

This Greater Honeyguide was first described in the eighteenth century by Anders Sparrman, a Swedish medical doctor and student of Carl Linnaeus, based in Cape Town, from a specimen he had collected a year earlier near the Great Fish River. Sparrman put the bird into the cuckoo family, naming it *Cuculus indicator*. This he did, not on account of his knowing that the honeyguide also laid its eggs in other birds' nests (which he didn't), but rather because, like all the cuckoos, it has zygodactylous toes – the second and third pointing forwards and first and fourth backwards. His journey into the eastern Cape was described in the *Philosophical Transactions of the Royal Society* published on 1st January 1777 under the title 'Dr Sparrman's Account of his journey into Africa from the Cape of Good Hope, and a Description of a new Species of Cuckow'. And there, on page 43 of this little A5-sized publication, is 'The History of the Honey-guide, or *Cuculus indicator*'.

Sparrman's charming narration gives a good idea of how, in those days, one introduced a new bird to science, before he later goes on to set out the bird's physical attributes in Latin: 'The Dutch settlers thereabouts have given this bird the name of *Honig-wyzer* or Honey-guide, from its quality of discovering wild honey to travellers. Its colour has nothing striking or beautiful ... and its size is considerably smaller than that of our Cuckow in Europe: but in return, the instinct which prompts it to seek its food in a singular manner, is truly admirable. Not only the Dutch and Hottentots, but likewise a species of quadruped, which the Dutch name a *Ratel*, are frequently conducted to wild bee-hives by this bird, which as it were pilots them to the very spot. The honey being its favourite food, its own interest prompts it to be instrumental in robbing the hive as some scraps are commonly left for its support.'

More of *Indicator indicator* later, but of the other nine species of *Indicator*, all are endemic to Africa except for two: the Yellow-rumped from the mountainous strip of Himalayan foothills, and the Malay, which ranges through most of Malaysia and Indonesia. With very little white in their tails, these two species most likely derived from an eastern movement of African honeyguides into Asia, which, because they are both still in *Indicator* (and so not vastly different from a lot of the African species), was perhaps relatively recently.

There are three more genera of honeyguide. *Prodotiscus* comprises three small, thinner-beaked honeyguides, also known as 'honeybirds' (Cassin's, Green-backed and Brown-backed). These are very flycatcher-like, both in habits and looks, until their white outer tail feathers become apparent. *Melignomon* contains only two species, Zenker's and Yellow-footed, both inhabitants of dense West and Central African forest; while in *Melichneutes* rests a single, and extraordinary species – the Lyre-tailed Honeyguide.

This bird is particularly remarkable for its display flights above the tree tops, during which air rushes through its feathers producing sounds audible nearly half a kilometre away. James Chapin spent four years, from 1910 to 1914, hearing the noise but being unable to identify the source, above the canopy, that emitted this extraordinary sound he describes as '*nyete, nyete*'. The 'call' was well known to the native inhabitants of the Ituri Forest, who assumed it was made by a bird, although none could identify which one. In the Semliki Valley in eastern Congo in 1926, Chapin heard 'this unmistakable note' again, but still 'all efforts to see the maker were vain, it seemed to be high over the tree-tops'. Part II of his *Birds of the Belgian Congo* was not published until 1939, by which time Chapin was able to write that, although still expressing personal opinion rather than scientific certainty, 'now I feel so sure it must be the lyre-tailed honey-guide'.

Even less scientific certainty attended the bird's breeding habits, which Chapin admitted 'may take many more years to discover', thereby highlighting one of the real difficulties of researching the habits of any

138

bird that lays its egg in another bird's nest, and takes no part in bringing up its young. Confusion and longstanding ignorance are inevitable, as is a failure to connect the young bird with the old, and the Lyre-tailed Honeyguide was no exception. It had been first officially described by another American, George Latimer Bates, from a specimen he obtained in Bitye in lowland Cameroon in 1909, and named *Melignomon robustus*. Yet, at more or less the same time, in the Berlin Museum Anton Reichenow was giving the name of *Indicator sommerfeldi* to another bird, submitted to him by fellow German, Von Sommerfeld, that actually turned out to be an immature Lyre-tailed Honeyguide.

Similar difficulties assailed taxonomists with *Indicator indicator*, originally known as the Black-throated Honeyguide, after the plumage of the male. The young birds, with their yellow throat, are dramatically different from either of the adults, and were for long regarded as a different species, *Indicator major*.

Chapin probably researched forest honeyguides more than anyone, and was quite convinced that 'none of the forest honey-guides leads mankind to the stores of bees, even though the pygmies are said to be so expert at collecting honey'. And this seems to be how it is. Why only Greater Honeyguides guide is not clear, nor how the habit evolved. Other species busily investigate human activity, particularly if this is accompanied by fires and smoke, which probably all honeyguides associate with the efforts of honey hunters. They may flit around bees' nests too, most likely having followed Greater Honeyguides there, but they seemingly do not decoy humans to them.

What all honeyguides are after from a bees' nest is not honey, but wax. 'Cerophagy' is the term for wax eating, and the prime sources of such wax are the colonial nests of the African honeybee, *Apis mellifera scutellata*. The wax-eating habit was first apparently noted by Catholic monks in Mozambique who watched the birds pecking at altar candles. Such a diet requires considerable modifications to the birds' physiology: a thick skin and slit-like nostrils to withstand not only bee stings but also attacks from other species of bird if honeyguides are caught leaving eggs in their nests. Despite these modifications, the doyens of honeyguide research in East Africa, Lester Short and Jennifer Horne, who also authored the section in *HBW* on the Indicatoridae family, report finding honeyguides stung to death below hives. Their digestive system also probably needs to be modified to cope with the unusual diet, which also forces the birds to drink a lot of water. Chapin remarked how 'wax is so often found in their stomachs that I believe it must resist digestion for some time, probably breaking up eventually in fine particles and passing down the intestine'.

To reach the wax, what the birds really want is an easy access hole to a large nest, preferably one that has been deserted by the bees, whether or not following major human disturbance. If honey hunters have been led to the nest by a honeyguide they will leave some of the comb there for the bird as an acknowledgement of its efforts – and perhaps also in deference to superstition. In his inimitable way, Sparrman remarks on their not leaving too much for the bird so its enthusiasm for guiding remains undimmed! 'Whilst the hunters are busy in taking the honey, the bird is seen looking on attentively to what is going forward, and waiting for its share of the spoil. The bee-hunters never fail to leave a small portion for their conductor, but commonly take care not to leave so much as would satisfy its hunger. The bird's appetite being only whetted by this parsimony, it is obliged to commit a second treason, by discovering another bees-nest in hopes of better salary.'

Unrewarded honeyguides are believed by some to ensure that next time the hunter's hand feels its way into a bees' nest, the first contact will be with the smooth, dry skin of a poisonous snake, rather than the sticky surface of honeycomb. Indeed, there is a Zulu folk tale loosely entitled *The Honeyguide's Revenge*, in which an unrewarded honeyguide called Ngede (*gede* means 'to chatter incessantly' in Zulu) seeks to avenge the failure of Gingile, the hunter, to reward it for leading him to a bees' nest. The next time Ngede entices Gingile to follow him, it is up a thorn tree in which, rather than bees nesting, a fierce leopard is sleeping, which then swipes Gingile across the face with its paw, scarring him for life.

David Livingstone had heard enough stories about honeyguides luring hunters to avenge rather than reward them for him to conduct a survey among his retinue. As he describes in *Missionary Travels and Researches in South Africa*, on 2nd December 1855 in the Zambezi Valley: 'We remained near a small hill, called Maundo, where we began to be frequently invited by the honeyguide (*Cuculus indicator*). Wishing to ascertain the truth of the native assertion that this bird is a deceiver, and by its call sometimes leads to a wild beast and not to honey, I inquired if any of my men had ever been led by this friendly little bird to any thing else than what its name implies. Only one of the 114 could say he had been led to an elephant instead of a hive ... . I am quite convinced that the majority of people who commit themselves to its guidance are led to the honey, and to it alone.'

While the needs of both bird and human are satisfied once the bees' nest is plundered, such satisfaction is only obtained at the bees' expense, as Sparrman readily recognised. 'I have had frequent opportunities of seeing this bird, and have been witness of the destruction of several republicks of bees, by means of its treachery.' Folk tales also acknowledge the rotten lot of the bee, and Ila-speaking people of Zambia tell how a honeyguide went to Bee-town to look for a wife, which he soon found; but his luck was short lived and, before long, the bees took her away from him. 'All right', he said, 'if that's the game, since you refuse me my wife, I will go and spread tales about you and your nests all along the roadside.' And since that day he has been doing his best to lead as many people as possible to rob the nests of the bees.

The relationship between bird and human may go even further, in that certain communities seem to use specific calls to attract the honeyguide first, rather than just hoping the bird will initiate the interaction. Recent, much publicised research by respected evolutionary biologist Claire Spottiswoode and colleagues K.M. and C.S. Begg in a 2016 paper in *Science* entitled 'Reciprocal Signalling in Honeyguide-human Mutualism' presented the results of research among hunters in the Yao communities of Mozambique. These use a specific 'trill-grunt' to attract the attention of the birds, which the hunters reportedly learnt from their fathers and to which the birds respond at least twice as often as they do to other arbitrary calls (another study reports the Hadza people of Tanzania using a more melodious whistle).

Many communities in Africa make artificial beehives, especially where trees with good holes are scarce, and honeyguides naturally often lead honey hunters to their own hives! In such less forested areas, baobab trunks make good homes for wild bees, with large entrance holes, and it is as well to keep a careful eye open when going anywhere near a big tree. The dark rim of waxy comb round a nest hole often betrays the presence of bees, as do hardwood sticks hammered into the shiny, grey baobab trunk by local honey hunters to make a ladder up to the nest – although these may have been long abandoned and the ladders used now only by baboons in search of the large hanging fruits.

Greater Honeyguides are often said to guide not only humans, but also honey badgers, or ratels, just as Sparrman had mentioned in his original description. Evidence is patchy, at best, and the belief may arise from humans finding both birds and ratels at the site of a nest and assuming one had led the other there. The lack of proof is not surprising as ratels have a poor sense of sight and are largely nocturnal, especially in areas of human habitation, and therefore not easily guided by the diurnal honeyguides. These mammals can climb trees but would struggle with the smooth trunk of a tree such as a baobab, so it may not even be worth the birds' investing time and energy in trying to guide them.

It is not just beeswax the birds are after, and once at the nest, they will also prey upon eggs, grubs or larvae. Those species that have been well researched (which the deep-forest species such as Zenker's, Yellow-footed and Dwarf have not) are also known to be keen flycatchers, especially after rain storms when termites swarm and the birds fly forth from perches. Other insects are picked off branches and tree trunks, and most species for which there is any evidence will not ignore spiders.

Despite our having three domestic beehives on our Nairobi plot, honeyguides are not common, and appearances by any of the four on the garden list – Greater, Lesser, Green-backed Honeybird and Brown-backed (once Wahlberg's) Honeybird – are all noteworthy. Post-honey harvest servings of wax are inevitably left untouched, whether placed prominently out in the open or under good cover, close to or far from the hives. Clearly I am doing something wrong, evidenced by my reading that Chapin, having placed some comb in the fork of a tree for a pair of Greater Honeyguides, the next day 'watched both birds, one after the other, come silently to seize a piece of the comb and fly off with it'.

Short and Horne have recorded, in a single day, over 50 individual honeyguides, of four species, on beeswax feeders! They did most of their research in northern Kenya, far from the road between Nairobi and Mombasa, halfway down which Frederick Jackson was based in his earlier years, and found 'the attentions and incessant chattering call [of the Greater Honeyguide] are little less than maddening to the weary and perhaps footsore traveller'. The calls were also a disturbance to early big-game hunters, making it clear to any nearby animal, particularly elephants, that there were humans not far away.

Having no contact with their biological parents, the guiding behaviour of *Indicator indicator* must be inherited. As their adopted parents feed young honeyguides mostly with insects, their strange predisposition to eat wax must also be inherited. Which brings us to the breeding habits of the family. Of these, incidentally, Sparrman had no idea, writing: 'Whilst I staid in the interior parts of Africa, a nest was shown to me, which some peasants assured me was the nest of a Honey-guide. It was woven of slender filaments of fibres of bark, in the form of a bottle.' Not only would this not be the nest of a honeyguide, none of which builds nests, but nor would it be of any host.

Most birds that nest in holes lay white eggs, and so do honeyguides. Visibility in the tree hole is poor, so minor mismatches in shape probably get ignored. Unlike many parasitic birds, or races thereof, the birds are far from being anywhere near host-specific, and some 20 hosts have been recorded receiving Lesser Honeyguide eggs, and double that number for the Greater. Barbets are the prime target for the Lesser, and both honeyguide species are partial to laying in the cavity nests of woodpeckers, bee-eaters and starlings. Sometimes, like other brood parasites, honeyguides may be forced to dump their eggs in less appropriate nests, for want of the availability of ideal hosts. Indeed, this may be how honeyguide parasitism evolved, the birds being pushed into using other species' nests because of a shortage of holes in which to construct their own. Holes are often in short supply, and many birds require them, so occasional efforts to drop an egg into one already occupied may have been successful and so, slowly, became the norm.

Parasitic birds have perfected the art of nipping in and out of the host's nest at high speed, not least to minimise the chances of being caught in the act, and possibly injured by a genuine occupant. Indeed, Chapin quotes a certain R.H. Ivy, 'well versed in South African birds ... shooting a female of [Lesser Honeyguide] *minor*, with an egg protruding from its vent as it tried to enter the nest of a barbet, *Lybius torquatus* [Black-collared Barbet], at Blue Krantz in Cape Province'. Sometimes the parasitic female needs to spend time not only laying her own eggs but also trying to eject the eggs already in the nest, or at least to puncture these.

The timing of egg laying is very important: the parasite chick should emerge from its shell either before or around the same time as the host's own offspring. Honeyguide eggs take, on average, around two weeks to hatch after laying, which is less than the incubation period of a lot of the hosts. As long as the parasite chick is about the same age or at least not much younger than its adopted siblings, it will be able to set about them with the fearsome hooked beak and spiny heels with which it is born, to such an extent that it pierces any other eggs in the nest or lacerates chicks to the point of death. The parents may then remove the corpses of their biological offspring from the nest, or otherwise just let them rot in the bottom. One of the *BoA* authors, Hilary Fry, added a personal comment about the Greater Honeyguide, to the effect that 'lacerated nestling Red-throated Bee-eaters die in a few hours and are then trampled into nest debris, not ejected from the nest'.

This instinctive behaviour is just as dramatic as it sounds. In an earlier 2011 paper entitled 'A stab in the dark: chick killing by brood parasitic honeyguides', Clare Spottiswoode described in great detail how a newly hatched Greater Honeyguide attacked the host chick with 'sustained biting, grasping and shaking motions', often shaking 'the host chick, either from side to side or up and down by rocking on their hind legs'. Attacks lasted anything from one to five minutes, inevitably causing the host chick's death, which took anything from nine minutes to over seven hours from first attack.

Within a couple of weeks, the membranous bill hook has disappeared and the young usurper continues to beg for food from its adopted parents, which bring it the mixed diet of fruit, seeds and insects they would naturally feed to their own young. Once fledged, usually within a month of hatching, the fattened, only-child honeyguide becomes the ultimate prodigal offspring: it takes no interest in learning how to forage from its adopting parents, nor in joining them back at their roosting site in the evening. Not for the young honeyguide a diet of ripe figs overhanging the river – rather, it seeks out the white flick of the tail of another honeyguide in order to follow it to a beehive.

There is surely no more intriguing honeyguide experience than actually being led to a bees' nest by a Greater Honeyguide. At the southern end of the rocky backbone of Tarangire National Park in northern Tanzania is a huge hollow baobab, known, like many others in different parts of Africa, as the 'Poacher's Hideout'. In April it was in full, luxuriant leaf, as was another tree 200 metres away, which provided perfect shade for a midday picnic. Up above us, in the branches of the lesser tree, a smallish, insignificantly plumaged bird began to fuss and flutter, and as soon as I reached for my binoculars, flew down onto the top of a nearby thorn bush. Leaving our picnic blanket and heading for its perch, I began to make out quite distinctive pale cheeks, but was still struggling with an identification when it took off again, this time into the dense foliage of the Poacher's Hideout, but still not showing me the distinctive white outer tail feathers. Assuming I would never catch sight of the bird again among the layers of leaves, I looked up for one last check – and there it was, fluttering away as if determined I should not lose it. Then everything suddenly fell into place. Right next to the branch where the bird revealed itself was a huge bees' nest, which it was desperately trying to show me, playing the perfect part of a Greater Honeyguide – and truly living up to its name, *Indicator indicator*.

That was 15 years ago, when I knew much less about honeyguides than I do now, and had yet to read Sparrman's account: '... if it should happen to have gained a considerable way before the men (who may easily be hindered in the pursuit by bushes, rivers, and the like) it returns to them again, and redoubles its note, as if to reproach them with their inactivity. At last the bird is observed to hover for a few moments over a certain spot, and then silently [retire] to a neighbouring bush or other resting-place; the hunters are sure of finding the bees nest in that identical spot, whether it be a tree, or in the crevice of a rock, or (as is most commonly the case) in the earth.'

Cisticolas
Cisticolidae

Rear Admiral Hubert Lynes deserved all the credit and decoration he received for his actions during the First World War to neutralise the German raids on British shipping out of Belgian coastal ports. He also deserves every accolade he received for a different form of bravery – embarking on an exhaustive study of the cisticolas. Awakened to the confusion surrounding the whole genus after an expedition to Darfur in the early 1920s, he, in his own words, 'became very interested in the fan-tailed warblers of the genus *Cisticola*'. The field researches and detailed examination of museum skins that followed culminated in the publication of an unprecedented 'Review of the Genus *Cisticola*' as a supplemental volume to the 1930 edition of *Ibis*.

Lynes's monograph, which basically split the genus into nine groups, earned him a prestigious Godman-Salvin Medal, awarded by the British Ornithological Union for distinguished research. Typical of the many other compliments he received was that from William Sclater, writing in his 1938 revision of Volume II of Frederick Jackson's *Birds of Kenya Colony and the Uganda Protectorate*: '... until recently the genus was one of the most difficult to deal with owing to the great number of described species and races, often based on seasonal plumages and differences in size. This has all been changed by the publication of Admiral H. Lynes's masterly volume, which has entirely reorganised our knowledge of this group of birds.'

145

Nearly 20 years later, in *Birds of Eastern and North Eastern Africa*, C.W. Mackworth-Praed and C.H.B. Grant acknowledged that 'through the researches of the late Admiral Hubert Lynes, more is known about the [cisticolas] than about any comparable group of African birds'. And still today Lynes's work remains an invaluable starting point for researchers. One such is Owen Davies, who acknowledged in his 2014 Ph.D. thesis for the University of Cape Town, 'Taxonomy, phylogeny and biogeography of cisticolas', that 'while subsequent authors have modified Lynes's original groupings, his work remains the basis for modern syntheses of cisticolas', and that '... without his huge effort and detailed descriptions, I would not have had a foundation upon which to build this thesis'.

So the Admiral's influence lives on, as does his name as the author of the Latin tags of many subspecies of cisticola. Perversely, for a few years there was a Lynes's Cisticola, which enjoyed recognition as a full species, at least in Sinclair and Ryan's 2003 *Birds of Africa South of the Sahara* and Zimmerman, Turner and Pearson's *Birds of Kenya and Northern Tanzania*. However, most current authorities consider it no longer deserving of specific status, and relegate it to a subspecies of the Wailing, so masking Lynes's huge contribution to ornithology from all but the most enthusiastic researchers.

Many other subspecies are candidates for the distinction of their own species. That highland duetter, Chubb's Cisticola, has two very disjunct populations, in East and West Africa, both perhaps deserving of specific status despite little difference in their songs; and with such a huge range, it may be surprising that the Zitting Cisticola has remained a single species for as long as it has (although the Socotra and Madagascan cisticolas are both closely related and, until comparatively recently, were probably subspecies of the Zitting). The Aberdare may be lucky to be out in a species of its own, saved from absorption into the Stout by more streaking on the nape of the neck, a sub-alpine homeland and a distinctly different voice.

Lynes recognised 40 species, and today there are 50 of these warblers on the list. All of these are in the genus *Cisticola*, although exactly where that rests has long been a matter of taxonomic debate. For the time being at least, it joins eremomelas, apalises, prinias, tailorbirds, camaropteras, Madagascar jerys and various African warblers in the rather catch-all family of Cisticolidae. Only three of the cisticolas – the Madagascan, Socotra and Golden-headed of southeast Asia and Australia – are not to be sighted on the African mainland.

Being so essentially African, the genus *Cisticola* fills many pages of any book on the continent's birds with descriptions of species that are almost all maddeningly difficult to identify. Field guides generally divide the birds first into those with either plain backs or streaked backs. This may be a good place to start, but risks confusion with the sometimes-streaky non-breeders of otherwise plain-backed species, as well as other seasonal or geographical differences in the plumage of individual species. Then the streaky ones can be split by size, which is often the same as saying they have long or short tails. Further identification pointers include red on the wing or not, red caps or not and streaky napes or not.

As one would expect with such an array of names like Croaking, Chirping, Wailing, Tinkling, Churring, Rattling, Trilling, Chattering, Whistling and Singing, it is often the calls that are meant to identify different species beyond doubt. The last of these is the most common one in many East and Central African gardens, and its name is particularly confusing because 'singing' fails to describe any of its range of vocalisations. However, thanks to having heard it at least every week for the last 20 years, and to my bird-guide friend Brian Finch having rechristened it 'Sneezing Cisticola', I can now safely identify it from its call. This would not necessarily be the case if I were relying on *Birds of Kenya and Northern Tanzania* to confirm identification for the first time: 'Song of loud emphatic 2- or 3-syllabled phrases, such as *wee-chew, tchew-whip, tchee-tchee-WHIP, o-ki-WEE*, etc., variously combined or a single phrase repeated ... Alarm call *srrt-srrt-srrt*.'

The volumes of *BoA* have never been ones to carry into the field, and in the absence of a tape-recorder, in the 1997 days of the publication of Volume V one presumably would have needed to try and memorise the call and then come home to check if it fitted with the description of: '2–3 loud, ringing, metallic notes, "wee-tyer", "kowee-chup", "ploo-wee", "plu-sip", "plotchit-tee", "pitch-chew", "tsoo-chew-wip", "trick-or-treat" ...'

All of which is to say that, if one has a good ear and an even better memory, the calls of cisticolas are indeed invaluable guides to identification. If not, an app with the calls on it would certainly help, but all is still not as straightforward as it could be: in different parts of Africa, different populations of the same species of, for example, Stout, Wing-snapping and Croaking have distinctly different songs.

The habitat where any particular cisticola is seen can often aid identification by narrowing down the range of possible species. Occasionally, names give clues as to where a species lives, either in terms of habitat (Desert or Coastal or even Cloud) or of geographical range (Aberdare or Ethiopian). Otherwise, a detailed search in the field guide may reveal a species' predilection for a particular environment, such as that of the Red-faced for streamside vegetation. Trying to find elements of plumage distinctive enough to be incorporated into a common name seems the very last resort of those who originally named the birds – Grey-backed, Rufous-winged, Pectoral-patch or Short-winged hardly focus on attributes that are truly distinctive and not shared by any other species in the genus. Nairobi National Park holds 10 species. Careful study of either of our local field guides makes it clear that both Red-faced and Winding are more likely to occur in damp areas, as it does that the Singing needs thick shrubbery and therefore will only be heard in the bushed or forested areas and not once the park flattens out into open grassland. Taller, rank grass is the province of the Stout, and shorter herbage of the Pectoral-patch and Zitting, as well as, belying its name, the Desert. Croaking, Rattling and Siffling make up the 10, all three of which prefer more bushed environments.

Males are often larger than females, perhaps more so in Croaking Cisticolas than in any other, but this is hardly an aid to identification. High flyers mostly have short tails, but short tails themselves are no sure indicator of flying high (one of Lynes's groups comprised six species of 'cloud-scrapers'). As a genus, cisticolas are generally solitary and monogamous, but after breeding, Stout will gather into small parties and sometimes males of both Zitting and Golden-headed may pair with several females, which together nest in the territory of the single male.

The construction of the spherical nests that all species build is usually a joint effort, the male often weaving the outer shell which, if it proves acceptable, his mate then lines. The Neddicky (from the Afrikaans *neddikie*), or Piping Cisticola, may be an exception, with the female doing most, if not all the nest building while the male serenades her from the top of a nearby bush. Somewhat surprisingly, given the size of the birds that built them, cisticola nests attract a range of different parasitic birds, some much larger than the host. Neddickies are the focus of the attentions of Klaas's Cuckoos, Brown-backed Honeybirds and Cuckoo-finches, all of which will also lay in the nests of other cisticola species if they get the chance. It is hard to imagine a Diederik Cuckoo squeezing into the low-lying nests of Stout Cisticolas, but they reportedly do; much easier to envisage is a female Pin-tailed Whydah slipping into the marshland construction of a Winding Cisticola.

Most cisticolas had to wait until the arrival of European ornithologists in Africa for their formal description: Hartlaub, Heuglin, Reichenow, Ruppell, Sharpe, Smith and Shelley had all named more than one species before Lynes's systematic analysis appeared in 1930. Given the essentially African composition of the genus, it is somewhat ironic that the first cisticola to be formally described was the Zitting, in 1810, from a specimen obtained in Sicily, in the Mediterranean. The credit for this goes to an extraordinary, multi-dimensional naturalist called Constantine Samuel Rafinesque-Schmaltz. Born in Turkey, he travelled to the United States but then returned to live in Europe, setting up a trading venture in Palermo in Sicily in 1805. While based on the island, he encountered the bird that would eventually become *Cisticola juncidis* (*juncidis* deriving from the Latin *iuncus* meaning 'a sedge'), but which at the time he ascribed to the warbler genus *Sylvia* – quite appropriate given that there was then no *Cisticola* genus, and understandable even now, when the habit of fanning their tails in flight gives rise to the alternative name of Fan-tailed Warbler.

Zitting Cisticolas are not known for their migratory instincts, and yet a glance at the map of their distribution sees them spread around the whole of southern Europe, throughout most of India and the Far East, as well as up into China and Japan and down into northern Australia. I well remember the astonishment of seeing my first non-African cisticola zigzagging over the grasslands around the edges of the magnificent southern Spanish sanctuary of Coto Doñana, forcing me to consult *Birds of Europe* to reassure myself that cisticolas could really be found there. The male's undulating display flight in the breeding season is designed to attract a mate down to check the nest he has built, and if this passes inspection, copulation seals the partnership. It is a good aid to Zitting identification, especially where there are other cisticolas around. Some years later, and still unaware of worldwide cisticola distribution, I was confirming my sighting of a Golden-headed Cisticola near Cairns, only to find the Zitting Cisticola there on the same page of Pizzey and Knight's *Birds of Australia*.

The species' widespread distribution is largely a consequence of its adaptability – be the conditions wet or dry, warm or cold, high or low, bush or cropland. Dispersal must also be aided by its preparedness to undertake local migrations into seasonally warmer or higher areas to breed, as in China, India or further north in Europe, and then to retreat downhill or further south in winter. Aiding this might be a breeding strategy that has the females often nesting in their first adult year, as well as laying two clutches a year, the eggs hatching in less than two weeks.

Evidence that this expansion is continuing is not hard to find. On 18th July 2006 Hungary's first Zitting Cisticola was heard and then seen on the reed stems of a swampy meadow near Lake Kolon. No doubt the bird had overshot its breeding range, as did those occasionals recorded in Denmark, Sweden, England, Ireland and Belgium. However, given our warming world and the bird's adaptability, there is little doubt that what start as visits from vagrants will evolve into visits to breed, before the birds finally establish themselves as year-round residents. Malta's first cisticola was recorded as a winter visitor as long ago as 1893, but the first nest was not found until 1973. Perhaps considered too small by the island's army of bird shooters to waste cartridges on it, the Zitting Cisticola is today a widespread breeding resident, far more so than either the Sardinian or Spectacled Warblers which have bred there for much longer. Next stop the UK?

Warmer, shorter winters are turning migrant birds into residents, and hotter, drier summers in Europe could well push Zitting Cisticolas northwards to breed in the increasingly temperate climes. Little Egrets are now firmly established breeders in the UK, as are Firecrests and Cetti's Warblers. Black-winged Stilts seem to be gaining a toehold, and Eurasian Bee-eaters have had several successes over the past decades. Will the time soon come when the breeding range of a single species of land bird stretches almost contiguously from South Africa to the south of England? Reg Moreau is frequently quoted as describing in his formidable compendium of information, *The Bird Faunas of Africa and its Islands* (and this was published in 1966), how the Zitting Cisticola '... qualifies as the most remarkable small bird in the world. Though tiny, short-winged and to all appearances everywhere sedentary, it has occupied nearly all the Ethiopian region, the coasts of the Mediterranean and a succession of stations right across the Oriental region to Japan and northeast Australia. This last, most easterly population is so like the most westerly, in West Africa, that in the words of the monographer of the genus "it is hard to find any difference" between these two extreme populations of *C. juncidis* (Lynes 1930). Whatever the inherent stability of the species and whatever the power of convergence, it seems necessary to accept that most of this bird's immense expansion has taken place in very recent evolutionary time.'

So, we began with Lynes and now we have ended with him, and Moreau's conclusion also needs to be repeated. Yes, a cisticola, one of those quintessential, largely ignored little brown jobs, could actually be the most remarkable small bird in the world!

Weavers & Widowbirds
Ploceidae

The weaver family is called Ploceidae, which includes anything with 'weaver' in its name, as well as birds such as sparrow-weavers or buffalo-weavers; and it also takes in queleas, bishops, widowbirds, fodys (of Madagascar and outlying Indian Ocean Islands) and malimbes. The 'true' weavers, if there are such birds, must be those of the *Ploceus* genus, which, with around 65 species, is one of the largest of all bird genera. Two species are in Madagascar and four in Asia, including the familiar Baya Weaver, whose map covers the whole of India as well as most of southeast Asia. The *Ploceus* males in breeding finery are generally a combination of black and yellow, but it is their nests as much as their plumage that define weavers and make them such an icon of the natural African landscape – each species' nest design as distinct and recognisable as its plumage. Many of the weavers are solitary breeders, especially the less conspicuous, forest-dwelling ones, but it is the frantic comings and goings of the colonial nesters that make such an impression.

One of the best studied of these communal breeders is the Village (Spotted-backed or Black-headed) Weaver, distinguished from most other masked weavers by its dark red eyes. It is widespread throughout sub-Saharan Africa, and extremely gregarious, whether in or out of the breeding season. On our road we are blessed with a colony of Speke's at one end and of Village Weavers at the other, both seeming to seek out human habitation as some sort of insurance against predation.

Nicholas and Elsie Collias were once in the forefront of research into weaverbird nest construction, taking it to the extent of fabricating one of their own, which looks pretty good, at least when its picture is compared to a real nest (in Volume 79 of 1962 *Auk*). A lot of their observations were of Village Weavers imported from Senegal into a well-treed aviary at the University of California in Los Angeles. Here they recorded the basic sequence of building steps, beginning with the male bird first creating a ring of long, coarse fibres, upon which he can then perch while he starts to add the roof, and then the breeding chamber. Thereafter, the antechamber is woven into the nest, from the outside, and finally a short, downwards-facing entrance tube. This is usually added after the female has accepted the nest, and before the male smoothes off the edges to complete the construction. The Colliases also tested the birds' affinity for colour. First, they offered them a variety of different-coloured toothpicks, followed later by real nesting material, finding that the males overwhelmingly opted for green in both. Fresh vegetation is much more flexible than dried and is therefore best suited for nest construction, so it pays the builders to go for green.

One of the first things anyone is told about a weaver nest is that it is built exclusively by the male, before he proudly shows it off to his prospective mate, who then more often than not rejects it. This is far from always being the case, but certainly among the polygamous colonial nesters the males do indeed build the nests, and any single female visiting a colony finds herself the subject of simultaneous mating displays from many different suitors. *BoA* charmingly describes how a male Village Weaver hangs, upside down, beneath the entrance to his nest, chirping nest-invitation calls and revealing the bright yellow linings to his wings as he flaps these wildly. If a female chooses to enter his nest, the male looks up inside and sings to her, and the female selects her mate based not only on the quality of the nest structure but also of his invitational displays. If his efforts are in vain, he may quickly pull it down and start again on the same site or otherwise shift to another, more favourable one. Both sexes of more solitary nesters like the Spectacled Weaver may join in nest building to the extent of putting the finishing touches to the breeding chamber at the top of what is probably the longest entrance tunnel in the weaver world; while sparrow-weaver females may share the whole job of nest construction with their mates.

Diederik cuckoos take their vernacular name from the high-pitched, multi-syllabic whistle uttered by the male when the time has come to establish a breeding territory. They are brood parasites, like other cuckoos, and particularly known for laying their eggs in the nests of weavers. Much the most frequented nests in southern Africa are those of Southern Masked Weavers and Southern Red Bishops (which are also weavers). The Masked Weaver's is an elaborate, onion-shaped construction with an entrance at the bottom. Male Red Bishops build hemispherical nests, usually woven around two reeds or bulrushes, with a porch added above the side entrance. Unlike open, cup-shaped nests, neither of these is easy for a cuckoo to nip into quickly, drop an egg and be out of again before the furore starts, although the darker interior of the nest will undoubtedly make it harder for the host female to discern differences between her own egg and that of a cuckoo.

Red Bishops nest in big, bustling, noisy colonies and it is difficult for a cuckoo to approach unmolested. The female cuckoo will usually first lurk in thick foliage close to the colony, perhaps trying to select a particular nest, before flying out, dropping her egg as quickly as she can, and possibly removing any host's egg in the process. It may happen that merciless mobbing by the bishops before she reaches the nest forces a retreat. In some instances, the male cuckoo has been known to play at least some post-coital attention to his mate by provoking attention to himself and so luring away the mobbing horde and allowing her to slip in less noticed.

The cuckoo's egg is usually a close match to that of the host. Detailed experiments, written up by M.J. Lawes and S. Kirkman in the 1996 *Journal of Animal Behaviour* to ascertain the likelihood of cuckoo eggs being rejected, were conducted at four South African colonies near Pietermaritzburg. The researchers used model eggs differing (in varying degrees) in size and colour from those of the bishops. Not surprisingly, they found that the closer the match to the host's light blue egg, the better the chances of acceptance, but differing egg size did not seem to increase the likelihood of rejection. From a timing perspective, to minimise the chances of rejection, cuckoos needed to drop their eggs after the host had started laying; attempts to discover whether eggs were more likely to be rejected if they were laid by the cuckoo after the bishops had finished laying their own clutch were inconclusive. The researchers also found that not only were cuckoos dropping eggs into bishops' nests, but some bishops themselves were laying eggs in their bishop neighbours' nests – 'intraspecific' as opposed to 'interspecific' parasitism, and probably much more widespread among the bishops than was originally supposed.

A number of other weaver species also find themselves hosting Diederiks. Many of these, like the Spectacled, build nests with long entrance tubes that severely restrict a cuckoo's speedy entrance. Long tubes are costly to build, in terms of energy, but this may be more than outweighed by the advantages in keeping out both predatory snakes and parasitic cuckoos. When filming *The Life of Birds*, David Attenborough and his team set up cameras near a colony of the shorter-tubed nests of Lesser Masked Weavers, around which several female cuckoos were lurking. Many times, as he relates in the book of the series, a particular cuckoo 'flew in to a weaver's nest, but each time, though she struggled hard, she failed to get inside. Later we heard that several nests had been found with a female cuckoo so firmly wedged in the entrance tube that she had been unable to extricate herself and had died.' He then added his own observation that the Lesser Masked Weavers seemed, over recent years, to have narrowed the diameter of the entrance to their nests and 'are currently winning what may be the final round in their contest with the cuckoos'.

Not only are weaver nests subject to parasitism, but also to predation. Weavers build their nests with a view to minimising this threat, often on the tip of an impossibly flimsy branch, which may at least deny larger snakes access. However, no matter how careful the birds are to avoid terrestrial predators, raptors are inevitable nest raiders. Gabar Goshawks try and rip open the grassy weave to get at its occupants, and there is no more dedicated raider than the Harrier-Hawk (or Gymnogene). Its long, almost double-jointed legs seem specifically designed to cling onto weaver nests or supporting branches, while the bird cranes its particularly small head inside to see if there are any chicks to pull out. Witnessing such an attack inevitably provokes conflicting emotions, where the urge to save the nestlings by scaring off the predator plays against the knowledge that the raptor, or its own offspring, will go hungry if it cannot feed.

Wherever there's a tree in Africa, one of the Ploceidae is not far away, but they certainly do not all merit the appellation of 'weaver'. Some of those on the family fringes, like buffalo- or sparrow-weavers, or social-weavers, make no effort to weave together grasses and fronds, instead just poking sticks or stems into a bulbous construction that emerges with the approximate shape of a nest. Some *Ploceus* species such as Vieillot's Black Weavers can build nests in a day, in their case often among a colony of Village Weavers with which they share promiscuous, polygamous habits. At the other end of both the nest-building and behaviour spectrum is the monogamous Spectacled Weaver, which may spend up to three weeks over his extravagant construction, with its long entrance tunnel.

My own prize for nest construction is awarded to the widespread, damp-dwelling Thick-billed (or Grosbeak) Weaver, a mildly gregarious bird and the only species in its own genus of *Amblyospiza*. The male links two or three uprights together, then begins building with the cup at the base of the nest, rather than the ring with which so many *Ploceus* weavers start. The nest is woven out of very fine grass, or strips of reed stems, over a period of between two and 12 days, and immaculately finished, with all loose ends tidied off. The whole construction often looks to have been fabricated from the same nesting material. No species better deserves to be described as a 'weaver', and if the female accepts a nest, she may at least make some contributions to the design of the entrance hole and the interior finishings.

With so many weavers having spent so much time and energy on nest construction, it is perhaps as well that their efforts have considerable second-hand value, and when the weavers have gone, lots of other creatures may move in. These are mostly other birds, which take over the nest chamber, often adding feather linings before laying their own eggs. For some, like the Cut-throat Finch and Orange-breasted Waxbill, using weaver nests is the rule rather than the exception, not least because the weaver nest is basically spherical, as theirs would be if they had to build one. In his treatise on 'The Biology of the Orange-breasted Waxbill', published in the *Ostrich*, Volume 53 of 1982, B.D. Colahan described examining 440 Southern Red Bishop nests in Zimbabwe, of which 318 were occupied by waxbills, these usurpers having built only 45 nests of their own. Sometimes more serious rehabilitation of the nests is required, as when Superb Starlings move in to the twiggy, spartan-looking nests of buffalo-weavers. Where species such as these, or Sociable Weavers, build a single structure containing many separate nests, large raptors occasionally use the communal roof as a ready-made nesting platform, which needs very little extra modification before they lay their own eggs on it.

Queleas, with three species – Cardinal, Red-headed and Red-billed – are the ultimate proponents of colonial life, famous for their massive flocks, especially of the Red-billed. These have sometimes been described as 'feathered locusts', and *BoA* conjectures that they 'may be the most abundant bird species in the world'. They collect together in enormous dry-season roosts, sometimes in their millions, and breed in dense colonies of almost contiguous nests. The birds are devastating consumers of sorghum, wheat, millet and rice, and different estimates have them eating between half and the whole of their 20-gram body weight in a day. Queleas are essentially seed-eaters but, like most weavers, they are also partial to insects and other arthropods.

Red-billed Queleas, in particular, are very migratory, some males even breeding successively in one colony after another. The flocks may break up and then regroup with different aggregations, and this continual movement must also help in disseminating information about food sources. Populations of queleas are robust, with individuals breeding up to three times a year, and perhaps they need to be particularly resilient, given some of the measures taken to reduce their numbers. These include taking flame-throwers to breeding colonies, spraying poison from aeroplanes or blowing up roosts with firebombs or even dynamite. The traditional means of control, involving humans banging tin pans in the middle of their crops to scare the birds away, worked admirably on small plots, as well as having no environmental downside, but was of little use on large-scale farms.

Widowbirds are far from being colonial, with the males defending established territories of grass or marsh in which more than one female may breed. Because they nest on the ground, the males must display well above it if they are to attract mates, and at this Jackson's and Long-tailed particularly excel. Jackson's certainly produces the most dramatic mating display, the males showing off in leks (as do bustards) in which they bounce up and down like puppets on strings. Thus, they lure females that are ready to mate into their dancing – and copulating – arenas, and, with one thing leading to another, the male fulfils and ends his role as a partner.

Long-tailed Widowbird males have an even longer tail than Jackson's – often up to half a metre – and are equally non-participatory in nest building, incubation and rearing of young, although they may bring a few token pieces of grass to a nest site. They were the subjects of a particularly bizarre experiment by Malte Andersson of the University of Gothenburg in Sweden to try and establish whether females really do prefer males with long tails. In 1982 *Nature* Volume 299 he told the story of his research on the Kinangop plateau, north of Nairobi.

Having found a patch of rough grassland much frequented by Long-tailed Widowbirds, Andersson caught nine groups of four males each. Then he treated each four-bird group by cutting off 14 centimetres of tail from one male and gluing that onto the tail of another; one male he left untouched, and, just to be sure that the gluing had no unforeseen effects, cut a length of tail from the fourth male and then glued it back onto its owner again. Then he watched. Yes, the males with add-on tails did much better at attracting brown, inconspicuous mates, mainly at the expense of those whose tails had been shortened. However, he never really got to address the downside to extravagant, mate-attracting plumage, which must be that it decreases mobility and so increases the chances of predation; he probably needed more time to show whether longer tails shortened chances of survival.

Much of what is written in the preceding pages concerns widespread species – colonial breeders with which many people are familiar. But, at the extreme other end of the weaver continuum are several species whose ranges are marked by tiny dots on the distribution maps, and about which very little is known – none more so than the Yellow-legged Weaver, described by Chapin in 1916 from a female specimen collected on 20th September in the Ituri Forest in the Congo, showing black plumage, yellowish feet and a yellow iris. 'All we can say is that this weaver inhabits high trees in the rain forest. I never saw it alive; the type was shot by my helper Nekuma. Its stomach contained a number of small caterpillars, and in the oviduct there was a developing egg.'This and eight other specimens are in museum drawers, and since the last was collected, there have been only two more sightings of the bird that Chapin named *Rhinoploceus flavipes*. Despite repeated suggestions that all the specimens are in fact hybrids of other black weavers, the bird has subsequently found its way onto most lists as *Ploceus flavipes*.

Nearly as localised, but with no doubts over its existence, is one of Kenya's very few endemic birds: Clarke's Weaver. This is found in coastal *Brachystegia* forest, the birds apparently feeding noisily in small flocks, sometimes of mixed species. In the last volume of *BoA*, published in 2004, the authors acknowledged that this bird's breeding habits were unrecorded and that it 'possibly nests high in trees'. Ten years later the bird finally revealed one of its breeding sites to a group of dedicated bird watchers in the Dakatcha Woodlands, not in tall trees but rather in the dense sedges of seasonal wetlands.

Never having set eyes on Clarke's Weaver, I determined to do so on my next visit to the Kenyan coast and thought I was sure of a sighting on its nesting grounds. However, I had failed to reckon on the El Niño cycle. 'Not a chance,' I was told when inquiring if one of the local coastal bird watchers would show me the weavers at Dakatcha.'The wetlands are no longer wet and there is not a weaver to be seen.'So for now I have to live by my own dictum of always leaving something for next time.

Chapter 4

SIX SPECIAL SPECIES

A lot of individual bird species from widespread families have come to epitomise Africa in different ways – some through rarity, others through familiarity. The Udzungwa Forest Partridge and Congo Peacock get ticks on very few bird watchers' lists, but the stories of their unveiling to the Western world are fascinating. So far in this book there is no mention of any wildfowl, hence the inclusion here of an account of the most fundamentally African of these, the Egyptian Goose. Similarly, I have reached chapter four with no more than a passing mention of endemic raptors, so now I write about two of the most widespread and instantly recognisable of these: the African Fish Eagle and Bateleur. Finally, the Hadada finds its way into this chapter in recognition of its being perhaps the best-known bird in the whole of the continent.

Egyptian Goose
Alopochen aegyptiaca

'You are worse than the goose of the shore that is busy with mischief. It spends the summer destroying the dates, the winter destroying the seed-grain. It spends the rest of the year chasing the cultivators, and allows not the seed to be thrown to the ground before it has got wind of it. It cannot be caught by snaring, nor is it offered up in the temple, that evil bird of piercing sight that does no work.'

This passage is from the ancient Egyptian document known as the *Papyrus Lansing*, written around 1500 BC, and is presumably describing what would eventually become known as *Alopochen* (*alopex* is Greek for 'fox', referring to its colour, and *chen* for 'goose') *aegyptiaca*. Much of the *Papyrus Lansing* takes the form of an educational diatribe, and this seems no exception.

The goose's range, until comparatively recently, extended up into Palestine and other parts of the Middle East, although any natural breeding outside Africa now seems unlikely. Escapees and feral birds confuse the limits of the bird's native range, but there is little doubt that in North Africa this has contracted significantly, as has that of the other ornithological icon of ancient Egyptian art, the Sacred Ibis.

At the other end of the continent the geese are rapidly becoming (as some would say) almost overly successful, with the population expanding to fill a similar niche to that exploited in America and Europe by Canada Geese. Perhaps perversely, both species relish human habitation for its freedom from predators, although one wonders if this is still the case in Europe, with the proliferation of urban foxes. These birds also seem aware that people don't generally carry shotguns in a suburban environment.

Egyptian Geese are now the most common waterfowl in South Africa, where, on top of the increased security provided by humanity, they also capitalise on many new expanses of grassland and, in some areas, more water-collection dams. The ideal combination of these resources is found on golf courses, where the birds moult and defecate on fairways, much to the annoyance of the golfers. In the July–August 2014 issue of *African Birdlife*, the results of a survey of golfing opinion showed clearly that over 80 per cent of golfers found the birds a nuisance. Keeping numbers down to reasonable levels seems sufficient to placate most of the golfers, but how best to achieve this?

The suburban surrounds of most courses mean that non-lethal methods are preferred. So, enter a fairly bewildering array of options including relocations, nest destruction and flushing with trained dogs, scarecrows or imitation predators – none of which has ever been particularly successful. In North America, playing the distress calls of Canada Geese cut numbers substantially until the birds began to associate the calls with a particular transmitting van. The survey's author, Rob Little, goes on to suggest modifying courses so they are less goose-friendly: build fewer ponds, cut down fairway size, and grow clumps of view-blocking vegetation to reduce the feeling of security engendered by wide-open spaces, where the birds can see far into the distance. He does not go so far as to advocate replacing greensward with Astroturf, which in addition to deterring the geese, would also save water!

Other reasons why Egyptian Geese flourish must surely derive from their habits. While they are principally vegetarian, feeding off grass, seeds, seedlings, leaves and a range of other vegetable matter not designed to endear them to farmers, they also take any easy animal matter that presents itself. On top of this, they are very adaptable in the times of year they breed, as described by *BoA*: 'Kenya, Lake Turkana April, May, Sept; rest of Kenya all months no pronounced peaks, Tanzania all months, no peaks ... Zimbabwe all months, peaking June–Sept; South Africa all months, peaking Aug–Sept'. Perhaps it is easier for wildfowl to be more flexible in their nesting schedules, especially if they live close to bodies of permanent water, and also in latitudes of less extreme temperatures. Nonetheless, in *Shot-gun and Sunlight*, B.G. Lynn-Allen raises one of the more bizarre consequences of always finding nests at different times of the year: it 'make[s] the nomination of a true and comprehensive close season so impossible'!

The geese have very catholic nesting habits, too, which go some way towards insuring populations against the effects of serious floods. In addition to breeding in or underneath thick waterside vegetation, according to *BoA* they also exploit 'holes in embankments, caves, cliff ledges, tree cavities, church steeples and other buildings up to 60 m above ground, in or on nests of other species, e.g. darters, herons, crows, eagles and Hamerkop'. V.G.L. van Someren added eagle-owl, vulture and fish eagle to the list of potential host nests; and in Holland, where there is now an established feral population, they seem to purloin old magpie, Carrion Crow or buzzard nests, and even usurp pole tops intended to attract White Storks.

During the breeding season, the males can be very vicious, showing a 'jealous and violent disposition' as Jean Delacour put it in *Waterfowl of the World*. He then goes on to caution their introduction into mixed aviaries 'because of their savage temper and extreme pugnacity'. So, while such aggression is no asset in a free-range waterfowl collection, it may be in the wild.

Typically for geese, the female (the sexes are indistinguishable except for her being slightly smaller) lays 5 to 10 smooth, shiny, cream-coloured eggs, usually one a day, in a down-lined nest. Incubation is her work too (although not every source agrees on this, and nor on whether the birds mate for life) and around four weeks after laying, all the eggs hatch more or less simultaneously. Then comes the first of many dangers in a young gosling's life, particularly if its parents have chosen to nest, for instance, in a church steeple. *BoA* continues: 'Young leave nest within 24 hours of hatching. In elevated sites called from nest by female below, all jump in quick succession over water or land.'

Terrifying as such a leap of faith sounds, in fact, because they weigh so little, are already covered in a layer of fluff, and are hormonally primed to leave the nest at once, it seems the chicks usually escape any serious injury. (Surprisingly, the editors of the third edition of *Roberts Birds of Southern Africa* seemed reluctant to believe, even in 1970, in such a seemingly suicidal exit strategy, and stated quite unequivocally that 'chicks are taken down from high nests in the bill'!)

One person to witness goslings leaving the nest was P. le S. Milstein, who recorded what he saw at the Free State's Allemanskraal Dam in the 1975 Witwatersrand Bird Club's newsletter, *Bokmakierie*. There he found that a pair of Egyptian Geese had taken over the abandoned nest of a White-breasted (now Great) Cormorant, on the edge of an active colony of these birds. From his boat, Milstein could see into the nest, which was relatively low down. One day, finding eight goslings already hatched and only a single egg left to go, he determined to witness their impending exit. Arriving there early next morning, he found the goose still sitting on the nest, with the gander keeping watch some distance away. All seemed quiet, and the female showed no concern at doves cooing and sparrows hopping above the nest, nor at moorhens and coots swimming below. Overflying pairs of Red-billed Teal and South African Shelduck gave no cause for concern either, although another pair of geese prompted the male to leave his post and fly off in angry pursuit.

Just before 8 a.m. the gander moved closer to the nest, called to his mate, then waded into the dam and began swimming around below, hissing softly. The goose then stood up and, after inspecting the view below, walked out onto the supporting branch, stood for some minutes and then plunged down into the water, honking as she went. As if this was a sign to the young, which it seems to have been, the first gosling immediately followed her, and then quickly the rest, embryonic wings flapping as they each fell from the nest. All the while the goose honked what seemed encouragement, and then immediately stopped as soon as the ninth hit the water – which brought Milstein to a further intriguing observation.

Did ceasing to call mean that the goose knew the ninth chick was the last? If so, did this mean she had been able to count to nine? That birds can count this far is contrary to much of the received wisdom as to their numerical abilities, even now, let alone in the 1970s. Researchers are still trying to decide whether birds can spot an extra egg in their nest, or crows can count (at least to five or six), but the proof seems elusive. Or is it? Pamela Egremont and Miriam Rothschild told their story of the 'Calculating Cormorants' in the September 1979 *Biological Journal of the Linnean Society*. On the River Li, they had watched Chinese fishermen who would let their trained cormorants (actually the same species as the one in whose nest the Egyptian Geese hatched their brood) eat every eighth fish they caught. Once the cormorants had caught seven, they would blatantly refuse to fish any longer until their neck ring was loosened and they were allowed their reward.

Not long after the 1975 publication of Milstein's description, in the course of making *The Legend of the Lightning Bird*, Alan Root twice filmed goslings leaving their homes, one on top of an abandoned Hamerkop's nest and the other in its down-lined interior. Potential disaster struck ahead of time, when one of the chicks fell out of the nest while reconnoitering the outside world from its edge; but by some benevolent quirk of fate, when the rest followed the next day, it was still alive to be reunited with its family. The launching of the other batch was trouble-free, with the female cackling encouragement and the chicks plopping down one after the other into the water beside her, along with bits of broken eggshell.

The baby goslings' reward for reaching the ground is to be cared for assiduously by both parents, often until long after fledging. Ensuring that multiple hungry young are well looked after, which often seems to entail frantically paddling off to rescue stragglers, certainly needs the attentions of both parents. Predators are waiting to grab errant chicks and *BoA* even records barbel preying on young in the water, where monitor lizards might also seize chicks. Other predators include various birds of prey, as well as snakes, mongooses and a variety of other mammals.

Egyptian Geese are not, in fact, true geese, and their close relatives include the seven species of shelduck. These geese have escaped or been released into a number of alien environments, although any artificial expansion of their range is somewhat curtailed by temperature. Perhaps still influenced by some genetic clock, they tend to lay early, and so a cold spring may kill the chicks. Where both the Egyptian Goose and Ruddy Shelduck are well established, the two species are said to interbreed; but there is still a question mark over reported offspring from a cross with a Mallard.

When many of Britain's breeding birds have moved south for the winter, it is time for others to arrive on the Gulf Stream-washed isles. Greylags and Canada Geese are both breeding residents now, but they are joined in the autumn by huge numbers of 'grey' or 'black' geese from further north. Early one November, on the Solway Firth, where my brother lives, we witnessed gaggles of Barnacle Geese tumbling down onto the salt marshes. A few days later I was further south, outside Oxford, where seeing a pure white goose among a lot of Greylags almost gave me a heart attack, until my hosts told me it was not a vagrant Snow Goose, but rather a Ross's Goose escaped from a nearby country house. Finally, I found myself near the north Norfolk coast, where a friend took me to watch Brent Geese far out on the mud, awaiting the high tides that would push them onto inland pastures. On marshy grassland behind the sand dunes grazed a flock of Pink-footed Geese and, just as I had put down my binoculars, we both noticed a pair of Egyptian Geese – familiar to me because they often fly over my garden, and familiar to him for just the same reason! These birds are feral now, self-sustaining, and originally derived from birds brought in to nearby Holkham Hall when its grounds were extensively remodelled at the end of the eighteenth century.

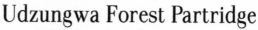

Udzungwa Forest Partridge
Xenoperdix udzungwensis

'This doesn't look like a chicken's foot,' might have exclaimed the researcher examining the bird's limb on the edge of his plate in the lantern light. 'It's yellow and there's no spur on it?' Turning to the cook, perhaps he inquired where his supper had come from, and on receiving a mumbled, scarcely audible response, he might have asked if the cook could find another of the creatures he had just stewed for them. And perhaps, some days later, on returning from the field, the researcher found a dead, fully-feathered francolin-like bird hanging from one of his tent's guy ropes. Or so might the story have gone, revealing to the world of ornithology the existence of the Udzungwa Forest Partridge. Long known to the Wahehe from the surrounding area of southern Tanzania, it was, until July 1991, yet to be recognised by science.

The Eastern Arc Mountains are comprised of a chain of generally smaller forested montane patches, the most southerly massif of which are the Udzungwa Mountains – and it is here that the partridge lives. The mountains were once a continuous chain of forested highlands, but drier times have turned the intervening lowland areas into savanna, leaving the forest to flourish on the higher massifs, continually dampened by warm, wet winds blowing off the Indian Ocean.

The isolation of each patch of mountains has led to the formation of a particularly large number of endemic species. In the botanical world, the mountains are famous for being the natural home of *Impatiens wallerina* (busy Lizzies) and African violets, whose *Saintpaulia* genus is now cultivated all over the world. The mammalian highlights of the Udzungwa Mountains themselves include the Sanje crested mangabey and Udzungwa red colobus, as well as six species of bushbaby. Birdlife is prolific, with at least 20 endemics in the Eastern Arc Mountains as a whole, some, like the Taita Apalis, confined to a single massif, and others, such as Mrs Moreau's Warbler, spread across two or more. Many other birds are near-endemic, like the Spot-throat, Dapple-throat and Red-capped Forest Warbler (once known as the African Tailorbird), their distribution edging out into other nearby areas of forest.

With such a spectacular range of biodiversity, researchers are always prepared for the unusual. But when, on 2nd August 1981, a completely new, and very distinctive male sunbird flew into Flemming Jensen's mist net set in the Udzungwa Mountains, it was still a big surprise – as it was again six weeks later, when a female was obtained, also showing distinctive rufous wing patches. (Female sunbirds are usually distinguished only by their lack of any distinctive features, and for both sexes to exhibit the same critical characteristic was unusual in itself – as, incidentally, do both sexes of the Golden-winged Sunbird.) Jensen published his formal description of the aptly named Rufous-winged Sunbird (*Nectarinia rufipennis*) in the 1983 edition of *Ibis*, Volume 125(4), although now it takes the generic name of *Cinnyris*, which it shares with over 50 other species. That such a very distinctive bird could have remained unknown to science for so long shows only how little researched are these extraordinary mountains.

Just as surprising was discovering the existence of the Udzungwa Forest Partridge. The bird was formally described in a paper by Dinesen, Lehmberg, Svendsen, Hansen and Fjeldsa from the University of Copenhagen in the 1994 *Ibis* entitled 'A new genus and species of perdicine bird (Phasianidae, Perdicini) from Tanzania; a relict form with Indo-Malayan affinities'. They gave it the name *Xenoperdix udzungwensis*, from *xenos*, meaning 'strange' in Greek, and *perdix*, a 'partridge'. Again, that such a large bird should have remained hidden for so long is testimony to the lack of scientific exploration in the area, and to the bird's very restricted range. Within this, the partridge is actually not that rare: anyone prepared to slog up the mountain slopes to their known habitat has a good chance of seeing two or three of them scratching their way through the leaves on the forest floor, having perhaps been alerted first by their muted, high-pitched 'peeps'. During roughly six months of study, the researchers saw a total of 246 birds on 85 occasions, making it what they described as 'locally common'. The Congo Peacock, by comparison, is distributed through a large area of Congo forest, but is incredibly hard to find, and were it not for its raucous call – and James Chapin's powers of observation – it might still be known only to those that live among it.

So why did the taxonomists give it a name meaning 'strange'? Their first thoughts were that the bird must be a francolin of the genus *Francolinus*. The nearly trans-African Scaly Francolins were found in the Udzungwas too, and both Latham's (now Forest) Francolin and Nahan's Partridge had evolved to occupy tropical African forests and were about the same size. However, the Udzungwa bird ticked only some of the relationship boxes, and the combination of yellow, unspurred legs, grey underparts with a very distinctive spotting pattern, and the habit of roosting in trees set them thinking outside the jagged outline of Africa's edges to the *Arborophila* genus, whose 22 members inhabit the thick tropical forests of the Indo-Malayan region. So, after weighing up the evidence, like Chapin before them, Dinesen et al. felt that the closest relatives of the bird they were identifying were not the local francolins but those denizens of the Far East. Unlike Chapin, though, they were able to call on evidence from DNA analysis to support their contention that 'opportunities for interchange of forest biota between tropical Africa and the Orient may well have existed in the mid-Miocene [23m–5m years ago], before desertification and rifting of the Red Sea isolated the two regions'.

In the *Journal of East African Natural History* in 2005, R.C.K. Bowie and Jon Fjeldsa attempted to convince readers that there was both genetic and morphological evidence for two species of the Udzungwa Forest Partridge, following the discovery of a second population of partridges in the Rubeho Highland Forests. These are relatively distant, perhaps 200 kilometres, from the forests where the original population was found, and on the other side of the Great Ruaha River. With the help of DNA analysis, the scientists estimated the two populations to have split some 200,000 years ago, and argued convincingly that conferring specific status on a population is likely to raise its conservation profile far higher than if it remained an outlying population of an existing species. And they have persuaded at least the compilers of the IOC Checklist that the Rubeho Forest Partridge, *Xenoperdix obscuratus*, should be its own species.

Congo Peacock
Afropavo congensis

In 1913, young American ornithologist James Chapin was exploring the then Belgian Congo with a zoological expedition from the American Museum of Natural History (AMNH). Near Avakubi in the Ituri forest in the northeast of the country he spotted one of its inhabitants wearing a traditional headdress adorned with a distinctive brown banded feather. Curious as to the plume's origins, the American immediately asked if he could keep it.

Among the 23,000 vertebrate specimens collected by the six-year expedition were many birds, but on returning to New York two years later, it became clear that none of their skins sported a feather remotely like the one Chapin had acquired.

From 1923 to 1948 Chapin served as associate curator of ornithology in the AMNH. His employers were magnanimous in granting him time to research what was to be his magnum opus, published over the course of 20 years – the four-part *Birds of the Belgian Congo*. In 1936 his research took him to Belgium's Tervuren Museum where, while poking around unlabelled specimens, he unearthed two large, bedraggled stuffed birds. They had little tufts on their crown, and an almost bare throat, with much bluey-green plumage that had once shone with iridescence but was now dulled by time and dust. Records showed them to have been presented to the museum by the rubber-trading Kasai Company in 1914. Victims of the staff's ignorance, the specimens had then been consigned to obscurity – the inevitable fate of exhibits for which no scientific description existed.

But Chapin saw at once that the brown secondary feathers of the female bird, flecked with distinctive black markings, perfectly matched the anonymous feather he had carefully preserved since collecting it from the Avakubi headdress over 20 years earlier.

The following year, having tested his employer's indulgence still further, Chapin was back in the Congo, where, from a forest mining camp east of Stanleyville (now Kisangani), he succeeded in obtaining several specimens of what he was to name the 'Congo Peacock' (*Afropavo congensis*, and now also known as the Congo Peafowl). As a member of the Phasianidae family (like the much more recently discovered Udzungwa Forest Partridge), the bird would rightly have belonged in Part I of his great work; but this had already appeared in 1932, so it had to wait until Part IV emerged in 1954 to be included in an addendum of 'Additional Species of Known or Probable Occurrence' (although a splendid illustration by bird artist G.E. Lodge provided the frontispiece for Part II).

'That the Congo Peacock should escape notice for so many years is still a cause for wonder' is how Chapin opened the species description, and 30 years later the authors of *BoA* endorsed his opinion. They considered that 'the discovery of *Afropavo* was one of the most sensational ornithological events of the 20th century, not merely because such a large and conspicuous bird had eluded discovery in an area reasonably well surveyed ornithologically, but also because of the implications of its probable Asiatic affinities'.

Common sense dictates that, despite its name, the peacock's closest relatives should also be in Africa, and therefore are most likely to be the guineafowl, which are endemic to the continent. Nevertheless, Chapin held out against both common sense and much scientific opinion, concluding that 'it is more closely allied to the true peacocks than to any other genus of Phasianidae, and we fail to see that it shows any tendency to approach the guinea fowls, as has been suggested by others'. DNA analysis now shows Chapin's conviction to have been fully vindicated, while at the same time raising a host of questions about the peacocks' common ancestors and their distribution at a time when both the map and climate of our planet were very different from those of today.

The Congo Peacock's very patchy distribution has now been better mapped, and shows it confined to the relatively undisturbed forests of the DRC. Hunting and habitat destruction have both taken their inevitable toll, and some seemingly ideal areas of forest are strangely devoid of peacocks. The bird's endemic status has given it special prestige in the DRC, which the primates, bonobos, also enjoy.

To reach the Réserve de Faune de Lomako-Yokokala in central DRC entails first taking the weekly plane to Basankusu, 800 kilometres northeast of Kinshasa. Helping the African Wildlife Foundation improve relations between the local communities and the Institut Congolais pour la Conservation de la Nature had provided me with a wonderful chance to visit the reserve, where both bonobos (the principal *raison d'être* for the reserve) and peacocks were supposedly locally common. Basankusu is the main outlet for produce from the upstream forest, which, if you live in, you live off. I dodged between the tea stalls to the covered market, off the main street, and the range of such produce was only too apparent. As if vetting visitors, a woman with a baby on her back wielded a large bloodied knife over the carcass of a crocodile; next door was the smoked monkey stand, tiny primate bodies splayed out on wooden frames, while the elongated hooves on the end of a dismembered carcass proclaimed the identity of that lovely aquatic antelope, a sitatunga. Further on, women dispensed cups full of caterpillars or wrapped slithering black catfish in banana leaves – but no one was selling dead birds of any description. And yes, I have to admit to a sneaking wish to find the carcass of a peacock on sale, and to be able to pluck out the same secondary wing feather that Chapin had nurtured for 20 years before his eureka moment in that Brussels museum.

From Basankusu up the Maringa River to the reserve usually takes about 14 hours in a dugout canoe. 'Going up that river was like traveling back to the earliest beginnings of the world when vegetation rioted on the earth and the big trees were kings.' So wrote Joseph Conrad of his own experiences in *Heart of Darkness* in 1899, and little has changed, except perhaps that some of those incredible big trees are no longer. Raffia palms drip over the banks, their leaves, nuts and sap providing sustenance or shelter for both human and animal inhabitants.

There are no peacocks around the headquarters of the Lomako Reserve – it is much too disturbed – but at the end of my assignment came the chance to visit Yemi, a research centre, half a day away. The incumbent scientist was Amy Cobden, who promised us bonobo sightings as long as we could get up at 3 a.m. and walk two hours to their nest sites. Amy was as good as her word, but when I asked about the peacocks her reply was dispiriting, and perhaps inevitable: 'Oh you should have been here last week'. Over the preceding months, Amy had captured several extraordinary photographs of Congo Peacocks (all the more extraordinary for their being taken in the daytime), and once I was back from the bonobos, I spent the rest of that day and the whole of the next searching around where she had last seen them – saw some splendid hornbills but no sign of peacocks.

If vocalising is a signal of activity, the birds seem most active at night, and many of the forest guards I spoke to told how they could set their watches by the 8 p.m. calls that began to penetrate the silence on the hour. And indeed, that third night, among the scrape and clatter of metal cutlery on metal plates, one of the Congolese researchers suddenly bade us be quiet. Yes, not far from the camp two peacocks were indulging in a raucous vocal exchange. I set off with torches, guides and good wishes, but the peacocks had flapped off into the distance and the dark. I should indeed have been there 10 minutes earlier this time.

The peacocks have gained a place on very few bird watchers' lists, and they were not to be added to mine. And even if hearing them doesn't count, at least I have those mysterious sounds in my memory. After all, Chapin's expedition spent six years in the Congo and emerged with only a feather, so what else could I expect in two days? Anyway, one always has to save something for the next visit – and this is where I have to admit to having gone back to Lomako a second time, and still not seen one!

However, there is an ornithologically successful postscript to this story. In September 2015 a group of eight intrepid bird watchers linked up with the African Wildlife Foundation and arranged for a 10-day stay in Yemi. Day after day went by, with much sound but no sight of the peacocks. Then, a week into their stay, returning in the dark from a visit to the bonobos, three of the party found, and photographed, a roosting female some 10 metres up in a tree. Not only that, but she stayed there long enough for the three to return to camp, collect up the rest of the incredulous group, and bring them all back to enjoy the sighting for themselves.

Bateleur
Terathopius ecaudatus

The Bateleur answers every bird watcher's prayer for a large, instantly recognisable raptor. The prayers must have been impassioned as it would take only one of its three most distinctive features of colour, shape or flight to identify the adult bird beyond any doubt.

The juvenile, just flown from its nest, is plain brown all over and takes up to seven years before attaining full grown-up brilliance. Then, unusually for large raptors, its gender is easily identifiable, even in flight, with the black band on the trailing edge of the male's wings much broader than that of the female. When the bird is perched, the vivid red face and legs, chestnut back and tiny tail are common to both, but the male shows all-black wings, while the female has a distinctive pale grey panel along its secondary wing feathers. There is also a pale-backed morph, not confined to any particular geographical area, in which a creamy brown replaces the chestnut.

The Bateleur's shape is something of a mystery. François Levaillant named the bird after the French word for 'juggler', and – by extension – tightrope walker, as an allusion to the bird's side-to-side rocking motion to compensate for its lack of tail. Surprisingly, both the Bateleur and the African Fish Eagle had to wait until 1800 to be formally described and given their Latin binomial; they were named by a 25-year-old Frenchman, François Marie Daudin, from specimens obtained, in the case of both birds, in the Knysna district of coastal southern African – where, sadly, it will take more than a miracle to spot a Bateleur today. The birds have suffered from a number of threats over the last two centuries; and, being partial to carrion, they have proved particularly susceptible to the poisoning of animal carcasses, intended to kill jackals and feral dogs during calving and lambing seasons.

The tail of a bird acts as a rudder to help it steer up, down, left, right – an appendage never put to better use than by the Black Kite, which can open, close and twist its broad, forked tail at will as it swoops down to pluck a morsel of road kill off the ground in front of an oncoming vehicle. The Bateleur has no such agility, with so stunted a tail that its bright red feet even protrude beyond it – and this despite these feet being on the end of particularly short legs! As so often, the taxonomic tag *Terathopius ecaudatus* finds the essence of the bird; the genus (of which this is the only species) *Terathopius* derives from the Greek *teras*, meaning a 'marvel', and *ops*, 'appearance'; *ecaudatus* is Latin, *ex* meaning 'lacking' and *cauda*, a 'tail'.

Strangely, the young birds start off with a slightly longer tail than their parents, this becoming progressively shorter with each moult, as if to help them gradually learn how to operate with their grown-up little stub. Perhaps in compensation, Bateleurs have 25 secondary flight feathers on each of their long wings, more than any other eagle and as many as most vultures. These, angled slightly upwards, give their wings greater rigidity, enabling the birds to glide far with scarcely a wing beat.

Bateleurs feed on a wide range of live prey, including birds as big as guineafowl, mammals weighing up to five kilograms (which would make most dik-dik worth going after), and creatures as small as termites, when these are hatching. They hunt in a very different way from other raptors, closer to the ground as they quarter back and forth over their territories. Flying slowly and relatively low allows them to spot much smaller prey, whether carrion or living. They are smaller than other carrion eaters such as vultures and Tawny Eagles, and so either avoid the larger carcasses, which these big birds focus on, or else visit them when the others are sated. Once the morning has warmed, Bateleurs take to the air, where they may spend most of the rest of the day, some estimates suggesting they travel well over 300 kilometres before the day is over. The birds sometimes follow road lines in search of dead animals or birds, and are said to have tracked old foot convoys in the hope of picking up discarded food remains, prey disturbed by the travellers or even snakes killed en route. Generally, though, with such catholic tastes it seems surprising that Bateleurs need to cover so much ground to find their food.

South African ornithologist Peter Steyn spent a long time studying Bateleurs, and recorded much of what he found in 'Breeding and Food of the Bateleur in Zimbabwe', published in *Ostrich*, Volume 51 of 1980. He monitored three nests in the savanna country round Essexvale (now Esigodini) for a total of 22 nestings. His records demonstrate only too well how varied are the birds' diets. Of the remains of 238 prey items, assessed from either pellets or prey pieces in the nest itself and on the ground below, birds made up 47 per cent, mammals 42 per cent, reptiles eight per cent and fish three per cent. At least half the animals were scrub hares, and while doves, guineafowl and francolin accounted for most of the birds, avian remains derived from a total of 26 species. It was not usually possible to tell whether a bird had been taken dead or alive, but the three species of nightjar he was able to identify most likely all derived from road kill. Of the 19 reptiles, 16 were snakes; and of the fish, five out of six were catfish, which the eagles could easily have picked out of drying pools. For all the number and range of prey, Steyn never once witnessed a Bateleur kill.

Most seasons, the female Bateleur lays only one egg – large for the size of the bird – in what is a much more substantial nest than that of any of its close relatives. Rick Watson studied Bateleurs in South Africa's Kruger National Park, and when researching nest sites, found the average height of the nest to be 15 metres off the ground, usually in a tree taller than most of the surrounding ones, which often meant one of the riparian trees along a watercourse. The same nest may be used for many years and, with only a single chick, there are no problems of sibling rivalry – but also no question of 'an heir and a spare'! During the 22 nestings Steyn monitored, he watched 17 young grow to maturity, usually taking their first flight aged around four months, giving an average of 0.77 offspring per pair per year.

Captive Bateleurs become very tractable. Respect him or not, Richard Meinertzhagen was a pillar of the English ornithological establishment, and a prolific writer. Born in 1878, his interest in birds began at a very early age, and he was particularly encouraged by his uncle Frederick. In 1885 the family leased Mottisfont Abbey in Hampshire, where Richard and his brother Daniel's enthusiasm progressed into collecting and keeping birds, particularly raptors. Among these was a pair of Bateleurs, shipped over from what is now Maputo in Mozambique, and in *Pirates and Predators* he relates: 'After a few weeks they became very tame and enjoyed being handled, performing the double or treble bow of pleasure or gratitude in anticipation of food or head-scratching; when they wanted food they would turn their head from side to side, gazing intently at one's face, balancing the body first on one leg and then on the other; but if they wanted their head scratched they would tuck it right down on their crop.'

Someone else who domesticated a Bateleur was Frederick Jackson's nephew, Geoffrey Archer, who went on to become, successively, Governor of British Somaliland, Uganda and Sudan, before finally retiring to co-author the four-volume *The Birds of British Somaliland and the Gulf of Aden.* In this he records: 'Taken young they are easily tamed. After keeping one young bird for a year at Sheikh I took it with me to England. It lived in the stables and spent the day at liberty in a Sussex park. In the evening it would return of its own accord to the stables and was so tame that my native henchman, Ibrahim Sayed, would pack it under his arm and take it with him by 'bus to spend the day in the neighbouring town.'

While we need the mind's eye to create an image of Ibrahim Sayed with a Bateleur under his arm, wandering around a Sussex village, no imagination is needed to visualise what are perhaps the best known of all illustrations of Bateleurs – those by Norman Lighton from the early editions of *Roberts Birds of Southern Africa.* Even seen on their own, out of the context of the book, they are instantly recognisable and have almost come to represent the oeuvre of the artist. Yet it is not so much the art of Lighton that these illustrations should epitomise, but rather that of the enigmatic and tragic British army major, Claude Gibney Finch-Davies.

Lighton was an architect, born near Pretoria, who launched himself onto a career ladder in the Public Works Department. His abilities as a bird painter rather than an architectural draughtsman were clearly in evidence early on because he first illustrated the four volumes of C.D. Priest's *Birds of Southern Rhodesia* before being seconded to the Transvaal Museum to produce 56 colour plates comprising 1,050 individual paintings for Austin Roberts's forthcoming book on South Africa's birds. This was published in June 1940, simultaneously in Johannesburg and London, complete with Lighton's illustrations, and has been continuously in print ever since, now under the name of *Birds of Southern Africa*.

Davies was born into a titled family in India in 1875, and after an undistinguished school career, emigrated to South Africa to join the Cape Mounted Riflemen. Army life seems to have comprised little more than an excuse for bird study, and his first known attempt at drawing birds was a rather amateurish picture of a snipe in his notebook entry of 4th August 1903. In 1908 he became a member of the British Ornithologists' Union, and his first opportunity to illustrate a book came when he was asked by Boyd Horsbrugh to produce the 69 plates for *The Game Birds and Waterfowl of South Africa*, a commission he successfully completed.

Around 1911 Davies began to focus on painting birds of prey, his bright, feather-perfect watercolours meticulously derived from studying museum skins or illustrations in printed works. Soon after the outbreak of the First World War he was posted to South West Africa (now Namibia), where the only sources of artistic inspiration were the wild birds themselves. Nevertheless, by 1916 he had almost completed a series of paintings of all South Africa's birds of prey, both nocturnal and diurnal and in varying plumages. That year, too, the wax-moustached 41-year-old lieutenant married Aileen Finch in Cape Town, adding her name to his.

By now, Finch-Davies was in frequent correspondence with Austin Roberts, then at the Transvaal Museum in Pretoria, who seems to have supplied the artist with bird skins and books to help him with his paintings. Finch-Davies saw out the last years of the war in Windhoek and was then posted, with his family, to Pretoria. There he had unrestricted access to the museum's whole collection of books and skins and it was now that things began to spiral out of control.

During 1919 Roberts discovered that a lot of coloured plates had been torn out of the Transvaal Museum's bird books. The police were alerted and a trap set, which snapped around Finch-Davies. In total, around 230 plates were found to be missing, and he was arrested on 5th January 1920. Having admitted his guilt, he wrote to the Director of the museum to say, 'I cannot explain why I should have done this but I can only put it down to the collector's madness ... God knows I have regretted this fatal blunder on my part.' He promised to return what he still had, and as security for doing so, deposited all his own art work with the museum. Court-martial was avoided, but his name and reputation were ruined beyond redemption and, with all hopes of promotion now gone, Finch-Davies transferred to Cape Town, where he was joined by his family, now comprising wife and three children.

The bearer of morning coffee to his room in the Castle on 8th August 1920 found Finch-Davies dead in bed. 'Angina pectoris' was recorded as the cause of death and he was given a military funeral and buried in the Maitland Cemetery. His wife tried unsuccessfully to recover the art work left with the Transvaal Museum before returning, near destitute, to live in Ireland.

Few knew of the existence of Finch-Davies's pledged paintings, and certainly not that they included at least four of Bateleurs. Even fewer were aware that Lighton had had access to them, and that his two pictures of mature and immature Bateleurs on Plate IX of the first edition of *Roberts Birds of Southern Africa* were feather-perfect copies of those of Finch-Davies. Lighton acknowledged Finch-Davies's influence on his work as a draughtsman. However, it was not until the Transvaal Museum allowed Finch-Davies's paintings into the public domain in Alan Kemp's 1980 *The Birds of Prey of Southern Africa* that the real extent of the influence of the soldier's work on that of the architect became generally apparent. In his article in the 1984:3 *Bokmakierie* entitled 'On the Bird Art of C.G. Finch-Davies and Norman C.K. Lighton', P.A. Clancey was particularly forthright, writing that 'many of Lighton's most convincing studies are no more than outright copies of the meticulous drawings, prepared decades earlier by Finch-Davies'.

And the most convincing of all these is surely that of the Bateleur.

Running through this tragic story are many ironies, not the least of which is that Finch-Davies painted far better than did any of the artists whose prints or pictures he stole. Further, had he never allowed his 'collector's madness' to get the better of him, would he have been the one to paint the illustrations for *Roberts Birds of Southern Africa*?

African Fish Eagle
Haliaeetus vocifer

The African Fish Eagle is likely to spend 10 times as much of its day perching and preening as it does flying and feeding – a significantly higher proportion of inactivity than that enjoyed by almost any other bird on the continent, and surely an indication of the success of this species. The Bateleur, in stark contrast, takes all sorts of animal flesh, alive or dead, but may have to glide almost all day and over 300 kilometres to find it. Insectivores have to work almost as hard, even in times of plenty, to catch insects equivalent to the protein of a 500-gram fish. Little wonder, then, that fish eagles thrive along the edges of most of the large watery expanses south of the Sahara.

Haliaeetus vocifer's closest relative is the very rare and Critically Endangered Madagascar Fish Eagle, confined to the northwest coast of its eponymous island, the two having split from a common ancestor relatively recently. Both these eagles also share their genus with the Bald Eagle of North America, and other large, dramatic birds, particularly the magnificent Steller's Sea Eagle. The genus is entirely absent from South America, and only the African Fish Eagle is found in Africa – and nowhere outside it. It bears a superficial similarity to the Bald Eagle but is easily distinguished, if it ever needs to be, by the grey-tipped beak, darker eyes and extensive white on the breast.

Unsurprisingly, like all its congeners, African Fish Eagles live primarily off fish, preferably taken live, although dead ones, which usually float, are an acceptable alternative. The hunt starts with the birds simply watching out for tell-tale signs of quarry from a high riparian branch, although sometimes they go out for sorties over open water, enabling them to cover a far wider area. Once something is spotted from on high that looks worth further investigation, the bird swoops down, then levels out, with legs stretched straight out in front, almost parallel to the surface, ready to pluck its prey from the water. Powerful talons, on the soles of which are raised barbs, help it grasp the prey, and usually the bird can be up and away without even dampening its plumage, other than with some spray.

Guides on many large African lakes entertain visitors by giving a loud, eagle-like call and then throwing a dead fish out onto the water; more often than not, a bird swoops down to pick the prey from the surface right in front of the boat. It is a remarkable spectacle, and allows a really good look at the fish eagle's mode of fishing. Some sport fishermen boast of a fish eagle taking their catch off the lure, or even the lure itself as it wobbles along the surface, with the possible consequence of having to try and disengage a treble hook from the bird's talons. I have hooked swallows, bats and a nightjar on flies, but none of these was difficult to return to the wild!

An average-sized catch may weigh 500 grams, and this is easily carried back to the tree. Larger fish up to about four times that weight can be lifted with much more effort, and a really big fish may have to be flapped ashore across the surface of the water. There is a lot of protein in a fish: a 500-gram catch, which is about 10 per cent of the bird's weight, can keep it going for a day; and where supplies are plentiful, the birds may hunt for only a few minutes to take their fill. Nesting males need to provide for their mates and young too, which might mean three or more successful fishing trips a day.

A.K. Whitfield and S.J.M. Blaber studied the 'Feeding ecology of piscivorous birds at Lake St Lucia', Part 1 of which appeared in *Ostrich*, Volume 49 in 1978. In this estuarine habitat they found that the Mugilidae family dominated the fish eagles' diets, particularly the flathead mullet, which can tolerate a wide spectrum of salinity and often shoals in the shallows, their backs breaking the surface. The second-favourite was the sharptooth catfish, perhaps the most widespread fish in Africa, and a freshwater staple of fish eagles' diets all over the continent. The researchers tested the birds' preferred size of fish by offering them dead ones on the surface, watching as they managed to grab a two-kilogram fish with one foot, and plane it back to dry land across the surface, but generally eschewing anything much bigger. Female fish eagles weigh up to a kilogram more than males, and so are more likely to take larger fish.

On top of a plentiful supply of fish, these eagles need the right conditions to catch them. A wind-ruffled surface makes for poor visibility, and, in some places, algal blooms caused by nutrient run-off can so colour the water that fishing becomes impossible. Sadly, these can also kill fish, which, though dead, may still satisfy the eagles' needs, but only in the short term. On rivers, fishing is easier in shallower water, and Chapin quotes one of his contributors as noting that the birds usually time their

breeding to coincide with these lower levels. The nesting season in South
Africa is mainly in the winter, when most of the country is dry and river
fishing easier. Eagles that forage in smaller rivers and swamps may have
brief spells of great plenty as fish mass to breed in the shallows or are
otherwise stranded in drying water pans.

If fishing gets hard and the rewards dwindle, there is nearly always a
range of other equally suitable prey. The BBC has shot some spectacular
footage at Kenya's Lake Nakuru, where the only fish are tiny *Tilapia
grahami*, more suited to being scooped up in pelicans' pouches than
taken individually by fish eagles. Here, eagles may try instead to grab
flamingos, usually singletons that peel off from the flock. In other lakes,
the eagles scoop up young coots or small grebes off the surface before
they can paddle into the reeds or dive out of harm's way. Eagles may
try for ibises, storks and herons, or their young, while these are on the
shore, or may even aim to catch cormorants out on the water. Of four
birds that Chapin cut open, three had been eating fish, while in the
fourth was a monitor lizard, as well as the hard, indigestible remains
of a lot of insects; these he assumed to have themselves been stomach
contents of the monitor or earlier lizard prey.

And if food of any kind is not easy to find, then fish eagles are well
used to taking it from other birds, or even, in one case captured on
camera, from a crocodile in the Kruger National Park. They are occasional
kleptoparasites – an ugly word for ugly behaviour. The ultimate
kleptoparasites are the frigatebirds, for which this is their primary means
of feeding. Skuas, gulls and crows are also inveterate thieves of other
birds' food, while for African Fish Eagles it is a very secondary means of
feeding. Bigger birds catch bigger fish, and eagles are on the lookout for
whatever Goliath Herons have just caught, and even the catch of Saddle-
billed Storks.

Fish eagles are also prepared to steal from birds on the wing. Pelicans
may be carrying beakloads of small fish back to their nests when they are
intercepted and forced to empty their pouch, and even Pied Kingfishers,
which would have only one small fish in their beak, have been similarly
deprived of their catch. However, the birds that provide the most suitable-
sized prey for both Bald Eagles and African Fish Eagles are Ospreys, which
are totally reliant on fresh fish for their food.

In most of Africa Ospreys are only migrants, breeding as far south as
the Red Sea but no further – something for which ornithologists have
yet to find any good explanation, because the conditions further south,

between the tropics, would seem ideal for year-round residency. Ospreys are smaller than fish eagles and their fishing techniques are very different: they hunt much more from the open sky than from a perch, quartering the water before stopping, perhaps hovering, and then plunging down near-vertically onto their prey; this is often in much deeper water than eagles ever fish, and the Ospreys may need to submerge almost completely before they can grasp their catch. They are more at home at the coast than are eagles, not least because they are much more practiced at fishing in the open, and less dependent on trees from which to watch the water. Having caught a fish, an Osprey carries it lengthwise, like a torpedo slung under an aeroplane, back to dry land to eat – unless the fish eagle's piratical attentions have forced it to drop its catch.

Fish eagles need tall trees to breed in, as well as from which to watch over the water, and the lack of these close to the sea makes them much less common there. At low tide, even a shore-edge tree would often be too far from the water for the birds to use as a lookout. In large estuaries, like Lake St Lucia, the water is less tidal and trees are more likely to be closer to its edge. There, as on so many other large expanses of African water, the birds' unmistakable cry may sound out from a high branch, accompanied sometimes with flapping wings, but nearly always an elegantly thrown-back head. It is variously described as a yelp, croak or laugh, but no single word does its call justice, whether it rings out to proclaim territory or in response to that of a mate. It has come to epitomise the African Fish Eagle's environment, and features far more than the bird itself in books, films or the minds of those who once lived in Africa but no longer do. Now the call can be retrieved at the press of a computer key, but years ago it would have been one of the sounds that needed to imprint itself on the memory of returning Englishmen – that is unless they had settled in Hampshire at the end of the nineteenth century.

Along with the Bateleurs that lodged at the Meinertzhagen family's rented abode at Mottisfont Abbey was also an African Fish Eagle, which '... was purchased for £10 from Jamrach's in the London Docks. She became perfectly tame and easily handled. She was given her liberty and remained at large for several years, being known as Lobengula [the name of a king, not queen, of the Ndebele people from Zimbabwe]. She would fish in the Test, always bringing her catch to a favourite chimney-pot on the old Abbey. To reach her fishing ground on the Test she had to run the gauntlet of two rookeries and a heronry, and these three communities would turn out in force to mob her; she disdained the rooks but took the herons seriously, turning over on her back if one came too close. During the mayfly season we had to shut her up as on one occasion she snatched a hooked fish from my father's rod, breaking the line. But trout were not her main prey; almost always roach, dace or perch, never pike or eel. Her wild call as she sat on her chimney-pot was a joy to hear; and whenever I heard it in Africa, I was reminded of my old home and Lobengula.'

Jamrach's was indeed a famous animal store on the Ratcliffe Highway in east London, and there are pictures of the Mottisfont eagles in the Hampshire Archives in Winchester. No matter, this time, whether Meinertzhagen embellished some of the detail of this story in *Pirates and Predators*: an African Fish Eagle throwing back its head to call from the rooftops of a Hampshire home, with a Test trout in its talons, is indeed a picture worth the painting.

Today African Fish Eagles seem to be holding their own, showing enormous resilience in the face of inevitable habitat degradation and overfishing. Perhaps such a successful hunter is less susceptible to fluctuations in food supply, and can afford to spend longer fishing if conditions deteriorate, easily surviving even if the ratio of perching to hunting time is halved. Lessons can be learnt from the much studied birds at Lake Naivasha, in Kenya's segment of the Great Rift Valley, which once held, and indeed may still hold, the highest density of African Fish Eagles in the world. With an average size of around 150 square kilometres, the lake's extent varies with the fluctuations in the water level, and in the late 1960s the renowned raptor expert, Leslie Brown, counted around 250 birds, with a very healthy ratio of young to old. At that time the dominant fish were local species of tilapia, as well as introduced largemouth bass, which swam in clear, clean water, fringed almost all the way round by tall, yellow-barked fever trees.

Fast-forward 30 years, and the count was down below 70. Hundreds of acres of plastic greenhouses – testimony to a thriving horticultural industry – pressed down on the lake's southern edge, and much water was being pumped out, while agrochemicals and human waste from the huge labour force found its way in. Water turbidity increased, not least as introduced Louisiana crayfish made major inroads into the aquatic vegetation, and algal blooms became an ever-present risk. The nearby geothermal power plants also extracted water and the lake edge receded so far from the riparian trees that the fringing rim of papyrus almost died off; eagles even moved out to perch on the backs of the resident hippos in order to be closer to their prey. The birds became extremely stressed, and dissipated much of their energy in territorial disputes. Could they survive?

Today, according to Munir Virani of The Peregrine Fund, who has spent half his life studying the birds, numbers are almost back up to 1960 levels. The lake's only outlets are underwater and, perhaps because of some tectonic shift, water levels have risen quite out of all proportion to rainfall; birds can now watch from dead trees surrounded by water on all sides. The horticultural industry has, in general, become much more aware of its environmental responsibilities, and common carp have invaded the lake from an upstream fish farm. The carp are bottom feeders, and, on the face of it, this should have a seriously negative impact on the underwater vegetation. However, this seems outweighed by the ease with which the eagles catch them, either as they bask or spawn in the shallows, or else come up to the surface to take in air. Judging by the size of the fish being offered for sale on the roadside, their average weight is around half a kilogram: a perfect catch for a fish eagle.

Who could have foreseen 30 years ago that the Naivasha birds would be flourishing today, and for quite unpredictable reasons? What the next 30 years have in store is anybody's guess, but it seems that non-scientists have just as good a chance of making the right one as the most highly qualified researchers.

Hadada Ibis
Bostrychia hagedash

The raucous call of *Bostrychia hagedash* enables almost anyone living in sub-Saharan Africa to claim knowledge of bird sounds. It invades the soundscape of town and country, even down telephones to announce its presence in the background of conversations, and its call is freely available as a ring-tone for mobile phones. It is not a musical call, and many residents of Africa indulge in a sort of love-hate relationship in which its noise is much missed when it isn't heard, but not much enjoyed when it is! Jackson describes the cry as resembling 'the wail of a child in distress, at other times the hideous mocking laughter attributed to witches in fairy-tales ... perhaps noisiest when five or six in line ahead are going to their roosting quarters shortly after sundown'. With this last observation I would certainly agree, although the birds are also very noisy when startled off the ground.

The Hadada's boundaries are truly sub-Saharan: it is found all over the whole region except for the dry lands of the southwest. Its best-known African relative (although of a different genus) is the Sacred Ibis (*Threskiornis aethiopicus*), almost equally widely distributed with, at least until very recently, a breeding outpost in Syria. All of the Hadada's congeners are in Africa – Olive, Spot-breasted, Wattled and Dwarf – but none is easy to find. To tick a Dwarf requires a trip to the islands of São Tomé, the Olive and Spot-breasted are birds of thick upland or equatorial forest, while the Wattled was endemic to Ethiopia until the creation of Eritrea, which then split the bird between two countries. Not only did Ethiopia lose access to the sea, but it could no longer claim several species of bird as endemic because, once the line was drawn, they occurred in two countries rather than one.

Other more distant relatives include one of the most widespread birds in the world, the much slimmer Glossy Ibis, and also the indescribably brilliant Scarlet Ibis, whose nightly return to its mangrove roosts on the northern coasts of South America must be one of the world's great ornithological spectacles. In southern Africa the Southern Bald Ibis is an inhabitant of remote mountain haunts. As a 17-year-old, working on a farm near Clocolan in the eastern Free State in the late summer, I watched Bald Ibises, which had flown over from the Maluti Mountains in Lesotho as part of their post-breeding dispersal, angle down to feed on a field of permanent pasture. This had never been chemically treated and the birds had visited every year for as long as my employer could remember.

Bostrychia is from the Greek, *bostrukhion*. This means 'a small curl of hair', which seems more appropriate for some of the other members of the genus, like Olive, Dwarf and Wattled – which all have crests of a sort – than for the smooth-crowned Hadada. The species name is apparently an onomatopoeic tag given to the bird by early settlers in South Africa, where it is spelt Hadeda. Enter Sparrman again, who in September 1775 in Outeniqualand shot 'a new species of *tantalus* called by the colonists hagedash, and also hadelde. This latter name has, in some measure, the same sound as the birds' note.' (*Tantalus* was the early word for some of the storks, with which ibises were once grouped.)

Linnaeus was dead by the time Sparrman acquired his Hadada, and its formal description was left to the English doctor and amateur naturalist John Latham, who named it *Tantalus hagedash*. Latham had initially been sceptical of the use of the binomial system of nomenclature but ultimately realised that only by embracing it would he be given true credit for all his museum research. So in 1790 he published *Index ornithologicus*, in which he finally gave scientific names to all the birds he had described in his earlier publications. By then, many of these had already been named by others, but the *Index* nevertheless includes around 80 new species, including the Emu, Black Swan and Sacred Ibis, as well as the Hadada, for describing which Latham is given the credit.

Since those days, while the Sacred Ibis's range has contracted, that of the Hadada has expanded considerably, helped in South Africa by protective legislation in the 1930s, more plantations of exotic tree species, more ponds, and perhaps more irrigation. After all, it is essentially a water bird, which explains its absence from the parched parts of sub-Saharan Africa. Actually, Egyptian Geese and Hadadas are spreading for much the same reasons, and with equally mixed receptions. A song by a South African group celebrates 'Harry the Hungry Hadeda', but the nickname of the 'Flying Vuvuzela', after the football supporters' plastic horns, is not entirely benevolent.

There is no distinction between the plumage of the sexes, but there are some features of the birds' colouring that can help in distinguishing individuals. The pair that regularly visited our lawn (at least I presume they were the same pair, and sometimes they were accompanied by a third, which I also presume to have been an offspring) were separable by the comparative brightness of the buffy-white stripe below their eyes. The red mark on the top of the upper mandible can also vary in hue and extent, and both had more or less distinctive eye rings. One had brown legs and pink feet, while the other had a touch of pink in the legs and feet; variations in the glossy green/purple/bronze sheen on their wing coverts was not a reliable guide, because this changed so much with the angle and intensity of the light.

There is a lot more to be learnt by watching Hadadas than is often revealed in the bird books. Particularly interesting is that they have another call, which is inevitably ignored in the course of focusing on its more strident notes. As the birds stalk around on the ground, they often utter a comforting hiss to one another, quite loud enough to be audible before they come into view. Then there is the question of food. The ones we entertained could scarcely wait for the dog to

183

finish her meal before they headed over to the bowl to peck away at the leftovers – usually grains of rice. Yet all the books have Hadadas down as almost exclusively consumers of animal flesh in the shape of insects, crustaceans, worms, frogs, fish and small reptiles, and make no mention of any vegetable matter in their diets.

Watching them feed on the parched patch of earth that passes for a lawn was also fascinating. No matter how dry it might be, they seem to find cracks in the soil into which to push their beaks, often right down as far as they will go. Do they know there is food there, or is it a question of probing around in the hope of finding nourishment? Most birds have a poor sense of smell, so if there is something down there, do they detect this by sight, touch or possibly even hearing? When they peck into the ground they seem to start with an open beak, rather than probing with it closed, then opening it; so how do they avoid taking in soil along with any food they find?

Hadadas are communal roosters, raucously announcing their arrivals and departures, after which they usually split up to feed in pairs or smaller parties. Some ibises, like Sacred and Glossy, are communal nesters too, which Hadadas are not, although they have quite often been observed nesting in the same trees as colonies of Southern Masked Weavers. Their simple constructions of interlocking sticks are built over land or water, between two and 12 metres off the ground; and there, after a touching courtship ritual, they lay two or three eggs. This, along with much else about the birds' breeding behaviour, was witnessed in the most unlikely setting of Disney's Animal Kingdom in Florida, and related by Josef Lindholm in the January/February 2001 issue of the American Federation of Aviculture's journal, *Watchbird*.

In August 1997, two Hadadas, a brother and sister bred in Atlanta five years earlier, were housed in the Animal Kingdom's Pangani Aviary. This had successfully raised broods of several African species of bird, including White-headed and Blue-naped mousebirds, Black Crakes and African Jacanas. The following spring the Hadadas began to show an inclination to breed by looking around for nesting materials, much of which they plundered from a nearby Hamerkop's nest. The site they selected was over water, in a tipu tree – the yellow-flowered 'pride of Bolivia' and almost as out of place as were the Hadadas. As nest building continued, the male spent time rearranging twigs, and they would both greet one another with affectionate bill rattling, like storks are wont to do. They also engaged in mutual preening, and would call out loudly

184

to each other at last light. There was time, too, to copulate, to such an extent that 'for most of the month of April, observed copulations were an almost daily entry in the keepers' log'.

The Hadadas were specifically fed a diet of horsemeat derivative and flamingo pellets, but also had access to the dishes specifically designed for other birds, including the mealworms thrown out for Carmine Bee-eaters. Reading about 'the male lunging at a Superb Starling' or how he 'chased a Hamerkop from the vicinity of the nest', one really begins to think this was all happening in Africa, and as with the valuable observations by Meade-Waldo on sandgrouse behaviour, shows how much can be learnt by carefully observing birds even in an artificial setting. And this in itself is surely one more good reason to support the careful and considerate keeping and breeding of birds in captivity.

Chapter 5

CONSERVATION & CELEBRATION

So, from peacocks to picathartes, ostriches to sugarbirds, Hadadas to honeyguides, the preceding chapters try to do some justice to the wondrous diversity of birds in Africa. Within the continent, some species are widespread and often common in much of their range – very few people in sub-Saharan Africa have never heard a Hadada Ibis and even fewer have never seen a Pied Crow. At the other extreme are species clinging so precariously to their existence on the planet that it would take very little to push them into extinction.

All the world's endangered birds (and many other creatures) are classified on the Red List maintained by the International Union for Conservation of Nature according to the risk of their extinction. The most threatened species are listed as being Critically Endangered; those for which the risk is not so great, as Endangered; and where the threat is real but less extreme, as Vulnerable.

Rats, humans and habitat destruction have annihilated Dodos and other birds on Africa's outlying islands, but over the past 500 years no bird species is known to have gone extinct on the mainland. This in itself is no cause for complacency, and there are still around 30 Critically Endangered species on the continent and surrounding islands. The populations of some of these have long been recognised as small and fragile, like those of White-winged Flufftails, Taita Thrush and Taita Apalis. Others, particularly vultures, have in the space of only a few years been catapulted onto the Critically Endangered list from the apparent security of being of Least Concern.

In 2004 Ruppell's Vultures were of Least Concern, the category where widespread and abundant birds rest; then in 2007 the danger of secondary poisoning pushed them onto the list of Near Threatened birds, then Endangered in 2012, and, in 2014, Critically Endangered. White-headed and White-backed vultures have suffered almost identical slides towards the edge of the abyss.

Such endangerment is usually down to human activity, as is the decline in numbers of so many other bird species. However, this book celebrates what we have in Africa here and now, without trying to measure this against the past. There is indeed a frightening range of threats to almost all wildlife and its habitat, but balanced against these are massive efforts – at local, national and international levels – to improve the protection afforded to birds and their environment. Once identified, dangers can be removed or at least mitigated, and several species on offshore islands, particularly on Mauritius and the Seychelles, have had their status reversed, moving from Critically Endangered to a less imperilled category. In 2018 the status of the Northern Bald Ibis was similarly changed from Critically Endangered to simply Endangered, human help having prompted an expansion of its breeding range in Morocco.

The BirdLife Africa Partnership has taken the lead in species conservation by the creation since 1993 of around 1,250 sites of importance for bird protection. These are known as Important Bird and Biodiversity Areas (IBAs), which raise the profile of particular areas and their avian inhabitants. The organisation's stated intention for such areas is 'for all of them to be looked after by community-based organisations with the commitment and expertise to conserve their sites and wildlife'. As the website adds: 'Conservation cannot succeed without the consent and participation of the people who live in or near, obtain their livelihoods from, or simply enjoy the sites that threatened bird species depend on. With limited resources for conservation work, the survival and recovery of species and ecosystems depend on the willingness and ability of local people to manage and protect them.'

One way to formalise the involvement of rural communities in IBA conservation is through the creation of specific Site Support Groups (SSGs), which BirdLife helps through its local partners. At the northern end of the Eastern Arc Mountains in southern Kenya are the Taita Hills. Nature Kenya has been in the forefront of promoting the formation of the Dawida Biodiversity Conservation Group, whose remit includes not only buying or leasing land for conservation but also its reafforestation. Both Taita Thrush and Taita Apalis are species endemic to the tiny relict patches of forest, and their future surely rests in the hands of the local communities who have long lived around these hills. That said, few SSGs can operate in a vacuum, and most continue to need the guiding hand of a larger parent organisation, particularly when it comes to direct conservation interventions such as removing snares, planting trees, erecting and maintaining fences or creating visitor facilities.

Throughout much of Africa, the management of natural resources is becoming ever more decentralised and devolved to those who depend upon them. Whether or not the establishment of a local community organisation is prompted by the specific need for an SSG or by some other impetus, the local avifauna is increasingly being perceived as having not only a conservation value, but also a financial one, which can bring benefits directly to those living in or around areas of special bird interest. Few communities are privileged enough to be able to claim the guardianship of species as distinctive as the White-necked Picathartes (as are the folk of Bonkro in Ghana and the Kambui Hills Forest Reserve in Sierra Leone), or even Beesley's Lark, which is cared for by the Beesley's Lark Conservation Program of Engikaret in northern Tanzania (see picathartes, pages 85–89; larks, pages 21–23). However, with some guidance from local Non-Governmental Organisations (NGOs) and with the basic components of relatively undisturbed habitat, a reasonably diverse avifauna and a secure environment, plenty of community projects are now trying to attract the attention of visitors.

The hope is that such visitors will, either directly or indirectly, make a substantial contribution at least to the recurring maintenance costs, and by their very presence promote an awareness of the greater value of conservation over consumption. It is a huge help to BirdLife's local partner NGOs and others if the carrot of ecotourism – specifically avitourism – can promise benefits to local communities. How well these projects work, and how much income they can generate, is primarily determined by the local conditions, particularly the raw materials comprising the birds and their habitat. Other variables also need to be factored in, such as the degree of support from local leadership, the nature and extent of community involvement and whether the financial benefits accrue to individuals (particularly guides or providers of accommodation) or to the communities at large.

Tourists, perhaps inspired to visit their destinations by watching high-quality television programmes, are helped by the availability of a wide range of flights making faraway places more accessible. For sure, overseas bird tours are expensive in terms of both money and carbon emissions, and beyond the reach of many enthusiasts; however, those who can indulge in these travels certainly stand to gain an international perspective on ornithology, as well as insight into the cultures of the human guardians of the environments they are visiting. Furthermore, avitourism is mostly low impact and the individuals involved are generally prepared to spend several days in a single destination in fairly basic accommodation, aided throughout by local people.

Professor Angelo Nicolaides, in 'Promoting Avitourism as a special niche area of Ecotourism in South Africa', published in the 2013 *African Journal of Hospitality, Tourism and Leisure*, wrote a neat summary of his conclusions: 'Avitourism is a branch of ecotourism, which shows great potential because bird watchers are usually from the ranks of the relatively well educated and wealthy individuals who are passionate about observing birds in their natural habitats. Avitourism also has huge potential to add value to local communities. Local communities could be educated on aspects such as biodiversity and ecology, and may be provided with socio-economic incentives for the successful protection, sustainability and preservation of natural areas in which they reside. If managed correctly, and partnerships are forged between NGOs and the government as well as external benefactors, avitourism has the potential to empower local communities, promote diverse cultures as well as further educate the avitourists that would grace our shores.'

Before attempts are made to attract visitors anywhere, the first crucial step in all conservation programmes is to find out exactly what there is to conserve. The need for this baseline knowledge is fundamental, and the technology for collecting it is improving exponentially. The days when retired army officers wrote to *The Times* in London to report hearing the first cuckoo, back from wherever they then thought it had spent the winter, are not quite gone – there are nearly always reports on our local *Kenyabirdsnet* of the arrival in Kenya of the first Eurasian Bee-eaters; rather it is the *means* of disseminating the news that has changed beyond recognition.

In 1913, Keeper of Paleontology at the British Museum, Richard Lydekker, reported from Harpenden Lodge in Hertfordshire that he had heard a cuckoo as early as on 4th February. Without today's email or social media, he had to write to *The Times*: 'While gardening this afternoon I heard a faint note, which led me to say to my under-gardener, who was working with me, "Was that the cuckoo?" Almost immediately afterwards we heard the full double note of a cuckoo, repeated either two or three times, I am not quite sure which. The time was 3.40 and the bird appeared to be about a quarter of a mile away. There was not the slightest doubt that the song was that of the cuckoo.'

Actually, there was indeed some doubt, and one week later he was forced to admit to the readers in a further letter: '... in common with many other persons, I have been completely deceived in the matter of the supposed cuckoo of February 4. The note was uttered by a bricklayer's labourer at work on a house in the neighbourhood of the spot whence the note appeared to come. I have interviewed the man, who tells me that he is able to draw cuckoos from considerable distances by the exactness of his imitation of their notes ...'

Neither Mr Lydekker nor any of the other early writers hearing the first cuckoo were participating in any recognised programme of information gathering. Nonetheless, they might still be regarded as the forerunners of today's 'citizen scientists' – members of the general public who, in the words of the Oxford Dictionary, undertake 'scientific work under the direction of professional scientists and scientific institutions'. Only within the last 20 or 30 years has the scientific community begun to appreciate the potential as data collectors of the thousands of non-scientist bird watchers who roam through their neighbourhoods with binoculars round their necks; and never could these emerging enthusiasts have predicted how rewarding they would find the actual process of data collection, or how much they would learn about birds in the course of their participation.

Few citizen-science undertakings in Africa make better use of amateur ornithologists than the Bird Atlas projects. In southern Africa, the first Southern African Bird Atlas Project (SABAP), launched in 1986, culminated 11 years later in the Atlas of Southern African Birds, covering six countries. Then in 2007 began SABAP 2, which is intended to run indefinitely. Kenya launched a nationwide study of bird distribution from published records, museum specimens and individual contributors in the early 1980s, leading up to the publication of Lewis and Pomeroy's A Bird Atlas of Kenya in 1989. Now the Kenya Bird Map project, with technical support from the Animal Demography Unit at the University of Cape Town, aims to map the current distribution of all the country's birds, so acting both as a comparison with the previous work as well as providing a baseline for ongoing research.

Both the Kenyan and Southern African atlases work through an app called BirdLasser, which, once downloaded, provides the basis for the submission of sightings. This requirement may deter older enthusiasts who are used to sending in written records, but in Kenya (at the time of writing), over 250 different observers have contributed computerised sightings from 16 per cent of the 6,817 9x9-kilometre pentads – this seemingly low figure a consequence of both the insecurity and inaccessibility of much of northern Kenya. A similar app for a Cornell/Audubon joint project is eBird, which covers sightings worldwide; and, as such, gets a lot of records that don't reach the computers of BirdLasser.

There are any number of other citizen-science projects, often involving looking out for breeding birds, or counting species in defined areas, even on bird tables, on specific days. World Migratory Bird Day is a global celebration, Euro Birdwatch is continent-wide, while other programmes work at national level, such as the monitoring schemes established by BirdLife through local partners in Botswana, Kenya and Uganda. Now bird watchers feel they can participate in scientific research by submitting records, which contribute to the greater good of birds, as well as serving their original purpose of generating personal pleasure and benefit.

The publicity surrounding these programmes and events, and the high level of lay participation, all help to create greater awareness of the birds and their habits, as well as their distribution or timing of migrations. The data can provide early warning of factors that may negatively affect species distribution, as well as monitoring numbers, from which, in turn, can be deduced positive or negative population trends. Collected data can also influence developmental decisions, such as where to site wind farms or power transmission lines, where to permit fracking for shale gas or oil exploration, whether to approve dams and hydroelectric or irrigation projects and how to mitigate the adverse consequences of such developments.

The information collected by citizen scientists has also played its part in increasing awareness of the need for a more holistic regard for the lives of birds. It is not enough just to count and care for Palearctic migrants on their wintering grounds, or post-breeding Madagascan Pratincoles on the shores of East Africa; more needs to be discovered about their journeys and how best to protect them along the way. Contributing hugely to the body of knowledge of migrant birds, in particular, whether these be intercontinental or intra-African migrants, are the efforts of dedicated enthusiasts who catch and ring (band) birds.

When, in the mid-1750s, Johann Frisch tied red thread round the legs of German swallows, their return the following year, thread intact, demonstrated with near certainty the homing abilities of the birds. To those who were aware of his experiment, the intact thread laid another ghost to rest. It dispelled any lingering doubts as to whether, when birds disappeared in late summer, it was to winter underwater, or otherwise metamorphose into some unrecognisable form in which they passed the cold, leafless northern months undetected. Since then, bird tracking techniques have become highly sophisticated, and ringing techniques have improved enormously, so enabling detailed investigations into bird movements.

Soon after Ngulia Lodge opened on the edge of an escarpment in Kenya's Tsavo West National Park in 1969, ornithologists discovered that a combination of moonless nights, midnight mist and bright lodge lights attracted masses of migrating birds down to ground level. It was December, and these were southward-bound migrants from Eurasia as well as intra-African migrants. Ringing quickly started in earnest, and 50 years later still continues; and the dramatic edge of the escarpment remains the premier site for ringing birds on their way through Africa.

The practical data garnered from ringing and recovering birds can contribute to a much deeper knowledge of their habits, behaviour, longevity and migration routes, thus influencing conservation measures. Most of the Ngulia birds seem to have paused in Ethiopia to gather up energy for the rest of their southward journey. This is invaluable information, particularly if translated into heightened protection for identified stopover areas. Of over 25,000 Barn Swallows ringed, none has been recovered in Europe (nor have any Red-backed Shrikes), suggesting that all the swallows overflying Tsavo derive from Asian populations. Sprossers and Marsh Warblers, on the other hand, are recovered far and wide, showing their numbers to come from a broad breeding range.

Ringing birds has three main objectives, each of which contributes to a greater understanding of their migrations. The first is to analyse the species composition of 'the catch', something that could never be recorded by watching through binoculars. The second aim is to net birds that someone, somewhere else has already caught and ringed. For example, in the 2016 two-week Ngulia session, there were three such recoveries: a Sprosser ringed in Sweden and two Marsh Warblers, one previously caught in Germany and the other in the Czech Republic. The third objective is to ring birds in the hope that they will be netted or otherwise identified elsewhere – although recoveries may also be of dead birds, and more Ngulia-ringed birds have been reported from Saudi Arabia, where they are trapped or shot, than from any other country. Rings are much lighter than they ever were, the numbers and letters on the rings are easier to read, and catching birds in order to ring them is now a much more sophisticated undertaking. Occasionally details of rings on the legs of larger birds can even be read with binoculars – particularly so with storks and waders pecking around on grassland or seashore.

The composition of the Ngulia catch is fascinating and over 40 per cent of birds ringed since the programme began are Marsh Warblers, with Sprossers and Common Whitethroats a close second and third at around 20 per cent each. These are followed far behind in descending order by Barn Swallows (mostly daytime ringed), River Warblers, Iranias, Willow Warblers, and Red-backed and Isabelline shrikes. A few intra-African migrants such as cuckoos turn up, and when I was there two years ago we even netted a nocturnal Wattled Starling.

There are many initiatives all over Africa involving ringing resident birds in an effort to obtain more information on breeding and local movements. However, recovered birds only inform the state and location of the bird at times of ringing and of recovery; what happened in between is confined to comparisons between the two sets of information. In the early days, the idea of actually tracking a bird on its journey was so remote as to be inconceivable, and remained so even when Marconi produced his first wireless telegraphy system. It would take 100 years of gradual refinement of transmitters and increasing the distance they could transmit before fitting one on a bird became a possibility – and many more years until it was a reality.

The first efforts entailed fitting birds with transmitters that could either record information to be accessed later, on recovery of the transmitter, or that emitted signals recognisable by receivers within their range. From here, technology made another leap, with transmitters that could broadcast radio waves up to satellites. These allow an animal's movement to be monitored from the comfort of the laboratory, rather than requiring one to bump around in a truck or plane, waving a large aerial in the hope of detecting a signal. Since then, devices have become ever smaller and lighter. Platform Transmitter Terminals (PTTs) are fitted with a solar panel, which constantly charges the battery, and operate by transmitting data to overhead satellites that allow precise calculations of the bird's position. When the weight of one of these was brought below five grams, the British Trust for Ornithology (BTO) reckoned this was small enough to fit onto Common Cuckoos without in any way impeding their flight. Now GPS technology devices are even lighter, and as technology improves, so commensurately does the recovery of vital information on bird migrations.

Common Cuckoos are fairly large birds, weighing well over 100 grams, unlike some of our smaller, but no less determined migrants, such as warblers, which weigh little more than 10 per cent of that. These cuckoos are actually not common and nor are they easy to catch, and the BTO's enthusiasm was fired by the fact that there was only one African recovery of a British-hatched cuckoo – a bird that was ringed in a pied wagtail's nest in the south of England in 1928 and recovered in Cameroon in January 1930. Exactly where the birds overwintered, or how they got there, was a big gap in ornithological knowledge. And, with cuckoo numbers in steep decline, there were questions to be answered about whether this was due to conditions at home, on the journey or at the destination in Africa.

BTO biologists trapped and tagged five males in early summer of 2011, with 'Chris', destined to be the star of the programme, having his tag fitted in Norfolk on 1st June. Four days later he moved south to Sussex for nearly two weeks before crossing the Channel and holing up in Belgium for another fortnight. Whether these local migrations were driven by a search for more suitable territories and more females, or simply better feeding, can only be guessed at – there is still a limit to what can be deduced from the transmitted information. By early July, Chris was down in the Po valley in northern Italy, again for about two weeks, until his migration began in earnest, and he set off over the Mediterranean, through Libya, across the Saharan wastes and down into southern Chad. There he spent over two months before moving south again into the savanna mosaic of the Central African Republic and then on into the 'Heart of Darkness' forests of the Congo, where he passed the winter.

Chris got back to England by a different route, arriving on 1st May, soon returning to Norfolk where he had been caught. Six weeks was more than long enough for him to undertake his breeding duties before he set off south, although who is to say he did not continue these duties in Belgium, where he stopped again. As before, he then headed down the leg of Italy, this time through Sicily and over the Mediterranean, finding himself almost within sight of the shrunken waters of Lake Chad on 19th July.

In the summer of both 2011 and 2012 Chris had flown through France and Italy on his way south; then, in 2013 and 2014, transmitter signals showed him deviating from what had come to be regarded as his normal route by returning to Africa through Spain. Birds' migratory journeys are clearly not fixed, either by inheritance or experience. Towards the end of his second and third southward journeys he also changed another of his habits: instead of spending the whole northern winter in the thick Congolese jungles, something spurred him to move still further south, out of the forest and into the savanna of Angola.

Chris's last journey in the summer of 2015 seems to have ended in the deserts north of Chad, just short of the Tibesti Mountains, which would have provided him with a stopping point and possibly some food. Here the signals grew weaker, although they continued being transmitted from the same place for almost four weeks before ceasing altogether. RIP, Chris. Now Victor, Thomas, Sylvester and Bowie have taken over your role as bearers of the transmitters, which may help tell us why cuckoo numbers are collapsing throughout so much of Europe.

Two years after Chris got his transmitter, Naga, a male Amur Falcon, was fitted with one in Nagaland in northeast India. The profile of these migrating falcons had been raised by their annual slaughter on a grand scale while stopping over on their way from breeding in China to wintering in southern Africa. This atrocity (thankfully now a horror of the past) prompted research to try and unravel the details of one of the longest migratory journeys in the avian world. On 9th November 2013 Naga was released, fitted with a satellite tag that showed him flying 5,600 kilometres non-stop for five and a half days, including over the whole of the Arabian Sea, before making landfall again in Somalia. From there he meandered down eastern Africa, reaching South Africa two months later. Thereafter, his and other recorded journeys showed clear parallels with Chris's travels, in that they followed completely different routes back to their breeding grounds from those they had taken on their way out.

People who participate in citizen science or bird-ringing projects are the converted; we already have a passion for the activity. Participation is not necessarily the province of the wealthy, and there are increasing numbers of local bird or wildlife clubs and educational programmes that will provide a way into the world of birds for anyone with a basic interest. Harder to reach, though, are the hearts and minds of those for whom the only good bird is a dead one being roasted over a fire, or who see little wrong in the destruction of indigenous habitat if it furthers their own interests. Poor, hungry people live for today, not tomorrow, and unless their livelihoods are improved, it will take a lot to encourage them to conserve the natural environment and respect fellow creatures if, by doing so, they forego sources of fuel or food. Traditional or religious beliefs may contribute to a sense of respect for nature, as can some form of education; however, until countries, whether in or outside Africa, include Natural History as a compulsory course in the national curriculum, such education will need to be provided by the non-government sector.

Education can also come from those who are already birders and nature lovers. Simple day trips to tracts of wilderness outside built-up areas are within the reach of most people, and during such trips, beginners can learn to identify different species of bird. Only by developing this ability, whether by ear or eye or both, can new enthusiasts start to make lists of what they have seen. This can bring enjoyment at any level, whether the lists be for birds seen in a day, a week, a year or a lifetime, and be they in a garden, a park, a country or the world. Lists are crucial. However scorned 'tickers' may be, however derided is the twitcher of birds by the self-styled watcher, lists comprise the databases against which change is measured. Lists of species names show biological prosperity or paucity, and – crucially – changes in these. Keeping lists can also create an element of competitiveness, for better or for worse!

We each have our own guidelines for what gets onto our lists. If wishful identification sometimes edges a few species onto the list that would not have got there on days of stricter adherence to codes, then does it really matter? Well yes, but only if we are headed for the record books or are submitting records for scientific purposes (or even competing with friends). So (and may she rest in peace), the wife of one of my fellow lawyers who had no qualms about adding species to her own life list that she extricated from the mist nets of Ngulia. With luck she might have seen a Nightingale or even a Sprosser in the wild, but how else would she get to tick a Basra Reed Warbler?

I have my own somewhat flexible criteria. Hartlaub's Duck is a really unusual bird – a forest duck with phrases like 'little known' or 'scarcely known' appearing in its description in *BoA*. On a journey into the Semliki Forest on the Uganda-DRC border, two duck silhouettes flew fast over the tree tops. That they were ducks was indisputable, as was the fact that Hartlaub's are the only ducks living in the forest, as opposed to possibly overflying it. Do those two certainties make a tick? (Yes!) On the way home, malimbes with red heads hopped around the tree tops among other unidentifiable birds, darkened against the sky. It was quite impossible to tell if they were Red-headed or Crested. Then guide Godfrey heard the sound of the Crested from somewhere up in the trees; does that confirm the identification, even though we were not certain if the 'harsh repeated nasal *scree, scree, scree*' was actually made by the malimbes we had been looking at? (Yes!)

And then what about the Olivaceous Warbler that sadly killed itself as it flew into one of the windows on our veranda? Yes, the bird was dead by the time I found it (and had to send it over in an envelope to my next door neighbour to confirm its identification – all during the middle of the bird flu scare, without my telling him how the bird had died!) but undoubtedly it had been on our plot when it hit the pane.

There is no need to undertake long journeys to find rare or special birds. After all, almost every bird is rare somewhere, and even the most widespread and abundant ones are hard to find on the edges of their ranges. At the right time of year, migrant species can spice up the day almost anywhere in Africa, and overflying birds often add to the unexpected. Seek out some different habitat and there will be different birds. Anyone living near the African coast can look out for a range of resident or migratory water birds, although few bird watchers have the opportunity for such a glut of pelagic species as those in the Cape, and most of the endemic birds of the southern tip of Africa are not far from Cape Town either. Several years ago, charged with flying there to collect a close friend's ashes and bring them back to Kenya, I determined to do something memorable on that day. So, having picked up the urn I had the taxi driver take me to Simon's Town and then carried it down to the beach and sat among the African (then Jackass) Penguins. Well, was that memorable!

Most people live within reasonable reach of green spaces even if these are urban parks. Weaver colonies can provide fascination in all but the most built-up environments, and several large birds are showing an increasing inclination to roost, and often nest, in busy cityscapes. Whether human proximity is, somewhat perversely, regarded by the birds as lessening the risk of predation, or perhaps for some other reason, Marabou Storks, Cattle Egrets and Sacred Ibis are colonising trees in East African city parks or even the central reservation of urban highways. The trend is marked enough to have merited discussion in a 2017 *Scopus*, Volume 37(1) by Esther Toloa et al. in 'The increasingly urban status of the Cattle Egret in Uganda'; while further south, the FitzPatrick Institute of African Ornithology in Cape Town is researching how the campus's Red-winged Starlings (which also live in Nairobi city centre) cope without student sandwiches over weekends and holidays.

My own observations of urban birds have had both highs and lows. Despite living within Nairobi city limits, I can still see over 100 species in a day. However, I ran into a lot of trouble with security officers when trying to add the Peregrine Falcon to my list: the bird was nesting in a sculpted decoration high up on the city-centre Office of the President. In the lovely patch of forest next to the Nairobi racecourse I lost my signet ring to thieves; and I fell very foul of armed guards when using binoculars in the grounds of Addis Ababa's Holy Trinity Cathedral, which I visited in pilgrimage to Sylvia Pankhurst's grave and also in the hope of spotting an Abyssinian Catbird. This, I was repeatedly told, was easily seen in the capital's green spaces (but, to this day, not by me).

While cities have much to offer any bird watcher, there is no denying that many of Africa's very special birds are hard to see, and also that more remote areas are often likely to host more birds, and more interesting ones. *Ol Donyo Orok* means 'Black Mountain' in the language of the Maasai people, and sits above Namanga on the Kenya-Tanzania border west of Amboseli National Park. It is little explored and, while it has yet to be designated an IBA, my friend Brian and I thought a visit down there might turn up some new records for the Kenya Bird Atlas.

On our last day we had made some exciting finds of species that were so far unrecorded by the Bird Atlas, including the Crowned Eagle that circled noisily up above us, a Little Rock Thrush, behaving more like a forest skulker than an inhabitant of cliffs and open slopes, and beautiful Cinnamon-chested Bee-eaters, easily found in most of the Kenyan uplands, but never before noted down here on the Tanzanian border. I had also added the Stripe-cheeked Greenbul to my personal list, and when it was time to set off back to the car so as to reach home before dark, we had to wrench ourselves away from following a flock of over 25 Hartlaub's Turacos moving noisily up a river bed, from one fruiting fig tree to another.

Heading downhill, we passed the huge skull of a long-dead Cape Buffalo. Had it died at the hands of humans, or the jaws of some predator? Moving lower, we emerged where the trees had been cleared to make space for some half-hearted attempts at agriculture, evidenced by the dried stalks of scattered maize plants and by that invader of disturbed ground, the sodom apple. We had heard the raucous chorus of a group of Crested Francolins elsewhere the previous evening, and sure enough, there they were as we approached these cleared fields, like a flock of bantams, pecking around on the bare soil, rushing hither and thither, dark crowns, tails in the air. But what were those other birds trying to make themselves heard? Rufous Chatterers, always on the move through thick bush, indulge in incessant chattering to keep in touch with others in their party. They are not rare by any means, but we had neither seen nor heard them in our three days; this time they were both audible and visible, even down to their distinctive pale eyes peeping through the dried-up maize stalks among which the francolins had been feeding.

Around us, children were driving sheep and goats back to their family enclosures, bells tinkling round the necks of favoured animals. Our guides, Benjamin and Singira (not part of any formal Site Support Group, but found for us by the hotel and fascinatingly knowledgeable about their own environment), acknowledged everyone they met, seemingly related to them all. The younger ones would then approach us with lowered heads, awaiting our hands upon these in traditional Maasai greeting.

By now the sun had dropped down behind the Black Mountain, although it still lit the faraway plains. The car was in distant sight, and while I feigned not seeing it, suggesting it had been stolen in our absence, Benjamin was clearly keen to be reunited with his family. He upped his speed and seemed, Pied Piper-like, to attract the homebound children and their dogs round our party. When we finally reached his hut, his mother, adorned in red and purple cloth, her neck ringed with beautiful, beaded Maasai jewellery, was there to greet us, having earlier spread a blanket over the windscreen to keep the car cool. She had spent much of the day making slim bracelets for Brian and me. These she presented 'as a gift', translated Benjamin, brushing aside our attempts to pay for them.

Then Brian, ever observant while I was still admiring the mother's jewellery, brought home the final trophy. Throughout the last three days we had seen lots of D'Arnaud's Barbets, but Red and Yellow ones had yet to show themselves, notwithstanding their usual cheery duets from bush tops. In Benjamin's family enclosure there were a couple of scrubby thorn trees, in the dirt below which children cavorted with some tiny puppies. And yes, in one of those trees was a silent, immobile Red and Yellow Barbet; and as if deliberately to facilitate comparison, a D'Arnaud's hopped around in the thorn scrub that fenced in the goats.

Next, we loaded Mother and children into the back of our truck, and together with Benjamin and Singira took them all to Milei Tisa to buy their supper. Saying our farewells, we dropped them at the village store, and then set off into the African dusk, back towards Namanga. Could things really get any better, seeing such wonderful birds in such a wonderful country in the company of its custodians? It was exactly then that I began to feel this to be one of those rare times when life seems so perfect and complete, with a sense of being so at ease, at peace and at one with all around you that the only thing left to wish for is to be able to bottle up that sensation forever.

Couldn't it be like this every day?

Chapter 6

INSPIRATION & INFORMATION

In writing this book I have drawn heavily on earlier works about African ornithology. My admiration for their pioneering authors is boundless, as is the pleasure in reading what they wrote. Some compiled their books long before the invention of binoculars, with little or no help from any other published sources, relying instead on their own and others' observations, and often on conclusions drawn from hundreds of hours spent poring over bird skins in museums. There are frequently links between these authors, and so rather than list them chronologically, I acknowledge their works by way of a brief introduction to the early writers on African birds, mostly in the English language. I then move on to recognise more contemporary sources of help.

The emergence of ornithology in Africa is generally seen as a by-product of the expansion of European influence into the continent. However, such an approach should not ignore the store of indigenous knowledge about birds, amassed by the inhabitants of Africa long before foreigners set sail around its coasts. The history of African exploration brims with 'discoveries', but these are often no more than revealing plants and animals to other Europeans with which local people had long been familiar. So it was that this local familiarity would often provide a base to which travellers would add their own observations.

As more and more people started reporting what they saw on their travels, as explorers stretched their horizons ever further, a growing number of plants and animals needed to find their place in a wider scientific context. Gradually, thanks to the efforts of these travellers and their increasingly reliable means of transport, museums and other research facilities in the explorers' home countries were able to build up natural history collections, and to compare reports and, later, specimens from a widening network of sources across Africa.

The Portuguese were first down the coast of Africa, with Bartolomeu Dias tentatively rounding what he called *Cabo das Tormentas* ('the Cape of Storms') in 1488. In due course they began to experience commercial competition from the Dutch, and in 1652, Jan van Riebeeck arrived in Table Bay to establish a staging post on behalf of the Dutch East India Company, which would govern what became known as the Cape Colony. This Dutch toe on the tip of Africa set in train the creeping colonisation of the surrounding area. Unsurprisingly, early immigrants were preoccupied with settlement and survival, and observations of the natural world were left to administrators, adventurers or dilettante collectors, most of whom came, saw and disappeared again, with boatloads of skins, specimens and notebooks.

One such adventurer, and by no means a dilettante, was a Frenchman, born in Dutch Guiana (now Surinam), who was to make an astonishing contribution to African ornithology at the southern end of the continent – be it all in French. **François Levaillant** (sometimes 'Le Vaillant') was remarkable in many ways, not least because he came to Africa not as a government functionary, but with the specific purpose of researching its birds. Having been born and raised in an exotic tropical environment, he developed an interest in natural history at a very early age, and this passion endured on the family's return to Europe. After study in Germany and France, a voyage to southern Africa was arranged for Levaillant by Jacob Temminck (a wealthy Dutch aristocrat and an avid collector of natural history specimens), and sponsored by the Dutch East India Company. He arrived in 1781 after a journey lasting more than a year, and soon encountered near disaster with the scuppering by its captain of the Dutch ship, *Middelburg*, on which he was quartered, to avoid capture by the British fleet. Having lost most of his possessions, he set about re-equipping himself in order to pursue the first of three major journeys inland. During his travels he collected many new species of bird, kept a tame baboon called Kees, and is said to have fallen in love with his servant, whom he christened Narina.

He returned to France after three years in the Cape. The six volumes of his *Histoire Naturelle des Oiseaux d'Afrique* were only finally published between 1801 and 1806, embellished with coloured illustrations by the highly skilled painter, Jacques Barraband. Levaillant is often criticised for refusing to adopt Carl Linnaeus's binomial system – so referring to the Secretarybird only as *Le Mangeur de Serpents* – as well as for some unreliable descriptions of non-existent species or even composites of more than one bird. Still, his was the first work to cover exclusively African birds, with no expense spared on the quality of the illustrations.

Britain was a late starter in the race for influence in Africa, and equally slow to contribute to the knowledge of its birds. This seems surprising when compared to its considerable ornithological output over the last 200 years, but also reflects the more amateurish approach to natural history study that characterised the British presence in Africa. Bird study, in particular, tended to be a by-product of military or administrative postings, no better exemplified than by **Andrew Smith**, who has a good claim to be the first Briton to make a substantial contribution to African ornithology.

Smith, a surgeon, was posted to Grahamstown in South Africa in 1820 to care for British soldiers. As well as exercising his medical duties, he also showed himself to be particularly capable of dealing very diplomatically with local people, not least because of his fascination with their traditional ways of life. He was also an observant zoologist and managed to collect and describe over 70 species of bird, including the Cape Shoveler, which, as *Spatula smithii*, still immortalises the Latinised version of his name, as does the Karoo Thrush, *Turdus smithi*. He wrote about many of these new species in South Africa's first independent newspaper, *The South African Commercial Advertiser*, and also in the first issue of the *South African Quarterly Journal*, launched in 1830, which opened with the initial instalment of what would be a several-part article entitled *A Description of the Birds Inhabiting the South of Africa*.

By the early nineteenth century Cape Town was a secure and settled community, serving as a stopping point for almost any ship heading further east. A lot of these vessels brought new settlers, traders and administrators, as well as explorers who planned to use the settlement as a base for their journeys into the interior. Cape Town was booming, and by 1825 could also boast of the opening of The South African Museum, of which Smith was nominated the first curator by the then governor of the Cape Colony, Sir Charles Somerset. Smith continued to work in South Africa until 1837, when his time came to return to England. Once there, he devoted much of his energy to the production of the five-volume

Illustrations of the Zoology of South Africa – and, sadly, also to conducting a furious row with Florence Nightingale over the organisation of medical services for troops fighting in the Crimean War.

Another curator of the Cape Town museum would be **Edgar Layard**, also British, who spent time in South Africa after a long spell in Ceylon. To him goes the accolade of producing the first book on African birds to be published in Africa. His *Birds of South Africa: A Descriptive Catalogue of all the Known Species Occurring South of the 28th Parallel of South Latitude* was published in 1867 in both Cape Town and London. For all its lack of illustrations and common names, and somewhat uncharitable references to his predecessors, with a list of 702 species it is something of an ornithological milestone. The opening of the Preface explains: 'The following Catalogue of The Birds of South Africa was commenced eleven years ago, for my own information, and without any idea of its ever being before the public. On my arrival at the Cape, in December 1854, I inquired in vain for any book which would give some insight into the ornithology of the country in which my lot had been cast. I was shown Le Vaillant's *Oiseaux D'Afrique* and Dr A Smith's *Illustrations of the Zoology of South Africa*, but these visibly bore the stamp of incompleteness.'

A second, and this time fully illustrated edition was produced in 1884 by **Richard Bowdler Sharpe**, who never got to Africa but still has a longclaw and an akalat to his name. He had a 37-year stint as curator of birds at the Natural History Museum in London, and his revision of Layard's work remained the standard book on the birds of South Africa for the next 30 years.

At much the same time, a further effort to document the whole of Africa's birdlife was being made by **George Shelley**, a nephew of the poet, Percy Bysshe Shelley. Educated at the Lycée de Versailles before joining the Grenadier Guards, he thereafter travelled and collected specimens in sub-Saharan Africa –'this metropolis of birds' where 'every bush resounds with their melody'. He is probably best remembered for a beautifully illustrated, limited-edition monograph on the sunbirds and also for *A Handbook to the Birds of Egypt* (1872). Hoping to be immortalised by another major work on the *Birds of Africa*, sadly – after writing the first four volumes – he suffered a debilitating heart attack, and it was left to **William Lutley Sclater** to complete a further volume and bring all their joint work (though still incomplete) to publication in 1912, two years after Shelley's death.

Sclater reappears as a major editor of much more than Shelley's work. Having obtained a first-class honours degree at Oxford, and then taught science at Eton College, he moved to Cape Town in 1896. There he followed the paths trodden by both Andrew Smith and Edgar Layard in taking over the curatorship of the South African Museum, instigating Sunday opening as well as the bilingual labelling of specimens in English and Dutch. This may or may not have had anything to do with his falling out with the trustees of the museum and leaving in 1906, but not before he had also completed a project begun by **Arthur Stark**, a medical doctor who had arrived in the Cape Colony four years before Sclater.

Stark had begun a major work on the *Birds of South Africa*, the first volume of which had just appeared in England, before he was killed by a shell in the Siege of Ladysmith in 1899, helping wounded soldiers in a war he bitterly opposed. Sclater had always intended to oversee the preparation of this magnum opus (there is an introduction by him in this first volume), and to him fell the task of its completion. Stark's notes from both Ladysmith and his home in Natal were collected up and entrusted to Sclater, who eventually completed the four volumes, well illustrated with both drawings and black-and-white photographs, the title page reading 'Commenced by Arthur Stark – By W L Sclater'.

Having left South Africa in 1906, Sclater travelled through East Africa on his way back to England, and in 1909 became curator of the Bird Room of the Natural History Museum in London, where he remained until his death in 1944. His involvements were extensive: editor of the British Ornithological Union's (BOU) journal *Ibis* (as had been his father P.L. Sclater), president of the BOU for five years and secretary of the Royal Geographical Society for 12. Seemingly destined to be for ever completing the works of others (he appears again finishing off Frederick Jackson's *Birds of Kenya Colony and Uganda Protectorate*), he nonetheless found time to produce his own much respected overview, *Systema Avium Aethiopicarum*, between 1924 and 1930. This was essentially a checklist of sub-Saharan birds, which also strayed into the relatively uncharted territory of describing subspecies using a trinomial system to denote localised differences in some of the more widespread species. For all that it was essentially only a checklist, it formed the systematic basis for the presentation of many other works to come.

One to take full advantage of Sclater's efforts was **Cecil Damer Priest**, who wrote prolifically about birds and their nests and whose four volumes of *The Birds of Southern Rhodesia* emerged with remarkable speed between 1933 and 1936. Full of black-and-white drawings by the author, as well as colour plates by Norman Lighton, it would have been a godsend to anyone living there at the time and who wished to know more about its birds.

Priest had published a *Guide to the Birds of Southern Rhodesia and a Record of their Nesting Habits* in 1929, but realised that, with the publication of Sclater's work a year later, his own 'from a scientific point of view was deplorably inaccurate, and also out of date'. As he also admits, it was his idea to make the four volumes 'more of a "History" of the Natural History of Southern Rhodesia, as in so doing it helps to make the book more readable' – and in this he certainly succeeded. He quotes other sources freely and adds the most colourful digressions on local folklore, or his journeys round the country to visit selected sites in search of particular birds, or how hard it was to climb the trees where they were nesting.

Frederick Jackson was another archetypal amateur naturalist whose interest in birds absorbed almost all his free time during the 30 years he spent, first in the service of the Imperial British East Africa Company (IBEAC), then of the British Government, which reluctantly took over the administration of East Africa from the IBEAC in 1894. He retired in 1917 from his last posting, as Governor of Uganda, but his life, and the completion of his activities, were sadly curtailed by the lingering consequences of an 1897 bullet wound in his right lung. Jackson died in 1929, well aware, as his wife writes in the foreword to his work, of the need for an accessible reference work on East African birds: 'It was in the quiet days of his retirement that this book came into being, although he had long had it in his mind, particularly as Shelley's work, *Birds of Africa*, was discontinued after the issue of Volume V, and there was no publication on Kenya and Uganda birds in book form, except Professor Reichenow's great work [*Die Vogel Afrikas* – 1900–1905].'

Lady Jackson was clearly not only well informed, but also very persuasive, and one cannot help but wonder whether Sclater ultimately regretted his decision to take on the editing and completion of her husband's work: 'When Lady Jackson first asked me to undertake the editing and completion of Sir Frederick's work ... I little realised how much remained to be done before the manuscript could be sent to the printers, and that the task would occupy most of my time for several years ... On receiving the copy I found that there was still much matter to be added, descriptions of many of the species had not been drawn up and there were no diagnoses of families or genera.'

And so again, thanks to Sclater, *Birds of Kenya Colony and the Uganda Protectorate* was published in 1938 in three bulky volumes, following Sclater's own systematics but retaining all of Jackson's charming personal observations, which remain one of its most appealing features. Meanwhile,

Sclater's family life continued on the tragic course begun when both his stepsons were killed in action in the First World War; his wife died of injuries sustained in the bombing of London in 1942 before he himself was killed in 1944 by a flying bomb exploding over his home in Chelsea.

George Shelley's *A Handbook to the Birds of Egypt* had appeared in 1872, and this was not all that guided **Richard Meinertzhagen**, officer, adventurer, specimen collector and suspected fraud, in the production of the next major book on the country's birds. Michael Nicoll was the Assistant Director of the Zoological Gardens at Giza, outside Cairo, during which time he had begun a comprehensive guide to the birds of Egypt. Like so many others engaged on major works on birds, he died before its completion, leaving this to Meinertzhagen, who published it in two volumes in 1930 'with the title that seems appropriate' as *Nicoll's Birds of Egypt* by Colonel R. Meinertzhagen. It does appear that he was asked by Nicoll's widow to complete the work, and in the Introduction, he gives Nicoll every credit. The final result is two volumes totalling 700 pages, and is something of which Nicoll would have been immensely proud.

Meinertzhagen came from a wealthy family, and no money was spared in the production of his bird books, nor on the quality of their illustrations. In 1954 he produced the enormous *Birds of Arabia,* which, it was suggested, owed more to the work of G.L. Bates than Meinertzhagen would acknowledge. Be that as it may, the end result was also very fine indeed, and his *Pirates and Predators,* published five years later, is an interesting potpourri on 'The Piratical and Predatory Habits of Birds'.

In Sudan, where British influence also prevailed, **Francis Cave**, formerly a colonel in the Equatorial Corps of the Sudan Defence Force, and **James D. Macdonald** of the British Museum bird collection produced in 1955 *Birds of the Sudan – Their Identification and Distribution.* The book is dedicated to 'The Sudanese people, particularly our personal servants, field assistants and Equatorial soldiers', and was intended as a guide 'to identification and distribution'. It describes 871 species in one very manageable volume, with attractive colour illustrations as well as many line drawings, bringing it as close to a modern handbook as most of that generation of bird books would get.

By the time Jackson's book emerged, two other ornithologists had already conceived the idea of collaborating on practical bird guides for Africa. **Cyril Winthrop Mackworth-Praed** (1891–1974) was of the true Corinthian mould, winning a gold and two silver medals for shooting in the 1924 Paris Olympic Games – and gathering far more fame for his Olympic feats than he ever did for producing six volumes of readily accessible bird books. He had tried farming in East Africa, but returned home in 1914 and joined the army, becoming a stockbroker after the war.

Claude Henry Baxter Grant (1878–1958), born in London and trained in field surveying at London University, was something of a natural scientist. His early African experiences included service in the South African War in 1899, collecting expeditions on behalf of the Natural History Museum, where he had worked as a taxidermist, then further service in East Africa in the First World War. After that he stayed on in the colonial administration of what was then Tanganyika, returning to England in 1932. Once home he began collaborating with Mackworth-Praed (who provided most of the finance, while Grant offered more of the scientific input), on what would turn out to be three handbooks. *The Birds of Eastern and North Eastern Africa* was the first to appear, in 1952, after 18 years' gestation; and, sadly, it was the only one whose publication Grant would survive. He died in 1958, his obituary in *Ibis* (which magazine he had earlier edited) fittingly written by his co-author.

To the surprise of many, Mackworth-Praed was able to carry on their work alone, with *Birds of the Southern Third of Africa* appearing in 1963 and *Birds of West Central & Western Africa* in 1970. Had Grant survived longer, these other volumes may have reached readers earlier, but their value in increasing the popularity of bird watching cannot be overstated. As they write together in the 1951 Preface to the first volume: 'This book is written by two ornithologists as an attempt to give to others what they themselves wanted when they first went to Eastern Africa ... This book is not meant for the library shelf; it is emphatically for use and reference in the field. Economy of space has been our chief object, and condensed descriptions and diagrams must be forgiven. For the same reason the introductory matter is cut to a minimum, and there is no bibliography. There is undoubtedly a great and growing interest in birds all over Africa among officials, settlers, and the natives of the country, and if, by this book, birds which would otherwise have had to be killed for identification can be recognized and observed in the field, the authors will feel that their labours have not been in vain.'

In the Introduction they remark that, with the finalisation of Sclater's *Systema Avium Aethiopicarum*, the ornithological exploration of Africa was largely complete, but that today 'ornithologists are not so much concerned with the collecting of skins for taxonomic purposes, as with the habits of the living bird, its migrations, distribution and ecological place in the scheme of things'. Illustrated with colour plates, line drawings and a distribution map for each species, these publications filled a huge void, and the authors undoubtedly succeeded in their avowed intent.

The birdlife of West Africa has generally received much less attention than that in the east or south of the continent, certainly from English-language writers. American-born **George Latimer Bates** (1863–1940) had actually settled in Cameroon, rather than just visiting to explore. There he cultivated potatoes, coffee, cocoa and rubber, wrote a dictionary of the local Bulu language, and perhaps persuaded his father, who had always wanted him to go into the church, that he was also converting the local people to Christianity. On top of this, he was a committed naturalist and consigned thousands of specimens to the Natural History Museum in London, which eventually helped him to write a *Handbook of the Birds of West Africa*, published in 1930. Bates went on to focus on Arabian ornithology, his unpublished works allegedly plagiarised by Richard Meinertzhagen in the latter's much praised *Birds of Arabia*.

This opened the way for **David Alexander Bannerman** (1886–1979) to produce the definitive *Birds of Tropical West Africa,* its eight volumes appearing over the course of 21 years (1930–1951), during which time the price of the first, 25 shillings, exactly doubled to 50 shillings for the last! Bannerman had visited West Africa in his early years, but the compilation of this work was all done from London, building on the writings of earlier field naturalists. The first five volumes of Bannerman's work followed one another with some rapidity (the fifth was out in 1939), but the turbulence of the war years of 1939–1945 meant the sixth only appeared 10 years later. Thus, users were forced to focus on the non-passerine birds, which were those covered in these early volumes. Bannerman was well aware that eight volumes would live on the library shelf rather than in the haversack and so, in 1953, he produced a two-volume condensation under the title *The Birds of West and Equatorial Africa*, which would remain the standard work for years to come. In the introduction Alan Burns, former governor of the Gold Coast, bemoaned having completed his tour as governor with only five of the eight volumes, adding that, while the last three had made the set complete, they compounded its bulkiness.

In Central Africa it was another American, **James Paul Chapin**, heading a six-year expedition starting in 1909 and sponsored by the American Museum of Natural History, who completed the task of researching and cataloguing the birds in by far the most inaccessible part of the continent. Working largely in French, and doing most of his museum research in Belgian or French centres of science, his seminal four-volume work on *The Birds of the Belgian Congo* was published in the USA from 1932–1954. Chapin is responsible for one of the greatest ornithological revelations of the twentieth century – that of the existence of a peacock, *Afropavo congensis*, in the Congo jungles.

The last words in this summary of what could be called the first generation of modern English-language handbooks and their authors must be reserved for **Austin Roberts** (1883–1948) of South Africa and his groundbreaking *Birds of Southern Africa*. Roberts was a product of his own country, born in Pretoria and employed in the Transvaal Museum for most of his working life. From there he amassed a huge collection of bird specimens, which both helped him to identify the species that should find their way into the book and also provided its original artist, Norman Lighton, with skins from which to paint.

Published in 1940, simultaneously in Johannesburg and London, the book truly was a handbook, and has been continuously in print ever since, now under the name of *Birds of Southern Africa*. It has been through seven editions, the latest involving a major upgrade both of text and illustrations, as well as considerable taxonomic revisions of the order in which birds appear. Over the last 75 years, Roberts must have made bird watchers out of tens of thousands of people who had no real interest in birds until they picked up his book.

Roberts can also be credited with helping to further the devolution of African ornithology from the capitals of Europe down onto African soil. Far more bird books are now produced in African cities, and the publishing and printing facilities in several of them are world class.

Many of the seminal publications on African ornithology have been subsumed by more recent, better informed and more profusely illustrated books, and these early authors – like François Levaillant, Andrew Smith, Anton Reichenow, George Shelley and Frederick Jackson – are now better remembered for the birds named after them than for their writings. However, each of their works should be seen in the context of the time of its creation and the challenges they then faced: how well could specimens be preserved, how easily could they be despatched back home, how good were written field descriptions, how advanced were the worlds of publishing and illustration?

Since these early works, culminating in the first of what were intended as field guides, like those of Priest, Roberts, and Mackworth-Praed and Grant, both quality and quantity have improved dramatically. Now handbooks on birds of individual countries are increasingly common, such as Peter

Hancock and Ingrid Weiersbye's *Birds of Botswana* or Nik Borrow and Ron Demey's *Birds of Ghana*, although at the same time there also seems to be a tendency to produce more regional works. Roberts covers southern Africa now, not just South Africa, as also do the Sasol and Princeton Field Guides. Further north, the *Field Guide to the Birds of East Africa* by Terry Stevenson and John Fanshawe details the birds of Kenya, Uganda, Tanzania, Rwanda and Burundi; and Zimmerman, Turner and Pearson edge over Kenya's border with their *Birds of Kenya & Northern Tanzania*.

The pan-African overview has been well maintained by the large-format *Birds of Africa* (*BoA*) inspired by the vision of Leslie Brown, who died before he could witness the publication of even the first of its seven volumes in 1982. Not surprisingly, given that the entire work took 22 years to be finalised, concluding with an eighth volume that was devoted to the birds of the Malagasy region, the quality of each successive volume was noticeably better than that of its predecessor. The space allotted to each species allows for far greater detail than most of the earlier works could include. *Birds of Africa south of the Sahara* by Ian Sinclair and Peter Ryan covers over 2,100 species and still remains a handbook, and is particularly useful in those few remaining parts of Africa, like central DRC, which more focused handbooks have yet to cover. More recently, Michael Mills' *The Birder's Guide to Africa* manages to combine in a single paperback volume a detailed guide to the birds of the whole continent, with notes on where to see them, as well as descriptions of each of Africa's countries.

Africa is only one of seven continents, and those naturalists with a particular interest in birds are increasingly looking beyond national or even continental boundaries. There is much greater awareness now of the extent of birds' migrations and the perils they face on their journeys. Ever-improving internet communications, as well as a rise in the popularity of bird tourism and a willingness on the part of many bird watchers to travel far and wide to indulge their passion, are creating a generation of enthusiastic bird watchers with an increasingly global view. So now there are also publications covering the entire world's birds, particularly the magnificent 17 volumes of Del Hoyo et al.'s *Handbook of the Birds of the World* (*HBW*). A more comprehensive, and better illustrated cornucopia of macro- and micro-information is unlikely to appear in paper for many decades to come, and the introductory essays to each family make wonderfully good reading.

Of more sustained use to many bird watchers, not least in the light of the increasing urge of many to record species seen in a lifetime, are several world checklists. Each has a different focus or taxonomic priority and there are ongoing efforts to streamline these. Until this happens, the lists of Clements; Howard and Moore; Sibley and Monroe; and Peters, among others, each have their own followers. To these was added, in 2016, the joint Lynx-Birdlife International two volumes of an *Illustrated Checklist of the Birds of the World* (*HBW Checklist*), which sought to follow on from the *HBW*.

The *HBW Checklist* was unique in providing both an illustration and map for each of its 10,964 species, divided between 2,346 genera and these among 241 families. From my point of view, being something of a technophobe, I find this paper publication invaluable. However, I was advised to avoid relying exclusively on this as my taxonomic bible, and to temper its opinions with those from at least one other source, and this has been the International Ornithological Congress (IOC) Checklist, which is regularly updated – 8.1 being that in use as I wrote, and whose English names I also generally use.

The principal function of any checklist is to list species, and it is these species that often create much controversy. Paraphrasing some of the opening words in the *HBW Checklist*'s introduction, 'the species problem derives not only from trying to estimate the degree of variation between subspecies, but also the variation in the preferences and perceptions of the taxonomists'. Often these preferences and perceptions coincide, but with determination of potential new species now taking account of a bird's physical characteristics, behaviour, calls and also propensity to hybridise, as well increasingly of the evidence provided by DNA analysis, there is inevitably room for subjectivity.

So, publications will continue to appear promoting the creation of new species. So too will handbooks, monographs, checklists and more, which can take full advantage, as I have done, of the works of others. To my mind, very little can surpass some of these earlier ornithological compilations, and even if these gradually fade into obscurity, they have provided the foundations upon which all of those who came later, in one way or another, built their own works. Thank you all.

BIBLIOGRAPHY & FURTHER READING

Andersson, Malte. (1982) 'Female choice selects for extreme tail length in a widowbird'. *Nature* 299:818–820.

Archer, Geoffrey & Goodman, Eva M. (1937–1961). *The Birds of British Somaliland and the Gulf of Aden*. Oliver & Boyd, London.

Aristotle (c. 350 BC) *Historia Animalium*.

Attenborough, David. (1998) *The Life of Birds*. BBC Books.

Austin, Oliver L. & Singer, A. (1961) *Birds of the World*. Golden Press, New York.

Ayres, Thomas. (1884) 'Additional Notes on the Ornithology of the Republic of Transvaal'. *Ibis*, Vol. 19(3).

Ayres, Thomas. (1884) 'Additional Notes on the Ornithology of the Republic of Transvaal'. *Ibis*, Vol. 26(3)

Backhurst, Graeme. (2019) 'Ngulia at 50'. *Kenya Birding*, Vol. 13.

Bannerman, David A. (1930–1951) *The Birds of Tropical West Africa*. Crown Agents for the Colonies, London.

Bates, George Latimer. (1930) *Handbook of the birds of West Africa*. John Bale, Sons & Danielsson, London.

Belcher, C.F. (1930) *The Birds of Nyasaland*. Crosby Lockwood & Son, London.

Benson, C.W. (1966) 'The Spike-heeled Lark in East Africa'. *Bulletin of the British Ornithologists' Club*, Vol. 86.

Benson, C.W. (1971) 'Further Notes on the Spike-heeled Lark in East Africa'. *Bulletin of the British Ornithologists' Club*, Vol. 91.

BirdLife South Africa. (1997) *Atlas of Southern African Birds*.

Borrow, Nik & Demey, Ron. (2010) *Birds of Ghana*. Christopher Helm, London.

Bowie, Rauri C.K. & Fjeldså, Jon. (2005) 'Genetic and morphological evidence for two species of Udzungwa Forest Partridge'. *Journal of East African Natural History*, Vol. 94(1).

Brehm, Alfred E. (1879) *Brehm's Life of Animals*. Leipzig.

British Broadcasting Corporation Natural History Unit. (2013) Africa: Episode 2.

British Broadcasting Corporation. (1998) *The Life of Birds*.

British Trust for Ornithology. 'Cuckoo Tracking Project'.

Cade, T.J. & Greenwald, L.I. (1966) 'Drinking behaviour of sandgrouse in the Namib and Kalahari deserts'. *The Auk* (83).

Cade, T.J. & Maclean, G.L. (1967) 'Transport of Water by Adult Sandgrouse to their Young'. *The Condor* (July–August).

Cave, F.O. & Macdonald, J.D. (1955) *Birds of the Sudan*. Oliver & Boyd, London.

Chapin, James Paul. (1932–1953) *The Birds of the Belgian Congo*. Bulletin of American Museum of Natural History.

Clancey, P.A. (1984) 'On the Bird Art of C G Finch-Davies and Norman C K Lighton'. *Bokmakierie*, Vol. 3.

Coetzee, H., Nell, W. & Van Rensburg, L. (2014) 'An exploration of cultural beliefs and practices across the Southern Ground-hornbill's Range in Africa'. *Journal of Ethnobiology and Ethnomedicine*, Vol. 10.

Colahan, B.D. (1982) 'The Biology of the Orangebreasted Waxbill'. *Ostrich*, Vol. 53(1).

Collias, Nicholas & Elsie. (1962) 'An experimental study of the mechanisms of nest building in a weaverbird'. *The Auk*.

Dale, James. (1992) 'The Effect of the Removal of Buffalo on the Host Selection of Yellow-billed Oxpeckers in Zimbabwe'. *Tropical Zoology*.

Davies, Owen. (2014) 'Taxonomy, phylogeny and biogeography of cisticolas'. Ph.D. thesis for the University of Cape Town.

Del Hoyo, J. & Collar, N.J. (2016) *HBW and Birdlife International Illustrated Checklist of the Birds of the World*. Lynx Editions, Barcelona.

Del Hoyo, J. et al. (eds). (1992–2013) *Handbook of the Birds of the World (HBW)*. Lynx Editions, Barcelona.

Delacour, Jean. (1954–1964) 'Waterfowl of the World'. *Country Life Ltd*, London.

Dinesen, L. et al. (1994) 'A new genus and species of perdicine bird (Phasianidae, Perdicini) from Tanzania; a relict form with Indo-Malayan affinities'. *Ibis*, Vol. 136(1).

Donald, P.F. & Collar, N.J. (2011) 'Notes on the Structure and Plumage of Beesley's Lark'. *African Bird Club Bulletin*, (18)2.

Egremont, Pamela & Rothschild, Miriam. (1979) 'Calculating Cormorants'. *Biological Journal of the Linnean Society*, Vol. 12(2).

Farinos-Celdran, Pablo et al. (2016) 'The Consumption of honey-bees by *Merops apiaster* ...'. *Journal of Apicultural Research*, Vol. 55(2).

Finch-Davies, C.G. & Kemp, A. (1980) *The Birds of Prey of Southern Africa*. Winchester Press, Johannesburg.

Fry, C.H. & Keith, S. (eds). (1982–2004) *The Birds of Africa* (Vols I–VII). Christopher Helm, London.

Galeotti, Paolo & Inglisa, Maria. (2001) 'Estimating predation impact on honeybees by European Bee-eaters'. *La Revue d'Ecologie*, Vol. 56(4).

Holmes, R.T., Frauenknecht, B.D. & Du Plessis, M.A. (2002) 'Breeding System of the Cape Rockjumper, a South African Fynbos Endemic'. *The Condor*, Vol. 104(1).

Hopkinson, G. & Masterson, A.N.B. (1977) 'On the occurrence near Salisbury of the White-winged Flufftail'. *Honeyguide* 91:25–28.

Horsburgh, Boyd. (1912) *The Game Birds and Waterfowl of South Africa*. Witherby & Co., London.

https://medium.com/@NWBCT/the-race-to-save-the-amur-falcons-in-nagaland-northeast-india-d0b306892b48

International Ornithological Congress World Bird List.

International Union for Conservation of Nature Red List of Threatened Species.

Jackson, F.J. & Sclater, W.L. (1938) *The Birds of Kenya Colony and the Uganda Protectorate*. Gurney and Jackson, London.

Kingdon, Jonathan et al. (2013) *Mammals of Africa*. Bloomsbury Natural History, London.

Kioko, J.M., Smith, D.A. & Kiffner, C. (2015) 'Uses of Birds for Ethno Medicine Among the Maasai People in Monduli District, Northern Tanzania'. *International Journal of Ethnobiology and Ethnomedicine*, Vol. 1.

Lawes, M.J. & Kirkman, S. (1996) 'Egg recognition and interspecific brood parasitism rates in red bishops'. *Journal of Animal Behaviour*, Vol. 52(3).

Layard, E.L. (1884) *The Birds of South Africa*, 2nd ed. revised and augmented by R. Bowdler Sharpe. Bernard Quaritch, London.

Lee, Alan & Barnard, Phoebe. (2016) 'Endemic birds of the Fynbos biome; a conservation assessment and impacts of climate change'. *Bird Conservation International*, Vol. 26(1).

Levaillant, François (1796–1808) *Histoire Naturelle des Oiseaux d'Afrique*.

Lewis, A. & Pomeroy, D. (1989) *A Bird Atlas of Kenya*. CRC Press.

Ligon, J.D. & Ligon, S.H. (1978) 'The Communal Social System of the Green Woodhoopoe in Kenya'. *Living Bird*, Vol. 17.

Lindholm, J. (2001) 'The Hadada Ibis'. American Federation of Aviculture journal, *Watchbird*, Vol. 28(1).

Linnaeus, Carl. (1758) *Systema Naturae*, 10th ed.

Little, Rob M. (2014) 'The bogey bird – managing Egyptian Geese on golf courses'. *African Birdlife*, July–August.

Liversidge, R. (1963) 'The Nesting of the Hamerkop'. *Ostrich*, Vol. 34(2).

Livingstone, David. (1858) *Missionary Travels and Researches in South Africa*. John Murray, London.

Lydekker, Richard. (1913) Letters to *The Times*, 4th and 11th February.

Lynes, Hubert. (1930) 'Review of the genus Cisticola'. Supplemental volume in *Ibis*.

Lynn-Allen, B.G. (1951) *Shot-gun and Sunlight: The Game Birds of East Africa*. The Batchworth Press, London.

Mackworth-Praed, C.W. & Grant, C.H.B. (1952–1955) *Birds of Eastern and North Eastern Africa*. Longmans, Green & Co., London.

Maddox, Max & Geering, David. (1994) 'Range expansion and migration of the Cattle Egret'. *Ostrich*, Vol. 65(2).

Marks, B.D. et al. (2004) 'Rediscovery of the White-necked Picathartes in Ghana'. *Bulletin of the British Ornithologists' Club*, Vol. 124.

McAtee, W.L. (1944) 'Birds Pickaback'. *The Scientific Monthly*, Vol. 58(3).

Meade-Waldo, E.G.B. (1896) 'Sand grouse breeding in captivity'. *The Zoologist*.

Meinertzhagen, Richard. (1954) *Birds of Arabia*. Oliver & Boyd, London.

Meinertzhagen, Richard. (1959) *Pirates and Predators: The piratical and predatory habits of birds*. Oliver & Boyd, London.

Miller, John Frederick. (1796) *Cimelia Physica: Figures of rare and curious quadrupeds, birds, etc. together with several of the most elegant plants*.

Mills, M. (2017) *The Birder's Guide to Africa*. Go-Away-Birding, Cape Town.

Milstein, P. le S. (1975) 'How baby Egyptian Geese leave a high nest'. *Bokmakierie*, Vol. 27(2).

Moreau, R.E. (1933) 'The Food of the Red-billed Oxpecker'. *Bulletin of Entomological Research*, Vol. 24(3).

Moreau, R.E. (1966) *The bird faunas of Africa and its Islands*. Academic Press, London.

Moreau, R.E. & W.M. (1937) 'Biological and other Notes on some East African Birds'. *Ibis*, Vol. 79(1).

Nagaland Wildlife & Biodiversity Trust. (2016) 'The Race to Save the Amur Falcons in Nagaland, Northeast India'.

Nicolaides, Angelo. (2013) 'Promoting Avitourism as a special niche area of Ecotourism in South Africa'. *African Journal of Hospitality, Tourism and Leisure*, Vol. 2(3).

Papyrus Lansing, translated in *The Journal of Egyptian Archaeology*, 1925, Vol. 11(1).

Parkyns, Mansfield. (1853) *Life in Abyssinia – being notes collected during three years residence and travels in that country*. John Murray, London.

Pizzey, G. & Knight, F. (1980) *Birds of Australia*. Harper Collins, Sydney.

Portugal, S.J. et al. (2016) 'The fast and forceful kicking strike of the secretary bird'. *Current Biology*, Vol. 26(2).

Priest, C.D. (1933–1936) *Birds of Southern Rhodesia*. William Clowes & Sons, London.

Roberts, Austin. (1907) 'Remarks on the Breeding-Habits of the Pin-tailed Widow Bird'. *Journal of the South African Ornithologists' Union*, Vol. III.

Roberts, Austin. (1917) 'Ornithological Notes'. *Annals of the Transvaal Museum*, Vol. 5(4).

Roberts, Austin. (1940) *Roberts Birds of Southern Africa*. Witherbys, London.

Root, Alan & Joan. (1998) *The Legend of the Lightning Bird*. Anglia Television.

Rowan, M.K. (1967) 'A Study of the Colies of South Africa'. *Ostrich*, Vol. 38(2).

Royal Society for the Protection of Birds (RSPB). (2002) *Birds of Britain and Europe*. Dorling Kindersley, London.

Shelley, George E. (1896–1912) *Birds of Africa*. R H Porter, London.

Short, Lester & Horne, Jennifer. (2002) 'Toucans, Barbets and Honeyguides'. Oxford University Press.

Sinclair, I. & Ryan, P. (2003) *Birds of Africa south of the Sahara*. Struik Nature, South Africa.

Smit, D.J. v Z. (1963) 'Ostrich farming in the Little Karoo'. *Bulletin of Department of Agricultural Technical Services*, South Africa.

Smith, Andrew. (1830) 'A Description of the Birds Inhabiting the South of Africa'. *South African Quarterly Journal*, Issue 1.

Southern African Bird Atlas Project 2

Sparrman, Andreas. (1777) 'An account of a journey into Africa from the Cape of Good Hope, and a Description of a new Species of Cuckow'. *Philosophical Transactions of The Royal Society*, Vol. 67.

Spottiswoode, C.N. & Koorevaar, J. (2011) 'A stab in the dark: chick killing by brood parasitic honeyguides'. *Royal Society, Biology Letters*, Vol. 8(2).

Spottiswoode, C.N., Begg, K.S. & Begg, C.M. (2016) 'Reciprocal signaling in honeyguide-human mutualism'. *Science*, Vol. 353.

Stark, A.C. & Slater, W.L. (1906) *Birds of South Africa*. R.H. Porter, London.

Stevenson, T. & Fanshawe, J. (2002) *Birds of East Africa*. T. & A.D. Poyser, London.

Steyn, Peter. (1980) 'Breeding and food of the Bateleur in Zimbabwe (Rhodesia)'. *Ostrich*, Vol. 51(3).

Toloa, Esther et al. (2017) 'The increasingly urban status of the Cattle Egret in Uganda ...'. *Scopus: Journal of East African Ornithology*, Vol. 37(1).

Van Someren, V.D. (1958) *A Bird Watcher in Kenya*. Oliver & Boyd, London.

Vernon, C.J. (1984) 'The Breeding biology of the thick-billed cuckoo'. *Proceedings of the 5th Pan-African Ornithological Congress*.

Victorin, Johan Fredrik. (1860) *Zoologiska anteckningar under en resa i sådra delarae af Caplandat åren 1853–1855*.

Watson, R.T. (1990) 'Population dynamics of the Bateleur in the Kruger National Park'. *Ostrich*, Vol. 61(1–2).

Whitfield, A.K. & Blaber, S.J.M. (1978) 'Food and Feeding ecology of piscivorous birds at Lake St Lucia: part 1, Diving Birds'. *Ostrich*, Vol. 49(4).

Wilson, R.T. & Wilson, M.P. (1986) 'Nest Building by the Hamerkop'. *Ostrich*, Vol. 57(4).

Zimmerman, D.A., Turner, D.A. & Pearson, D.J. (1999) *Birds of Kenya & Northern Tanzania*. Christopher Helm (Publishers) Ltd.